IMAGES
of America

FIRCREST

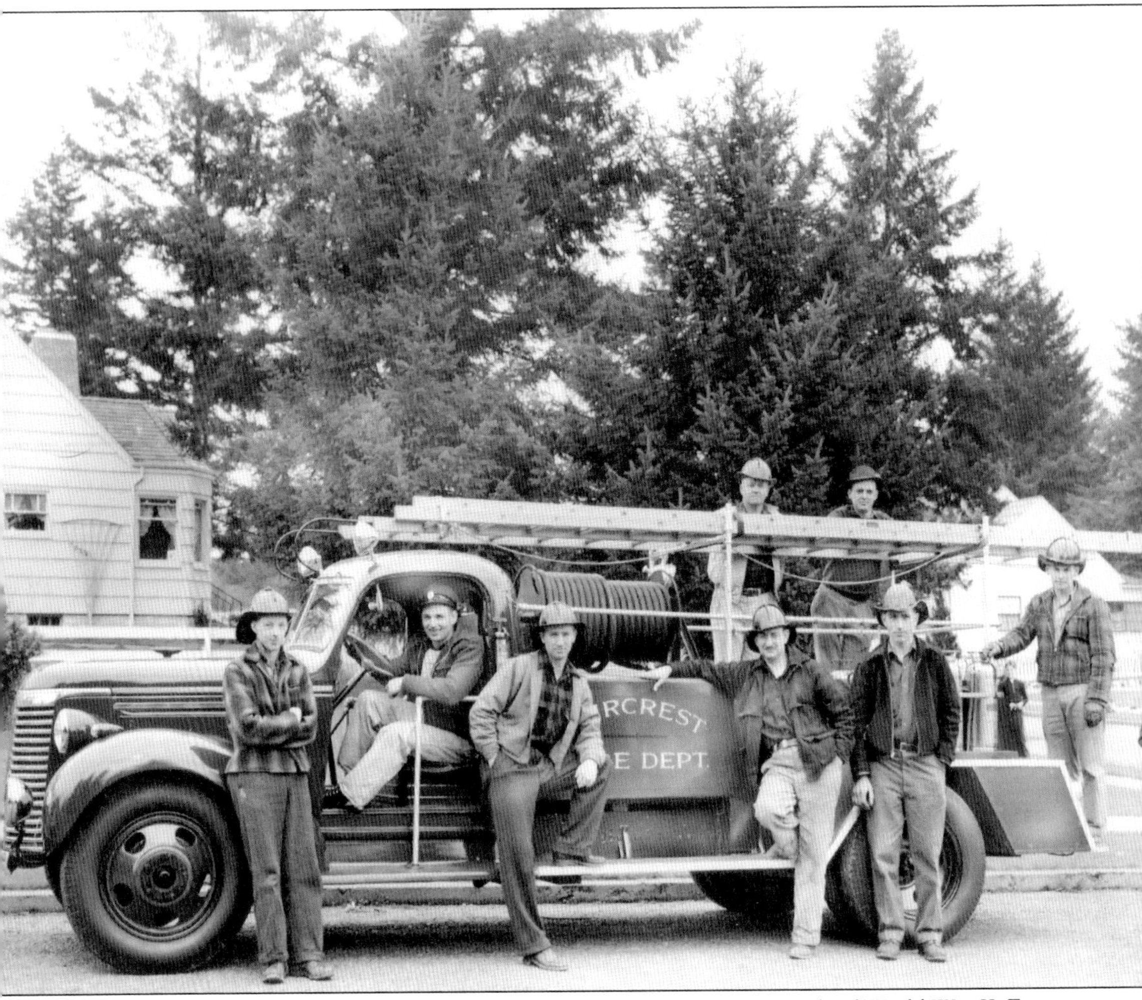

On the Cover: Municipal responsibility for civil defense grew as a result of World War II. Fircrest saw an urgent need for adequate firefighting equipment. With the availability of defense funds, the city was able to purchase its first fire truck, this red 1943 Chevrolet, and the Fircrest Volunteer Fire Department was formed. In July 1949, a large fire raged just north of the city. The volunteer firefighters stood by their truck and watched the fire grow, unable to fight a blaze outside of their jurisdiction unless asked. Suddenly, the wind changed, and the fire charged in, threatening to consume the city. As fir trees exploded into flame, the firefighters held the line, preventing the blaze from crossing Columbia Avenue. Today, the Fircrest Fire Department continues in this tradition, with one of the best records in the country. (Courtesy of the Tacoma Public Library, D12303-A.)

IMAGES
of America

FIRCREST

Ralph R. Colyer

ARCADIA
PUBLISHING

ISBN 978-1-4671-3390-6

Published by Arcadia Publishing
Charleston, South Carolina

Printed in the United States of America

Library of Congress Control Number: 2015933929

For all general information, please contact Arcadia Publishing:
Telephone 843-853-2070
Fax 843-853-0044
E-mail sales@arcadiapublishing.com
For customer service and orders:
Toll-Free 1-888-313-2665

Visit us on the Internet at www.arcadiapublishing.com

This book is dedicated to Marjorie, who has always been my best friend.

Contents

ACKNOWLEDGMENTS

My gratitude goes out to the builders and residents of the city of Fircrest and Regents Park for their vision and fidelity. They continue to build a forward-looking community dedicated to family, friend, and neighbor. Thanks also for your eagerness to share stories and images, especially the *Facebook* group Friends of Fircrest, without whose help this work might not have been possible.

Special thanks goes to Tacoma Historical Society's Dale Wirshing and Deb Freedman, who suggested I write this book. I also want to recommend the Tacoma Public Library's Northwest Room and staff to those interested in the local history of Pierce County and its communities.

I want to thank the City of Fircrest, particularly the city clerk, Lisa Keely, and the city manager, Rick Rosenbladt, as well as the Fircrest Golf Club and its general manager, Jeff Hilen.

It was a privilege to encounter so many people who do so much to keep our history alive. Albert Fisher of *The Original Amateur Hour* website was one, and I want to thank him especially. The men and women of our national parks are others.

Finally, I want to express my love and gratitude to my wife, Marjorie, for her encouragement and her great help in editing this book.

Introduction

At 5:12 a.m. on April 18, 1906, a tremor hit the city of San Francisco, followed 20 seconds later by the "Great Quake." The fires that broke out as a result of the earthquake lasted for four days. By the time the smoke cleared, over 3,000 people had lost their lives, and over 80 percent of San Francisco was in ruins.

As San Francisco began the process of rebuilding, a group of prominent businessmen, real estate financiers, and developers met at the Union Club for lunch. Among them were Edward J. Bowes, William A. Irwin, John H Spring, and William J. Hotchkiss. Of course, there was much talk of the earthquake, its aftermath, and their future prospects. Toward the end of the luncheon, an unidentified railroad man joined the four, and the conversation turned to the need for diversification of investments outside of San Francisco. In his book *Of Lions and Dreams, of Men and Realities*, Richard D. Osness writes: "The railroad man stated that if he had surplus money, he would invest it in Tacoma. I believe that city has the best immediate future of any on the Pacific Coast." That belief was well-founded, because the Union Pacific Railroad had chosen Tacoma, on Puget Sound, as the western terminus of the transcontinental railroad. By 1906, the area was booming.

The next day, Bowes, Irwin, and Spring boarded a train bound for the Pacific Northwest and arrived in Tacoma on Saturday, October 20, 1906. By Sunday, the men had toured the city, studied maps, and negotiated the sale of several hundred acres of forested land west of the city from the Tacoma Land & Improvement Company. The land was platted and designated as Regents Park and Regents Park No. 2. Less than seven months from the date of the men's luncheon at the Union Club, lots were being sold, and the development of Regents Park, later renamed Fircrest, had begun.

The entrepreneurs and engineers of Regents Park laid out the development with creativity and foresight. Anticipating America's transition to the automobile, the paved roads were wide and had concrete sidewalks and curbs. The streets, designed with aesthetics in mind, followed the natural contours of the site rather than the standard grid pattern that was popular at the time. Regents Park was designed as a residence park, a getaway from work, and a charming and healthy oasis, where one could enjoy life and raise a family. As such, "the Park" was one of the first designed suburban developments in the country.

As it turned out, the venture was too far ahead of its time. From the beginning, there was a lot of buzz about the development. Water, sewer, and power went in, and lots sold briskly. Well-designed and well-built homes began to dot the development. After the first few years, however, interest in the project and lot sales waned. Due in part to expensive infrastructure, the cost of land in Regents Park was relatively high. Also, to protect value, the developers supplied house plans and put a high minimum price on a home's construction, making building expensive. Finally, the community's main access to town was a single, unreliable trolley known as the "traction line." Regents Park was simply too far away from jobs, and cheap lots close to Tacoma were readily available.

The years between the world wars were hard on the community, and lot prices plummeted, with parcels going for $25 to $50. Some residents began to advocate a merger with neighboring Tacoma. Among the highlights of this period were the formation of the Fircrest Golf Club and the building of its 18-hole course. At this time, the homeowners joined together and decided to drop the name Regents Park. The new town, named Fircrest, was incorporated in 1925. These positive steps put an end to any talk of merger and brought residents together as a strong community. It set the stage for the realization of the builders' original vision. During the building boom following World War II, this quintessential suburbia of mid-century America blossomed.

Fircrest has been referred to as a "gem of suburbia." Currently, all of the original lots are sold, and several adjoining areas have been annexed into the city. There are over 6,500 residents in over 3,000 homes. But, more than this, the town possesses a very strong sense of community, security, and prosperity. Fircrest enjoys one of the highest ratios of parks per capita of any town in Washington State, and the city's many annual festivities are very popular, well supported, and well attended. A healthy, wholesome, and active community, the city of Fircrest continues today in the best traditions of its founders' early visions for the people who live here.

One

Regents Park

In the fall of 1906, in the wake of the Great Earthquake, a group of prominent San Francisco businessmen came to Tacoma in search of development opportunities as a means of diversifying their investments outside of the Bay Area.

Soon after their arrival in Tacoma, the four investors, Edward J. Bowes, William A. Irwin, John H. Spring, and William J. Hotchkiss, negotiated a purchase of several hundred acres west of the city from the Northern Pacific's Tacoma Land Company. Commencement Bay had been chosen by the Northern Pacific as the western terminus of the transcontinental railroad, and, as such, the city was experiencing rapid growth. After rejecting a brilliant but unorthodox plan for the city by Frederick Law Olmsted, Tacoma was growing linearly south along Pacific Avenue, and a standard grid pattern plan was being forced onto the hills and cliffs that hemmed in the city. The Regents Park investors believed that the time was ripe for development west of the city. The Narrows Land Company was formed on Halloween 1906, and plans for a new residential park called Regents Park began in earnest.

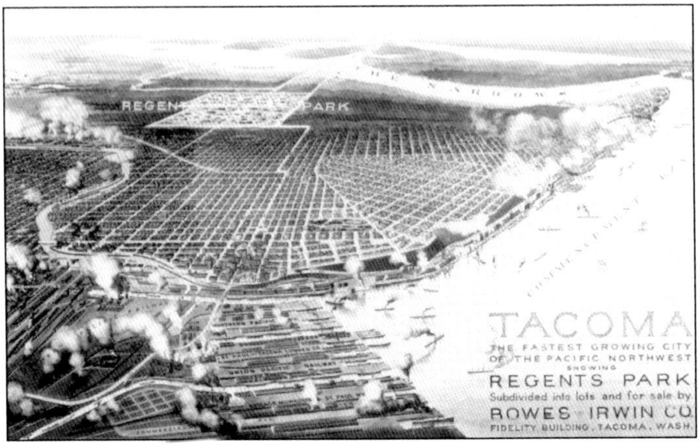

This c. 1907 advertisement for Regents Park is a bird's-eye view of the park in relation to Tacoma. Bowes-Irwin (the Narrows Land Co.) was selling lots within seven months of coming to Tacoma in the fall of 1906. (Courtesy of the Tacoma Public Library G72.1-108B.)

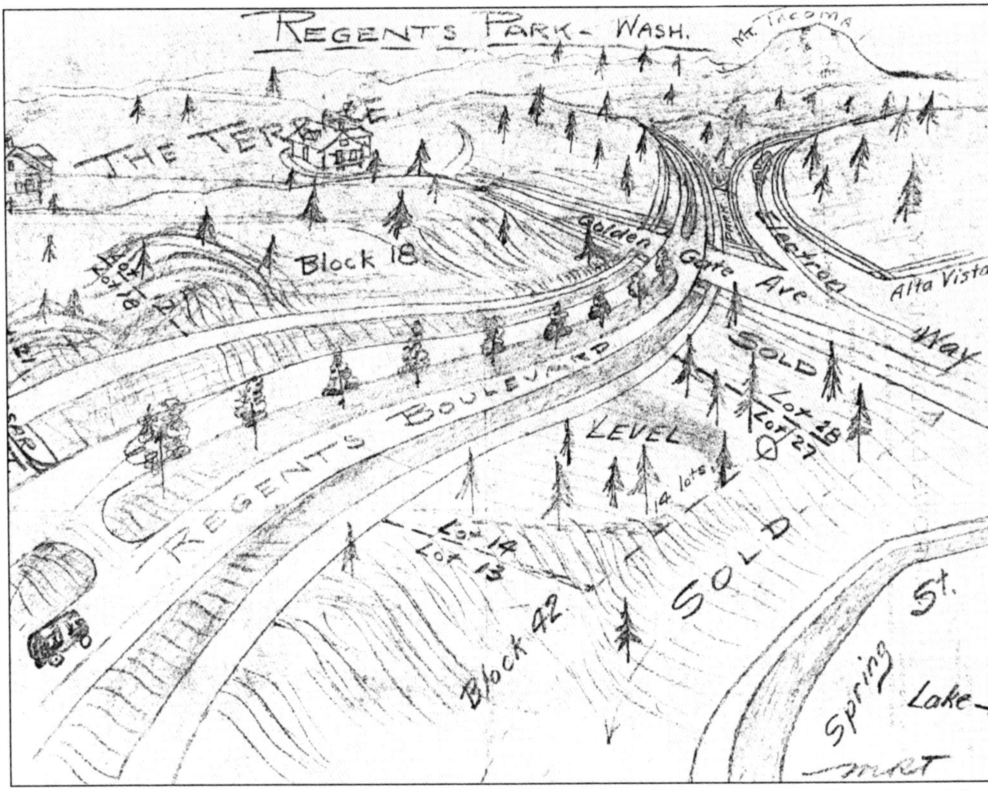

In the fall of 1907, Mrs. E.R. Dalton wrote the Narrows Land Company regarding several lots she was planning to purchase. She had concerns about the slope of the lots and questions about who would bear the cost of infrastructure improvements. In response, E.J. Bowes, vice president of the Narrows Land Company, wrote a lengthy letter addressing her concerns and enclosed this sketch drawn by his chief engineer, M.R. Thompson. The sketch shows a revolutionary concept in city planning: the standard grid pattern of the day had been developed for towns on the prairie. This new concept of streets, following the natural contours of the site, was 50 years ahead of its time. In fact, the suburban park concept developed for Regents Park would soon migrate to California. The well-known community of Thousand Oaks, near San Francisco, was inspired by Regents Park's plan and was designed by M.R. Thompson for John H. Spring, one of Regents Park's original investors. (Courtesy of the City of Fircrest.)

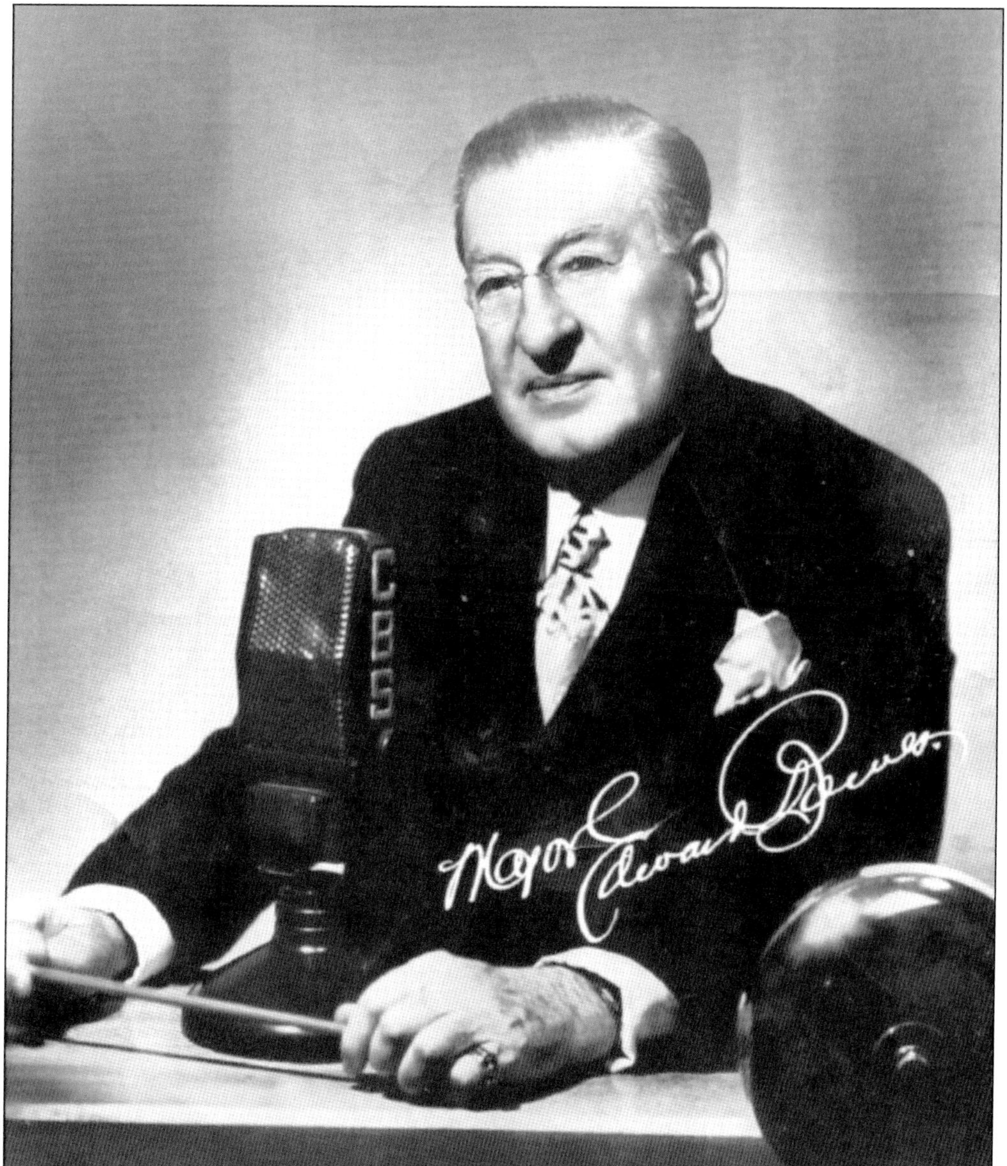

Famously known as "Major" Bowes, Edward J. Bowes was the most prominent of the original four investors in the Narrows Land Company. He was born in San Francisco of very modest means. According to Albert Fisher of *The Original Amateur Hour* website, "As a boy he learned calligraphy to help the family income." A self-made man, E.J. Bowes made his fortune in San Francisco real estate. He acquired his title "major" while serving in the US Army during World War I. Following the war, Bowes moved to New York, where he became a theater and radio personality. *Major Bowes' Amateur Hour* was one of the country's most popular radio programs from 1934 to 1952. It was the *American Idol* of its day. Celebrities whose careers began on the show include Frank Sinatra, Beverly Sills, Paul Winchell and Jerry Mahoney, and Maria Callas. *Major Bowes' Amateur Hour* was broadcast on both NBC and CBS. Bowes is seen here behind a CBS microphone with his famous gong, which he rang to cut bad acts. (Courtesy of *The Original Amateur Hour.*)

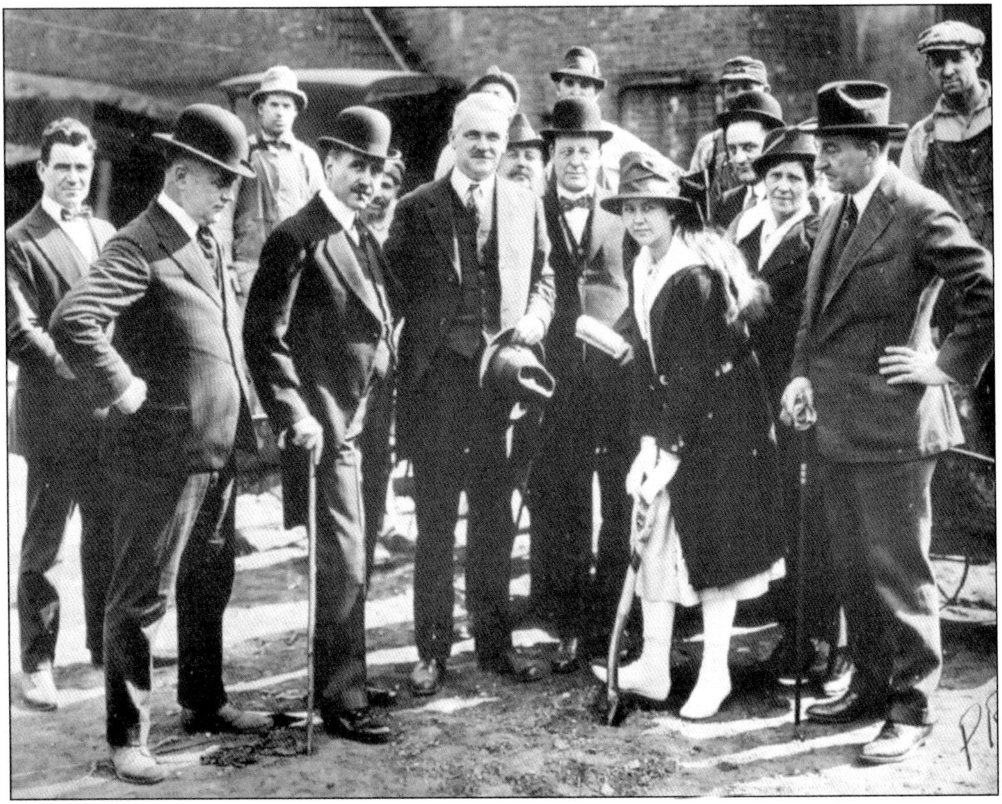

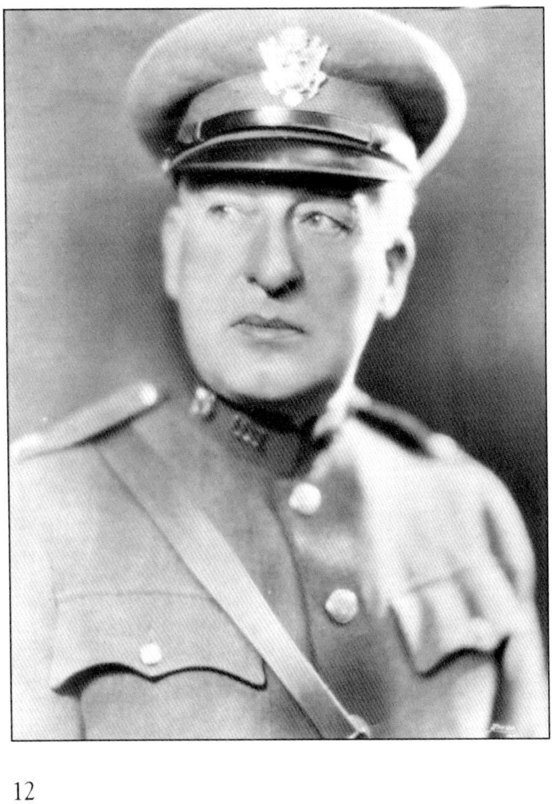

The photograph above shows a formal ground-breaking ceremony of the period. Edward J. Bowes is the gentleman on the right in the hat with a hand on his hip. Bowes is also pictured at left in his officer's uniform while serving in the US Army during World War I. After the Great War, Bowes added the title of major to his name and went on to become nationally famous as Major Bowes. (Both courtesy of *The Original Amateur Hour.*)

At right is a portrait of Edward "Major" Bowes drawn by the artist James Montgomery Flagg, whose best-known work is the iconic "Uncle Sam, I Want You!" recruitment poster. Shown below is a record of the land holdings west and south of Tacoma city limits in 1913. Regents Park and Regents Park No. 2 are at the upper right. While there are many prominent names on the map, two large areas of land in the center left are registered to John H. Spring. (At right, courtesy of the Original Amateur Hour; below, the City of Fircrest.)

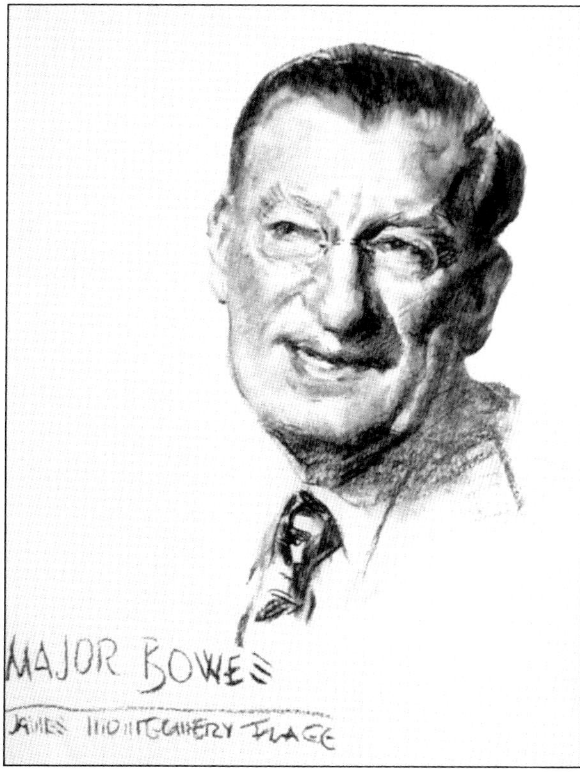

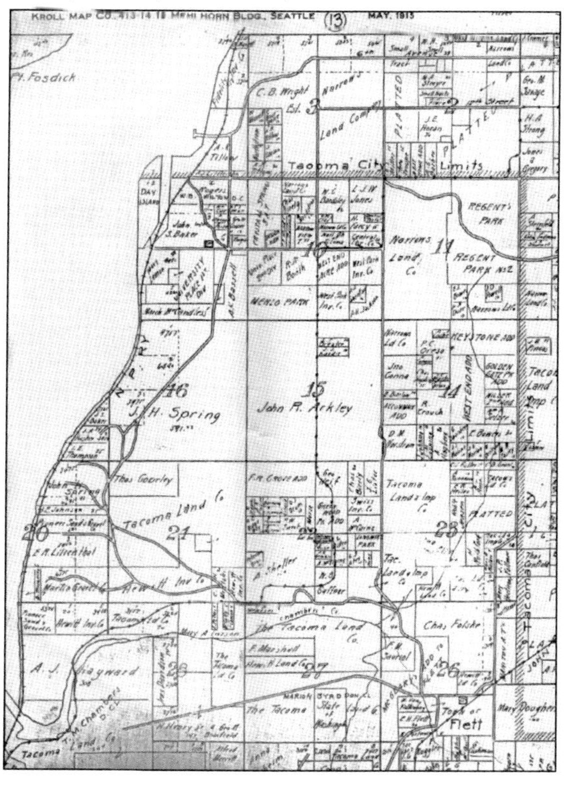

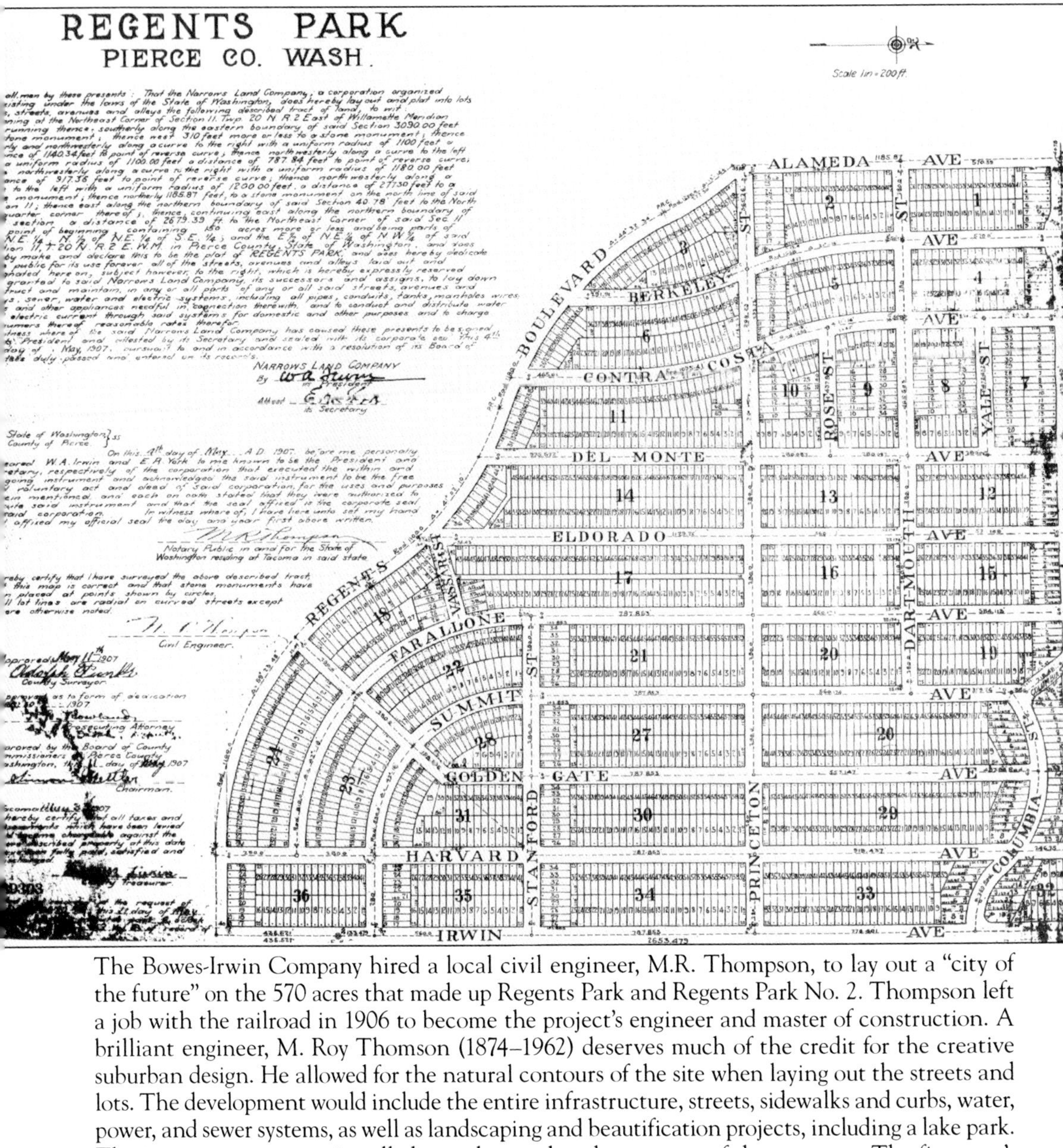

The Bowes-Irwin Company hired a local civil engineer, M.R. Thompson, to lay out a "city of the future" on the 570 acres that made up Regents Park and Regents Park No. 2. Thompson left a job with the railroad in 1906 to become the project's engineer and master of construction. A brilliant engineer, M. Roy Thomson (1874–1962) deserves much of the credit for the creative suburban design. He allowed for the natural contours of the site when laying out the streets and lots. The development would include the entire infrastructure, streets, sidewalks and curbs, water, power, and sewer systems, as well as landscaping and beautification projects, including a lake park. The improvements were installed complete and at the expense of the company. The first year's expenditures amounted to more than $350,000 in 1907. (Courtesy of the City of Fircrest.)

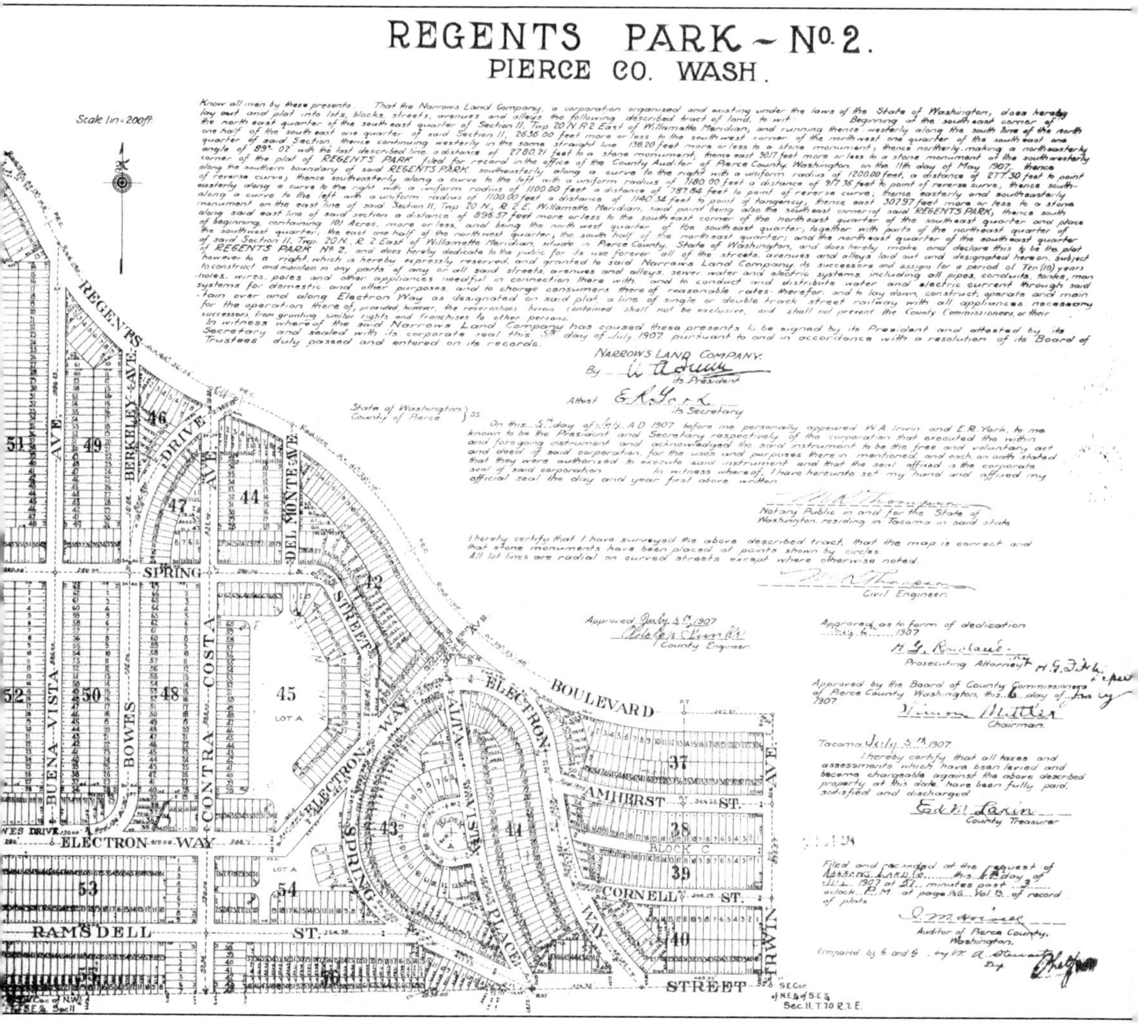

For reasons related to finance, the project was platted in two parts: Regents Park and Regents Park 2. In naming the streets, the designers and investors revealed something of their origins and values. The avenues running north and south are mostly San Francisco–area place-names (Contra Costa, Alameda, and Altadena). Those streets running east and west are mainly named for institutions of higher learning (Harvard, Princeton, Dartmouth). A few streets were named in recognition of the developers (Spring, Bowes, and Irwin). The grand Regents Boulevard bisected the two parks. John H. Spring (1862–1933) made a fortune in real estate following the San Francisco Earthquake. He and M.R. Thompson, the chief engineer of Regents Park, would return to San Francisco to build the housing development Thousand Oaks in Berkeley. William A. Irwin returned to California and was involved in building and real estate in Newport Beach. William J. Hotchkiss was the president of Central California Canneries. He later played a key role in the promotion of the bridge that spans San Francisco Bay, the Golden Gate Bridge. (Courtesy of the City of Fircrest.)

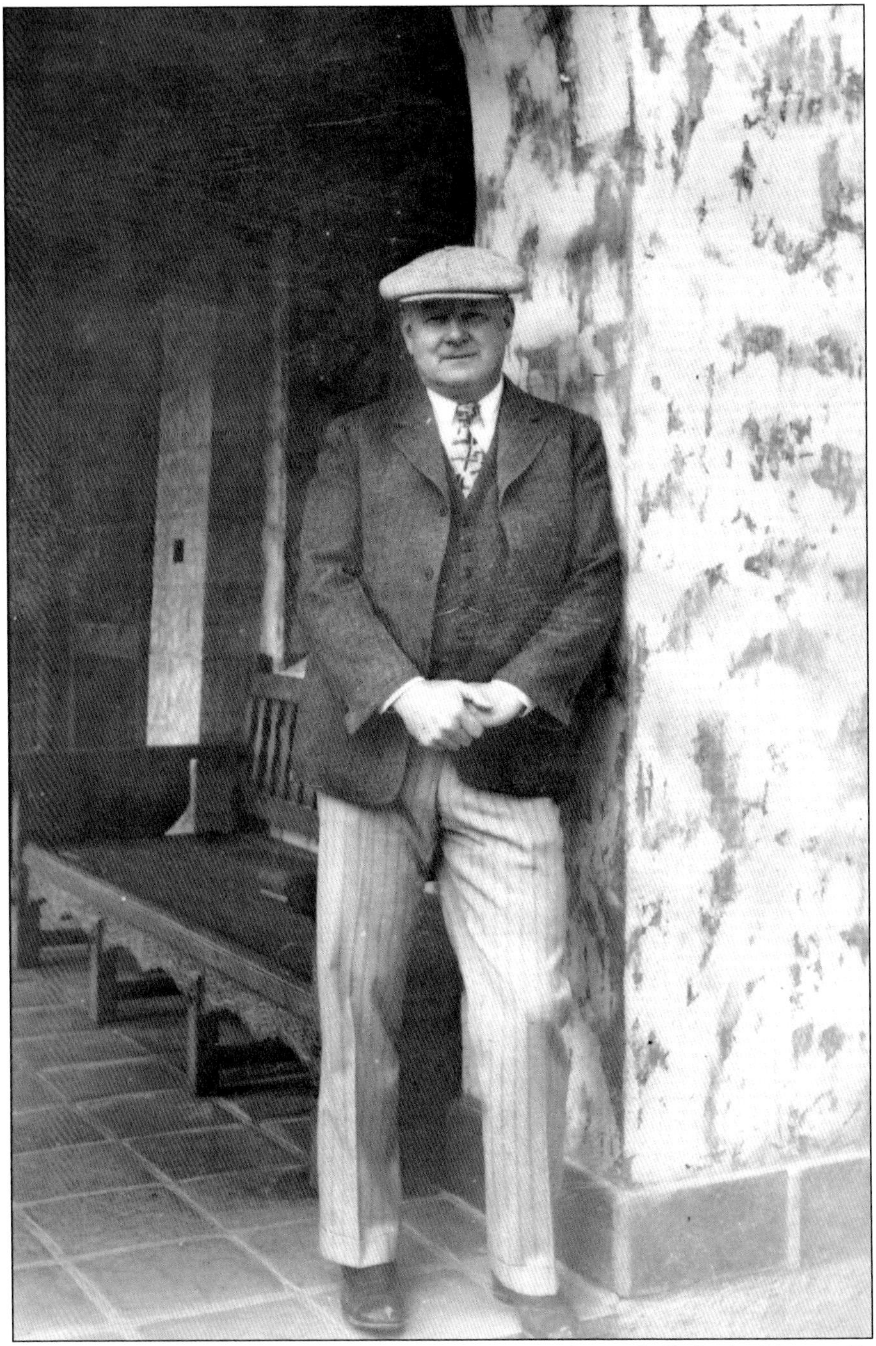

As engineer and master of construction, M.R. Thompson directed all the building in Regents Park (streets, water, and sewer systems) except for the construction of houses. Thompson, who was educated at Stanford, would return to the San Francisco area, working again with E.J. Bowes and J.H. Spring on the nationally recognized development Thousand Oaks. This photograph was taken at another famous project for which M.R. Thompson was engineer and head of construction: Scotty's Castle, also known as Death Valley Ranch, located in Death Valley National Park in California. (Courtesy of the National Park Service.)

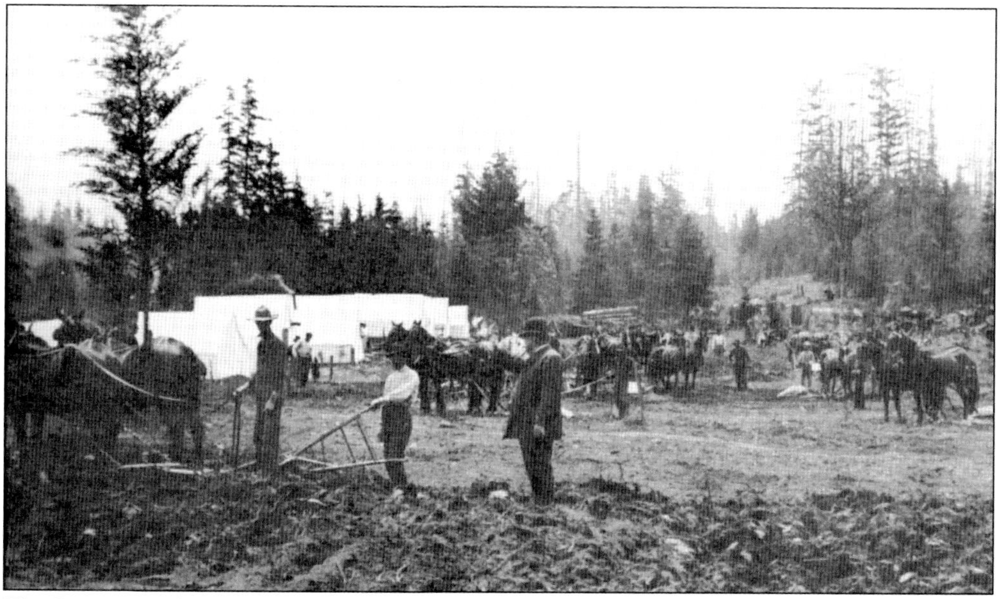

The Regents Park project began with clearing a space and building a tent city. A work camp of wood and canvas was put up to house the workers who surveyed and built the project's infrastructure systems, amenities, and landscape. Structures were also erected to house animals used in the construction. The vegetation seen in the background shows what the entire site looked like before clearing began. The first work camp was near the intersection of University Avenue (now Columbia Avenue) and Berkeley Avenue. (Courtesy of the City of Fircrest.)

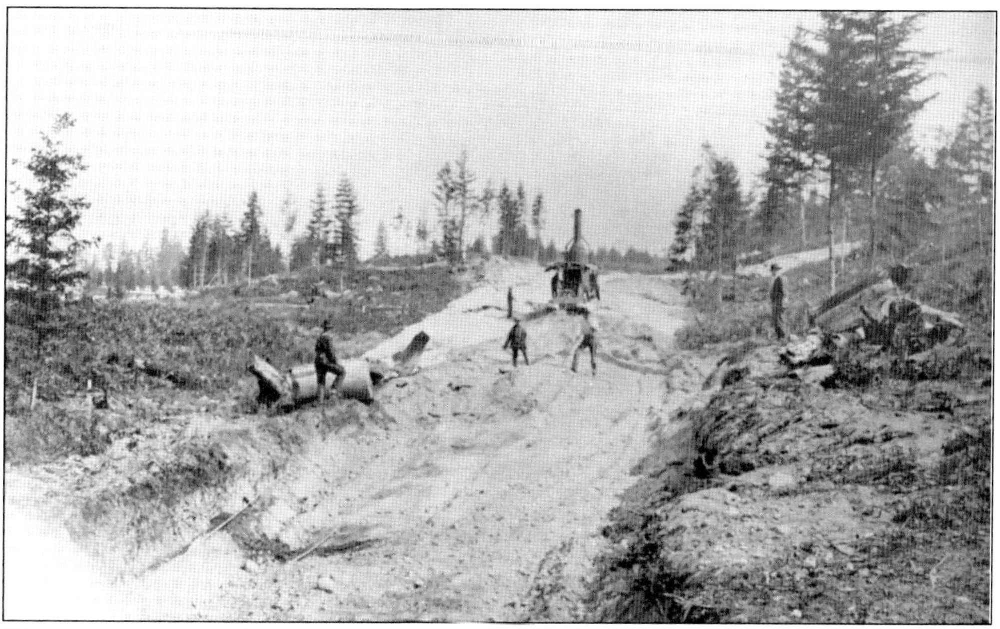

The survey crews set about measuring and setting stakes according to the plat maps of M.R. Thompson. This was followed by the clearing and grading of the streets. Here, a "steam donkey," a small steam engine mounted on a heavy timber sled, is used by a clearing crew to pull a stump with steel cables. The photograph's location is not known, but note the white lot stakes on the left, indicating lot lines. (Courtesy of the City of Fircrest.)

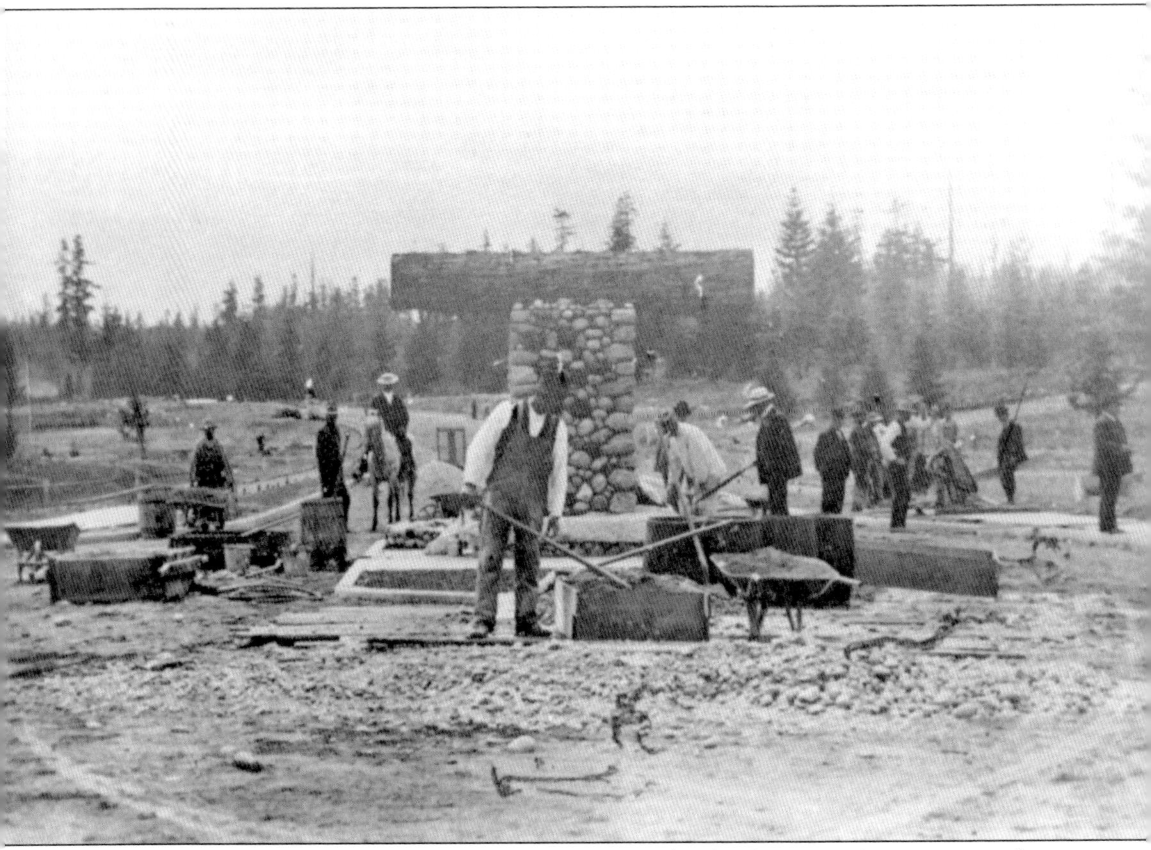

Visitors to the project watch as the first structures in the development, the entrance pylons at University Avenue (now Columbia Avenue), are being built. The rustic stone-and-log monuments were a popular architectural feature of the day. Note the fir trees dotting the landscape. A 1907 brochure from the Bowes-Irwin Company states, "Unlike other tracts of land that have been marketed in the City, instead of destroying the work of nature all desirable trees will be preserved so that every buyer will have his share of the beautiful park." (Courtesy of the City of Fircrest.)

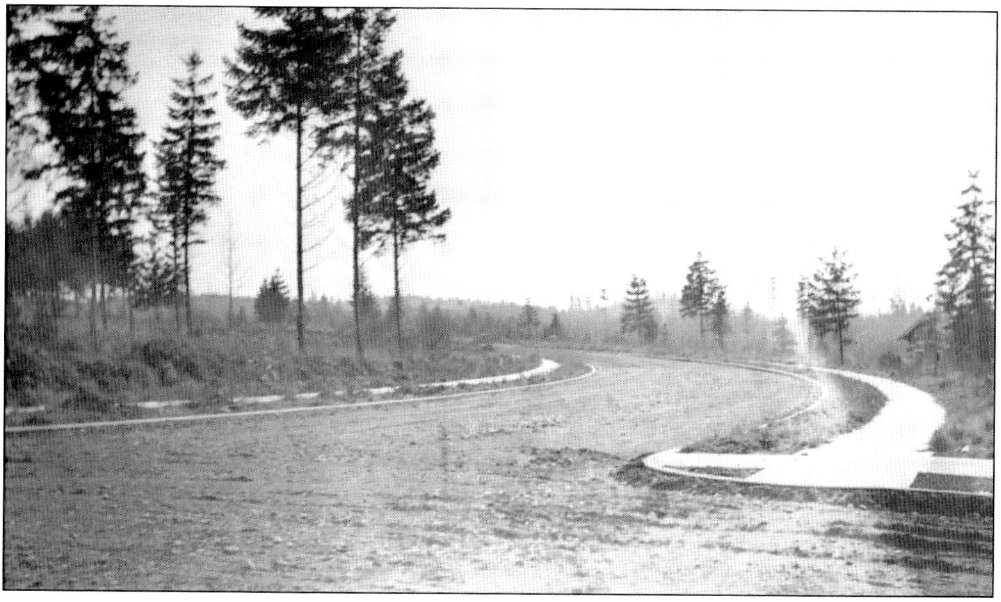

These c. 1910 photographs show Golden Gate Avenue from Summit Avenue (above) and Farallone Avenue, looking southwest from Harvard Avenue (below). The curvilinear streets and concrete curbs and sidewalks made Regents Park an innovative city plan at the time. (Both courtesy of the City of Fircrest.)

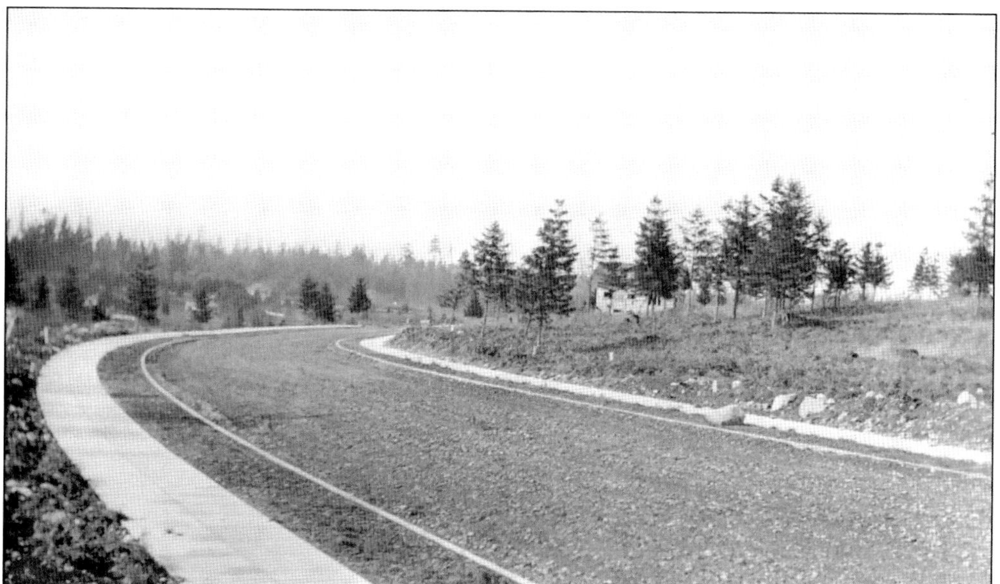

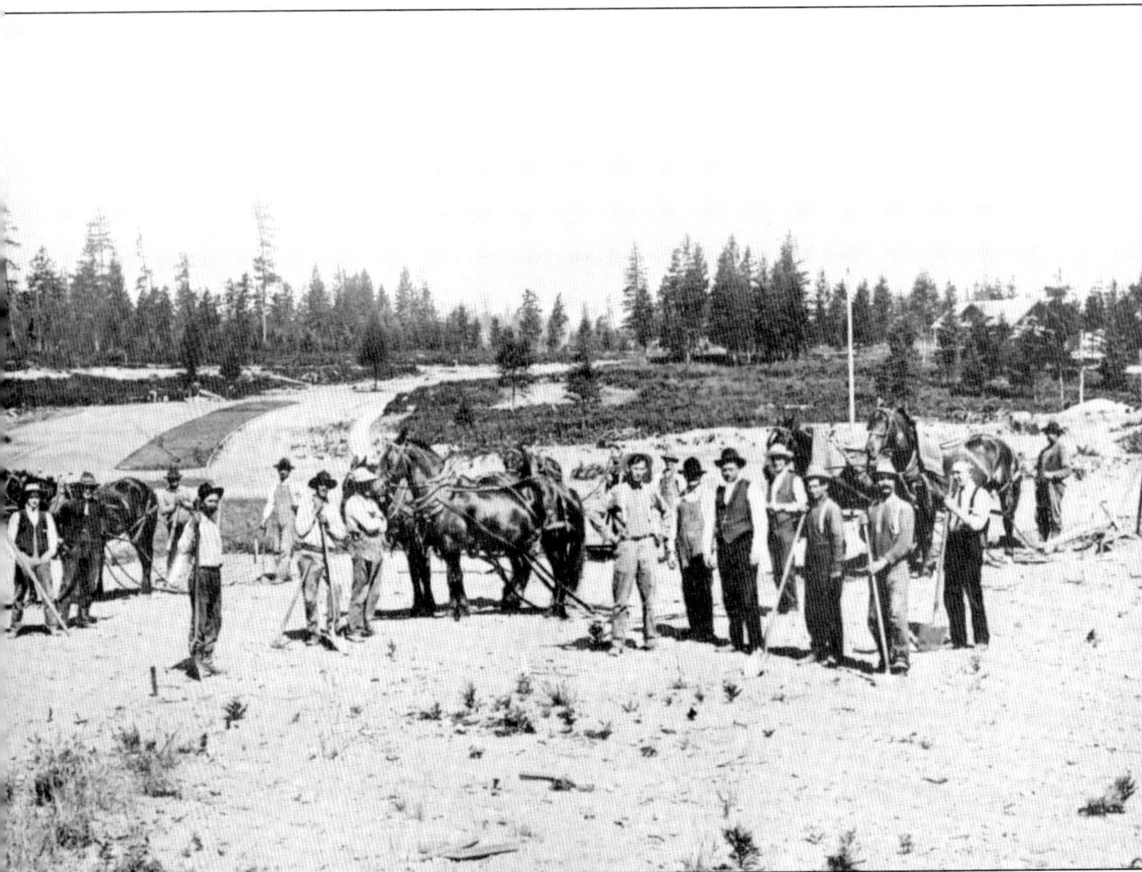

A survey crew and grading crew stop for a photograph at the intersection of Regents Boulevard and Contra Costa Avenue. The survey crew lays out Contra Costa, and the grading crew clears and grades the road. The west-facing photograph was taken from Regents Boulevard. Note the medians in the center of Regents. This feature denotes a boulevard, but Fircrest's medians have long since been replaced in favor of turning lanes. A classic boulevard no more, the name remains. (Courtesy of the City of Fircrest.)

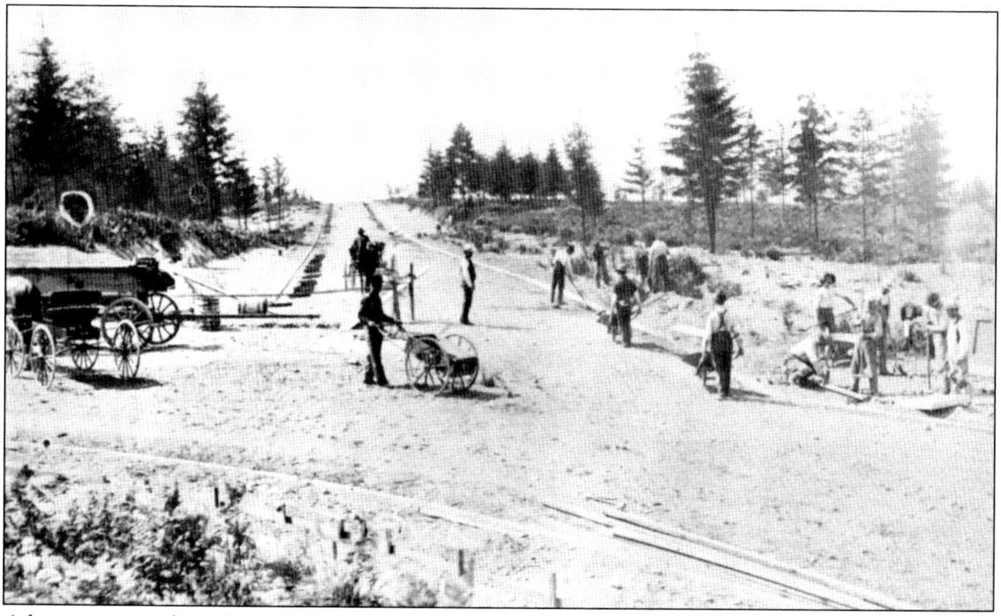

After survey and grading, the cement crews set the forms and poured cement for the street curb and sidewalk. This crew works on the crossing of University Way (now Columbia Avenue) and Summit Avenue. Note the wood water pipes lining the curbs of Summit Avenue. (Courtesy of the City of Fircrest.)

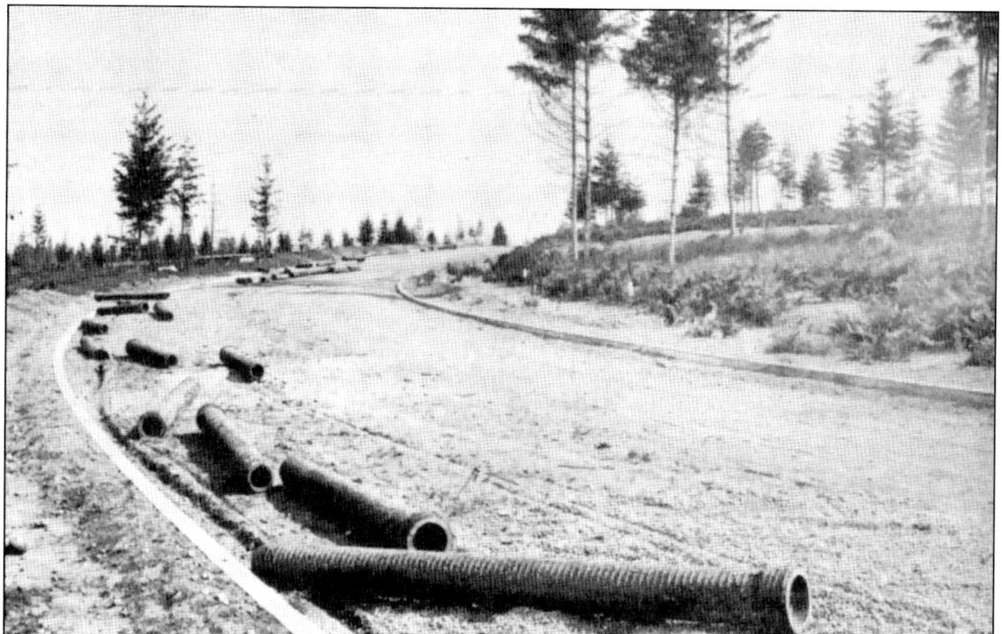

Wooden water pipes line Summit Avenue in 1907. The wooden pipes were a main component of the early infrastructure of Regents Park. During the lean years of the Great Depression, ruptured water mains were caulked and repaired multiple times. But, by the 1930s, they were in very poor shape. In 1935, Pres. Franklin Roosevelt and his WPA (Work Progress Administration) came to Fircrest's rescue. WPA workers uncovered and repaired neglected sidewalks and eventually replaced the wooden water lines with a new pipe system. (Courtesy of the City of Fircrest.)

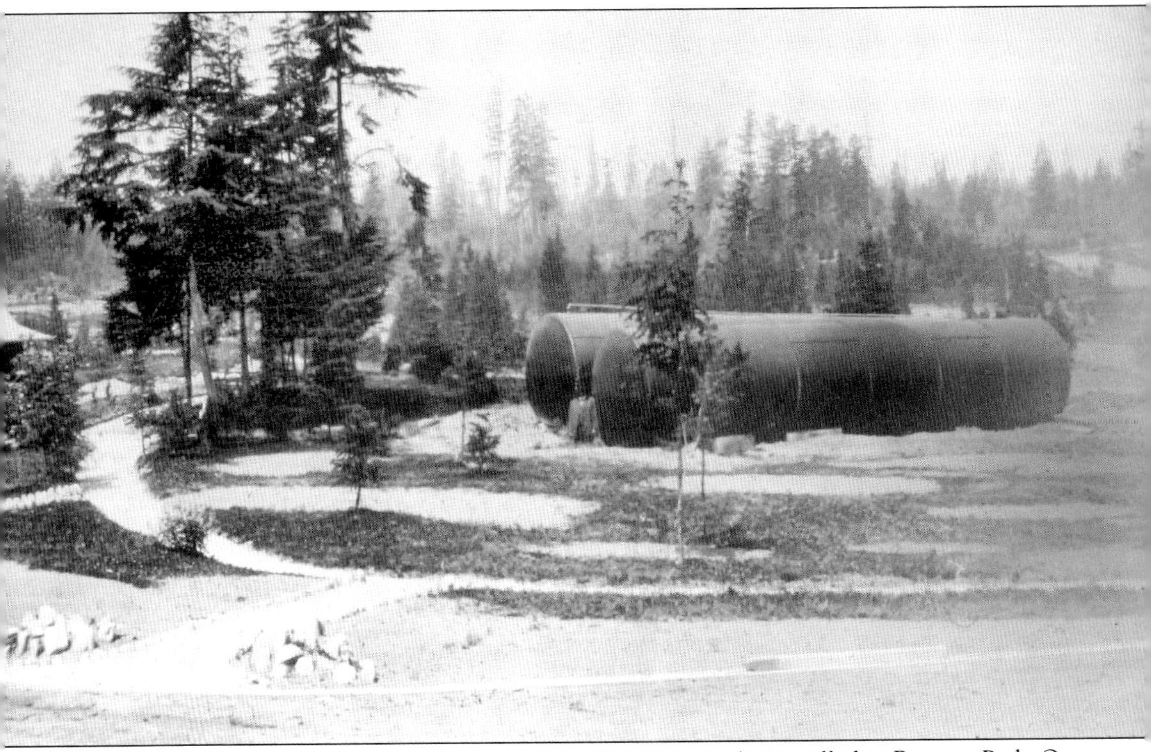

This early photograph shows two huge water tanks waiting to be installed in Regents Park. One of the things that made Regents Park such a desirable place to purchase a lot was the fact that the Narrows Land Company had invested in quality infrastructure: roads, sewers, and a water system. All of these amenities were included in the price of the lot. (Courtesy of the City of Fircrest.)

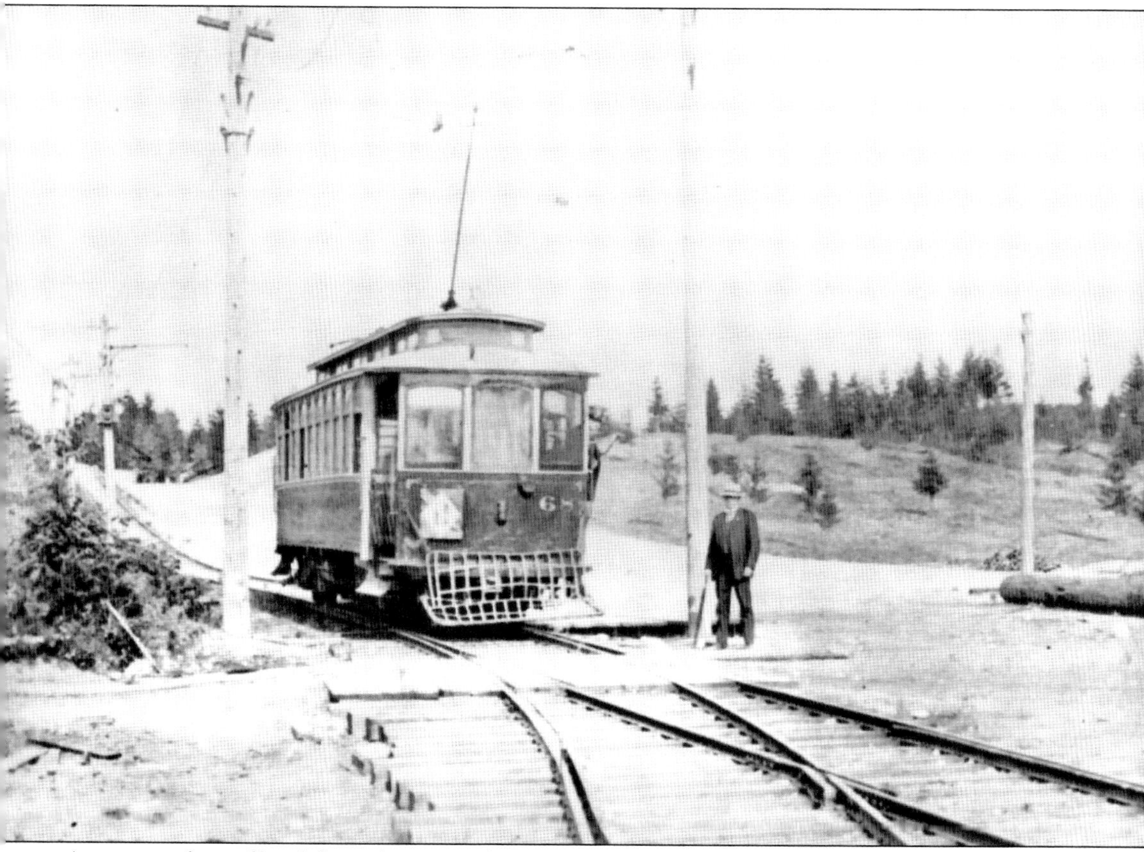

A streetcar line offered the only practical access to Regents Park. The line ran along University Avenue on the north side of the park. University Avenue is now Columbia Avenue on the Fircrest side and Nineteenth Avenue on the Tacoma side. The streetcar service, known as the "traction line," was notoriously unreliable. This photograph was taken from the intersection of Contra Costa Avenue, looking east toward Tacoma. The gentleman in the straw hat is Beecher McKenzie, who owned a large house that still stands on the corner of Columbia and Alameda Avenues. (Courtesy of the City of Fircrest.)

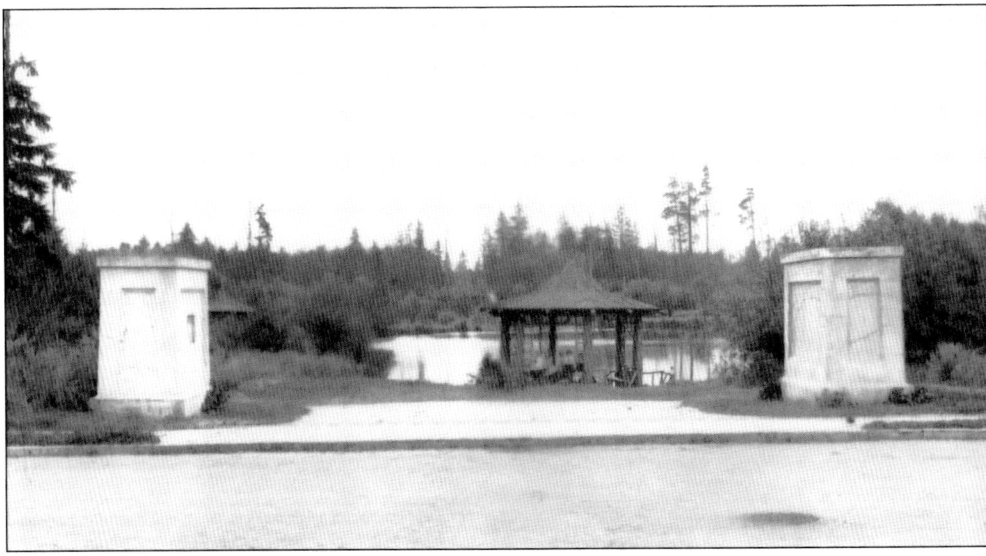

In the first year of the development, over $350,000 was spent on improvements. Along with infrastructure features, including roads, sewers, and waterlines, a relatively large amount of money was spent on beautification. Shown above is the entry to Spring Lake. Concrete monuments stand on either side of the main entry. The lake's stick-and-log pavilion can be seen between the monuments. Below, concrete pedestals with urns flank the main entry into Regents Park. Golden Gate Avenue stretches into the distance. (Above, courtesy of the Tacoma Public Library Boland-B1985; below, the City of Fircrest.)

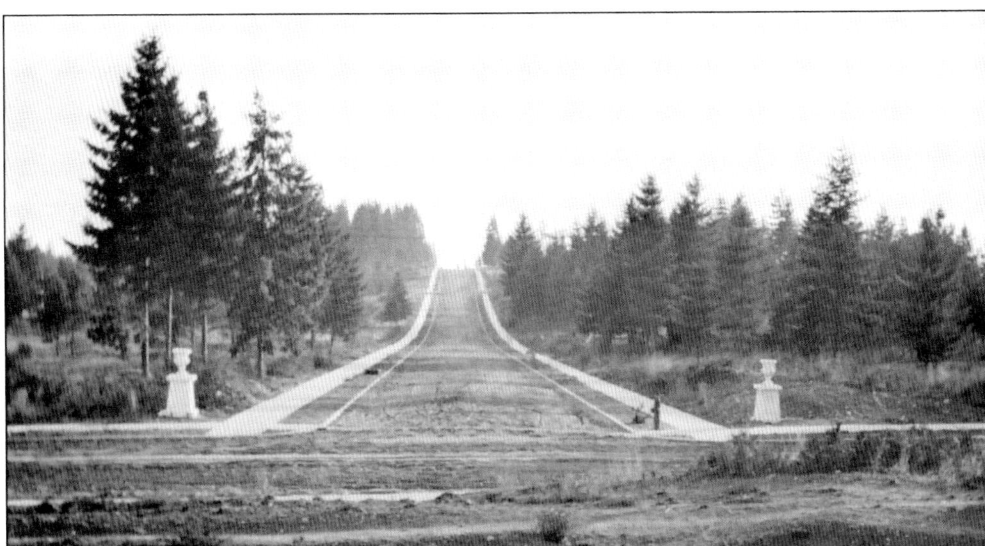

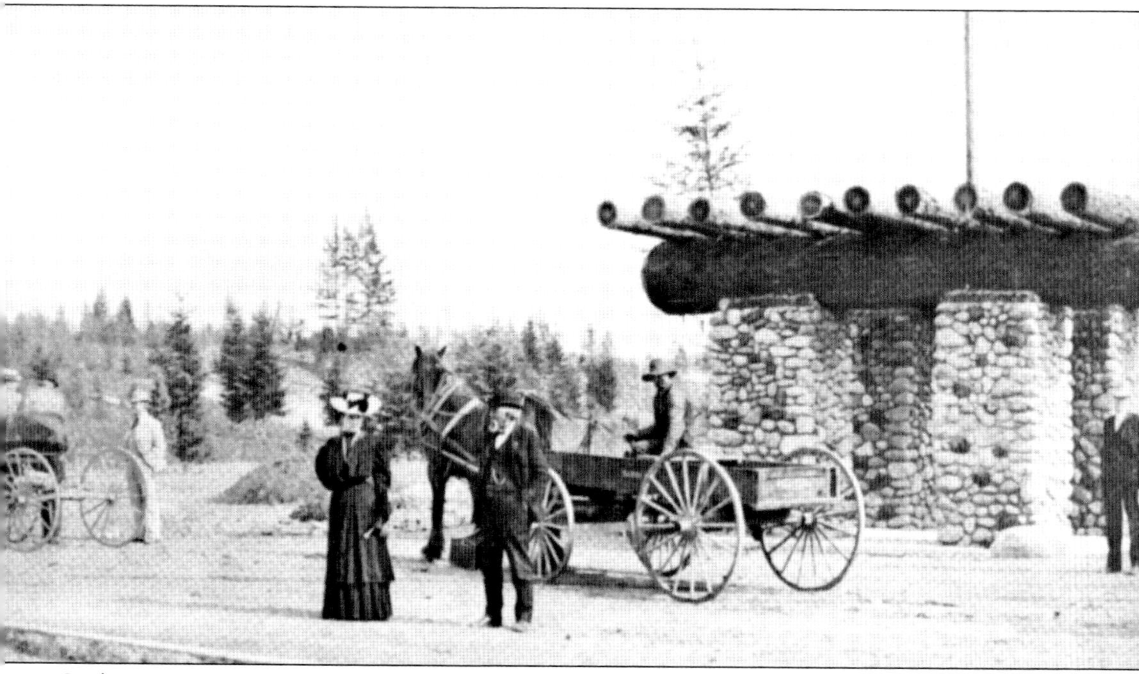

In the 1910s, the main entrance to Regents Park was located at the intersection of Berkeley Avenue and University Way (now Columbia Avenue). This was the main stop of the traction line streetcar. It was here that the developers concentrated their beautification efforts. This 1909 photograph shows the pylons, workmen, wagons, and visitors. (Courtesy of the City of Fircrest.)

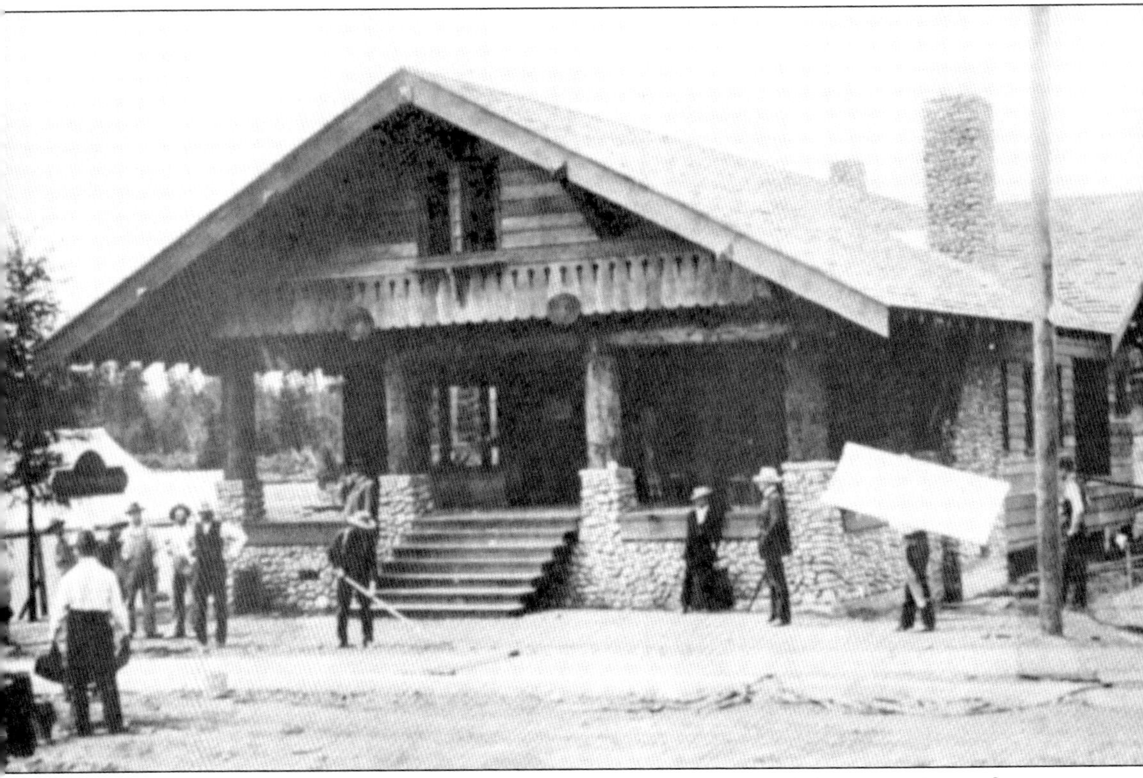

On the southwest corner of Columbia and Berkeley Avenues stood the Bowes-Irwin Company office and showroom, seen here during construction. It is interesting to note that the stereotypical architecture of rustic, heavy timber construction associated with the Pacific Northwest contradicts the forward-looking civil engineering of the streets and lots of Regents Park. Unfortunately, this building, then the Names family home, burned down around 1936. (Courtesy of the City of Fircrest.)

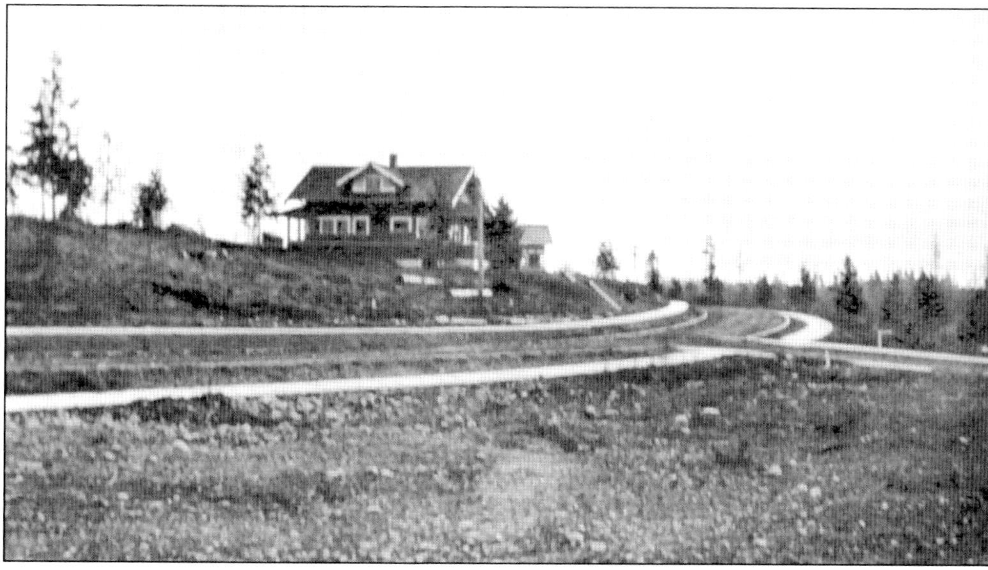

A 1907 advertisement brochure, printed by the Bowes-Irwin Company, seems to describe these photographs perfectly: "The land is of a rolling character; the streets are laid out with easy grade, affording views of Mt. Tahoma and the Olympic Range. Aside from this unrivaled view, Regents Park has surplus of all other elements of attractiveness, its own virgin beauty is heightened by the picturesque environment, and while located within a few minutes of the business center, it is far enough away from the manufacturing industries to preserve that purity of air which counts for so much in a distinctly residential district." (Both courtesy of the City of Fircrest.)

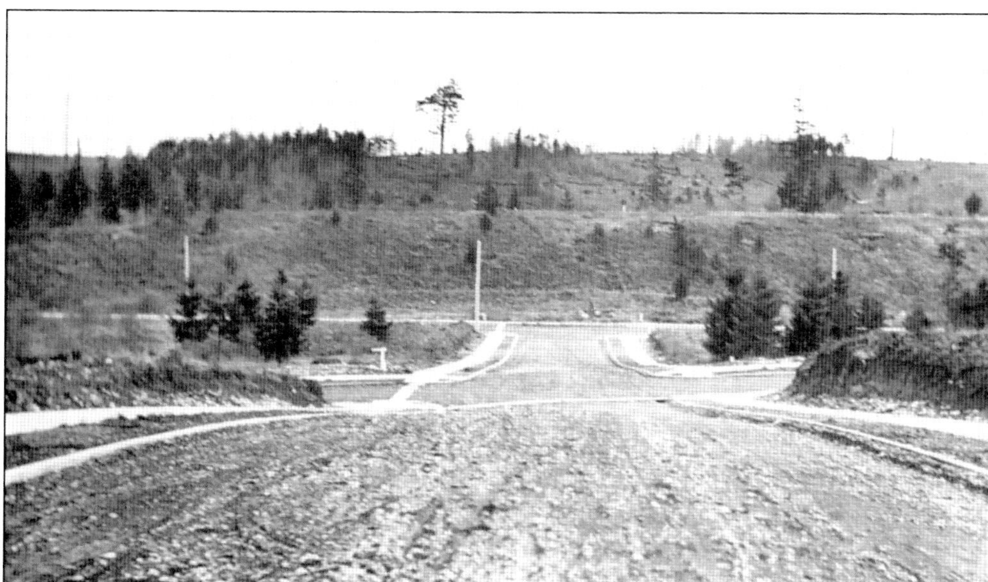

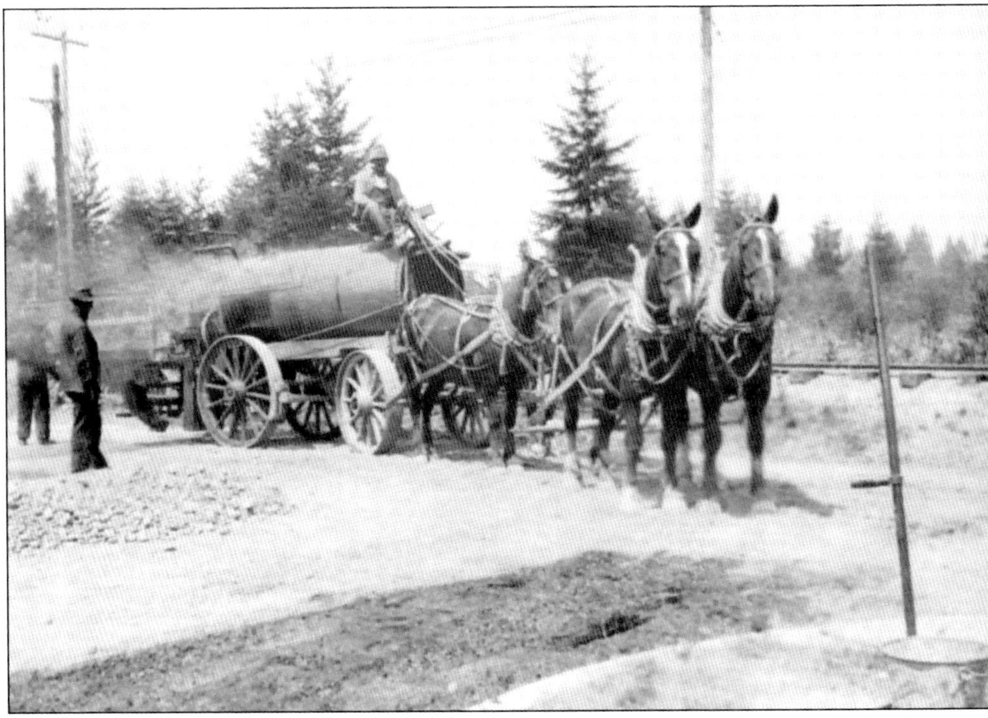

These images show the process used to oil the streets in preparation for liquid asphalt, which was promised to be used on all avenues and boulevards. Streets, sewers, and water mains were supposed to be supplied to every homeowner at no additional cost. Horses were used throughout the early development of Regents Park. They were stabled at the Bowes-Irwin Company office complex. It is interesting to note that during World War I horses were again stabled at this site and used for training by the National Guard. Fircrest children were often given the job of currying the horses. In exchange, they were allowed to ride the horses along the lanes of Regents Park. (Both courtesy of the City of Fircrest.)

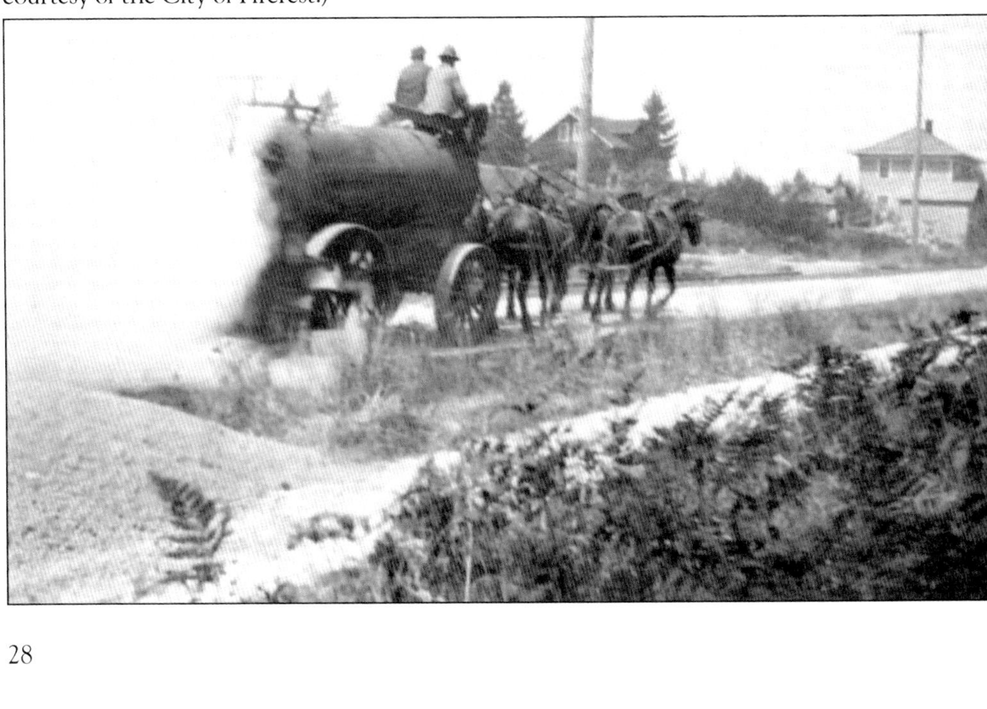

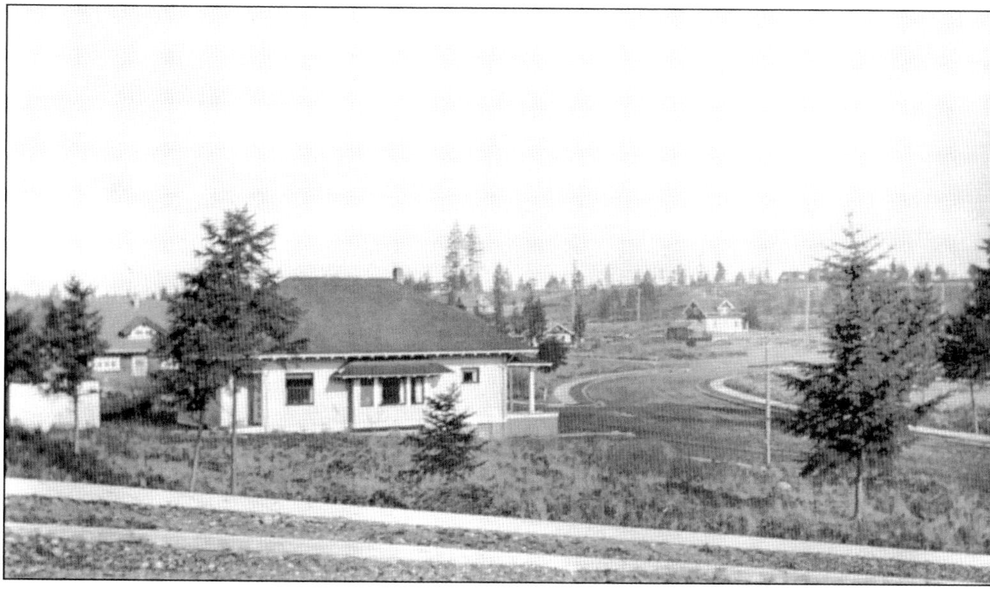

Even as the initial fervor slowed, homes began to dot the development. The photograph above shows Farallone Avenue looking southwest from Harvard Avenue. In the upper left is Spring Lake and Park. The image below shows Contra Costa Avenue as it looked in 1915. It was taken from the intersection of Princeton Street looking south. (Both courtesy of the City of Fircrest.)

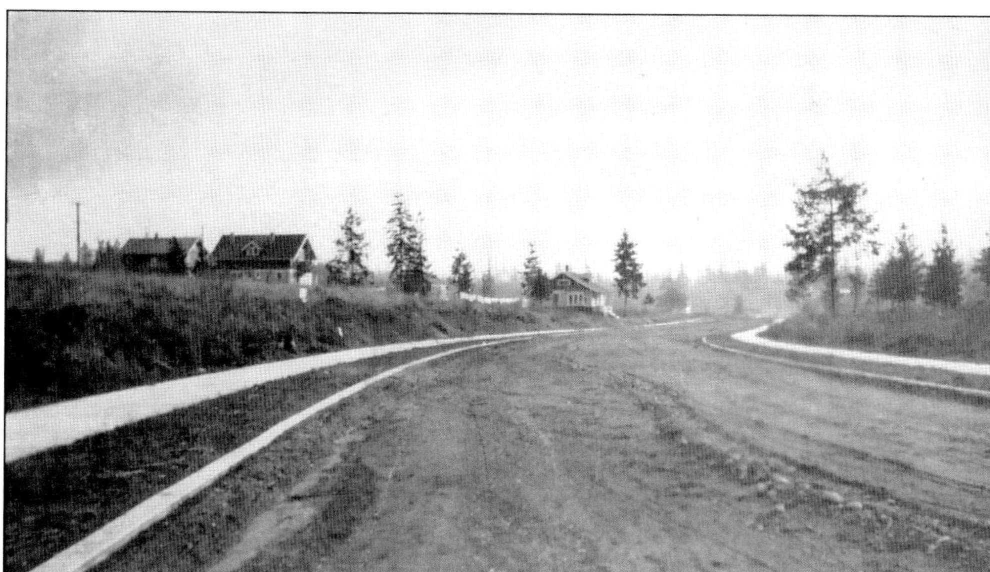

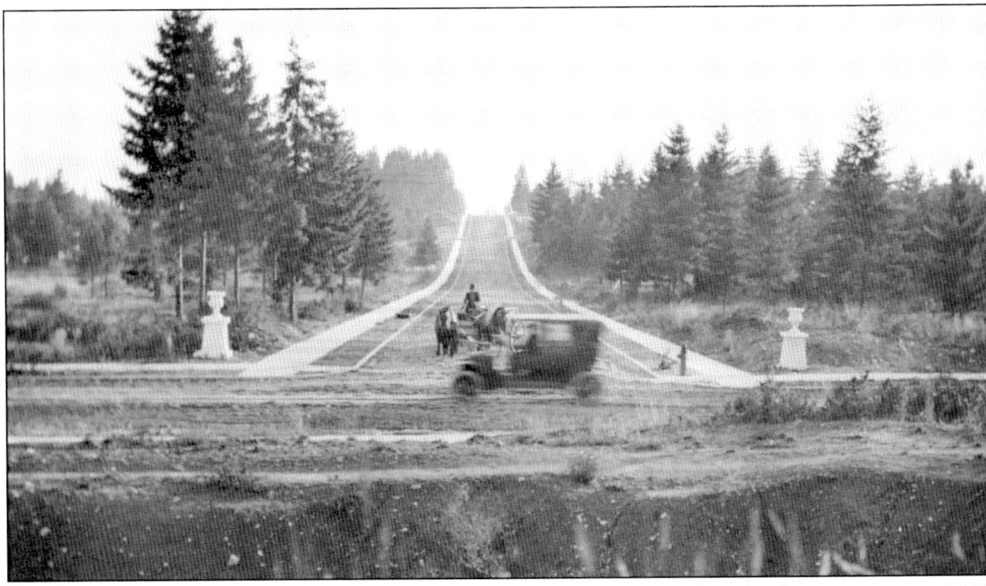

The past and the future intersect at the corner of Golden Gate and Columbia Avenues in 1912. The camera clearly captures the 19th-century mode of transportation of the horse-drawn wagon, but the photographic technology cannot contend with the speed of 20th-century transportation; the automobile is moving too fast to be captured in focus. (Courtesy of the City of Fircrest.)

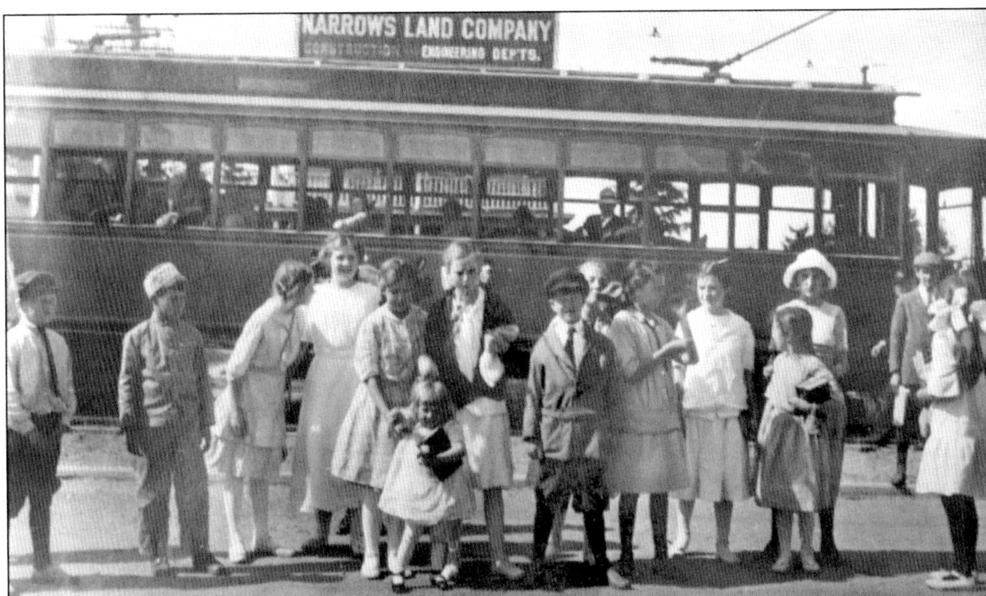

The streetcar trolley depot was located at the intersection of Columbia and Berkeley Avenues and featured a covered waiting area and benches. Children would ride the trolley to and from their schools in Tacoma. The main line went to Tacoma, but some streetcars also left the Regents Park depot and traveled to Steilacoom. The average pay for conductors at this time was 30¢ an hour. Across the street from the depot, visible in the background, is the two-story office building of the Narrows Land Company. (Courtesy of the City of Fircrest.)

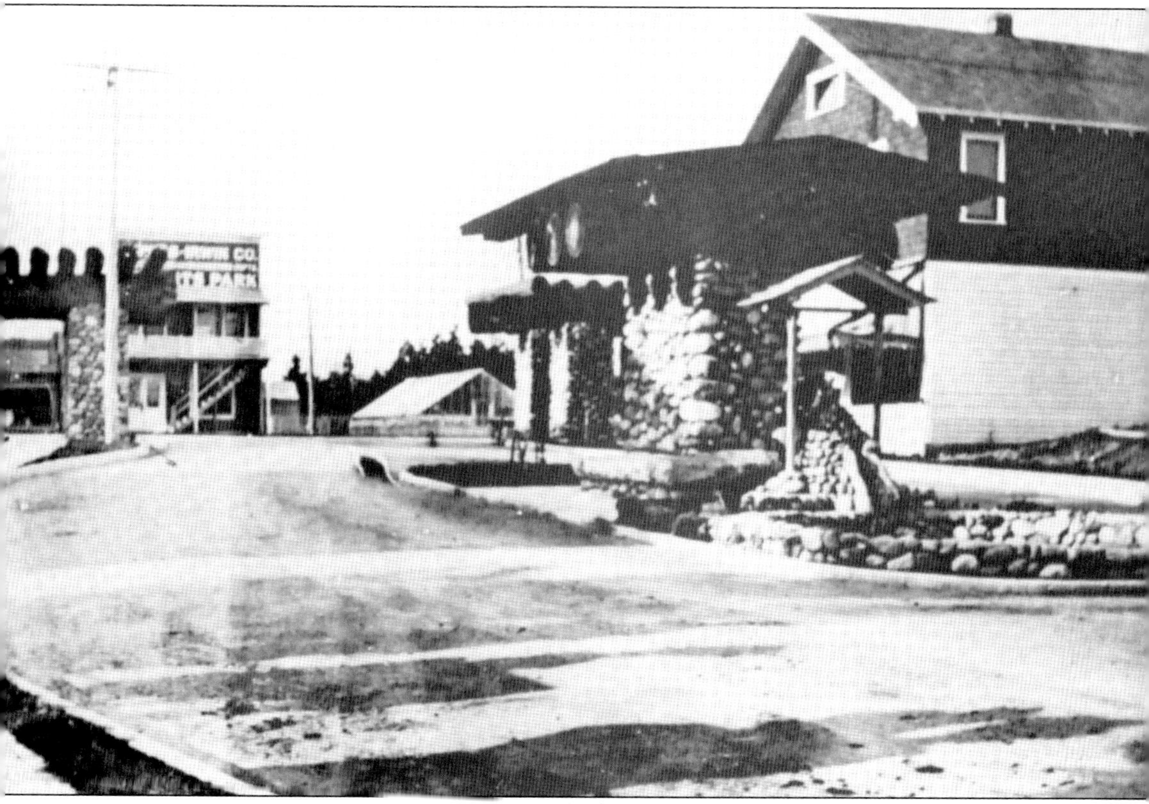

The main entry to Regents Park in 1909 stood where Berkeley Avenue runs into Columbia Avenue. On the far (north) side of Columbia Avenue stands the two-story Bowes-Irwin Company building, with its greenhouse left of center. The building on the right is Stephens Grocery, later Mclean's. Some of the beautification structures, seen in the right foreground, are, from left to right, the entry pylons, a wishing well, and the fishpond. A Bowes-Irwin advertisement brochure in 1907 reads, "At the main entrances and driveways stone pillars are being erected as designed by the well-known artist Mr. W.H. Bull of San Mateo, California, materially adding to its beauty." The grandeur of Regents Park was also enhanced by the design and construction of several large urns and two lion statues. The urns were designed to hold flowers to grace the development's entrance. Sadly, the lions did not survive for long and soon fell into rubble. John Gutzon Borglum was commissioned to create these statuaries, which were constructed on-site. Borglum went on to become a world-renowned sculptor and painter, best known for creating the presidential carvings on Mount Rushmore. (Courtesy of the City of Fircrest.)

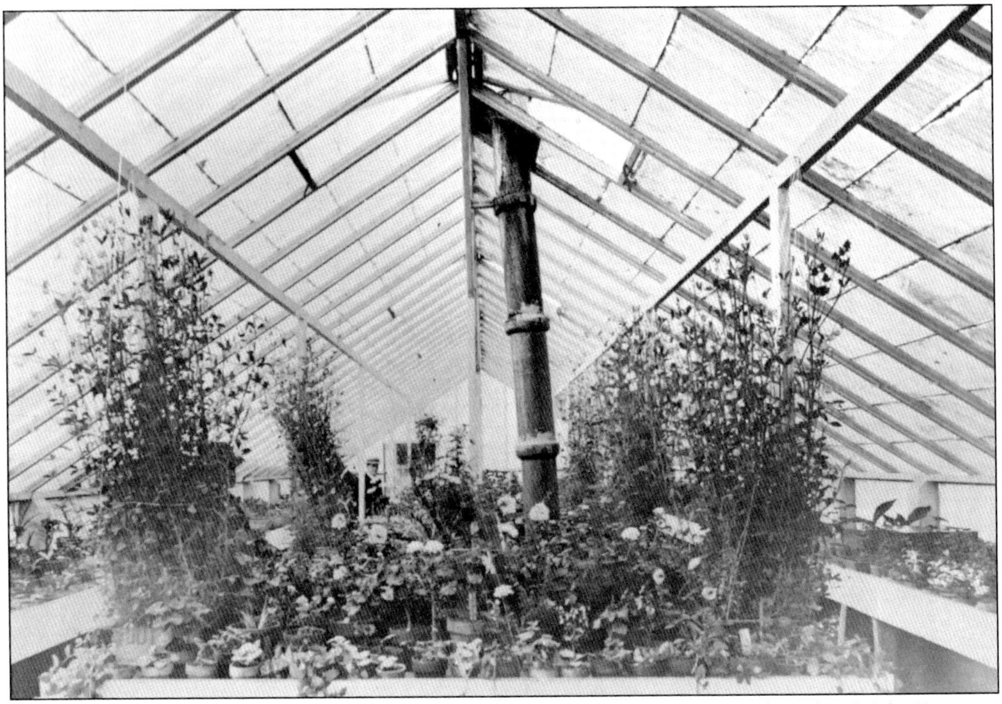

A Bowes-Irwin publication proclaimed, "Nature, Art and Enterprise Combined to Make Regents Park the Place to Live!" This greenhouse, built next to the Bowes-Irwin business office on Columbia and Berkeley Avenues, nurtured the flowers and plants used for landscaping to enhance the natural beauty of Regents Park. Each major roadway was lined with a different variety of ornamental tree. (Courtesy of the City of Fircrest.)

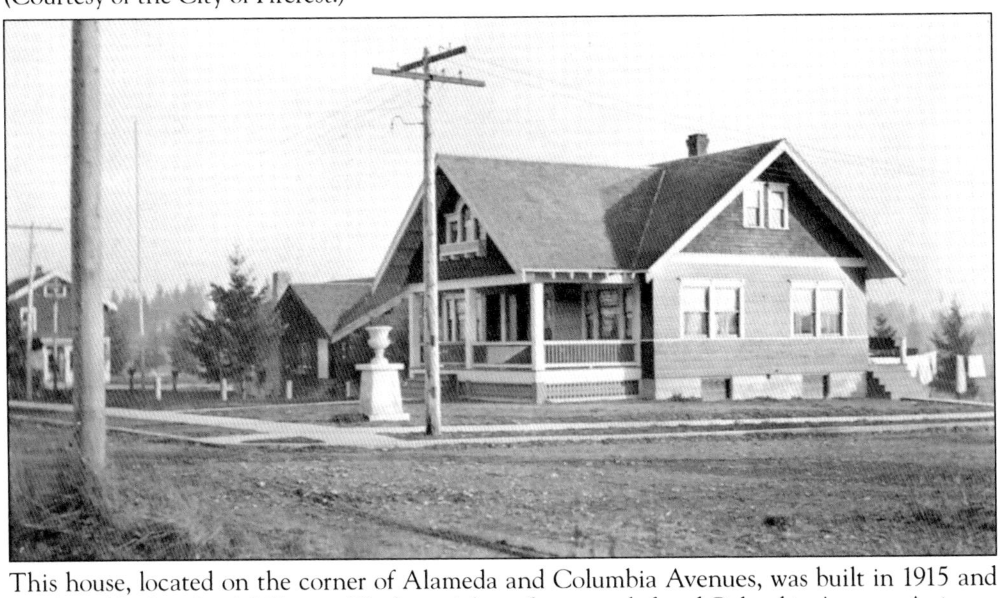

This house, located on the corner of Alameda and Columbia Avenues, was built in 1915 and purchased by Beecher McKenzie. The house's large front porch faced Columbia Avenue. As it was near the streetcar depot, many travelers would stop at the McKenzie house and leave their wagons and buggies while they rode the trolley to downtown Tacoma. Upon their return, they would pick up their vehicles and travel the rest of the way home on foot. (Courtesy of the City of Fircrest.)

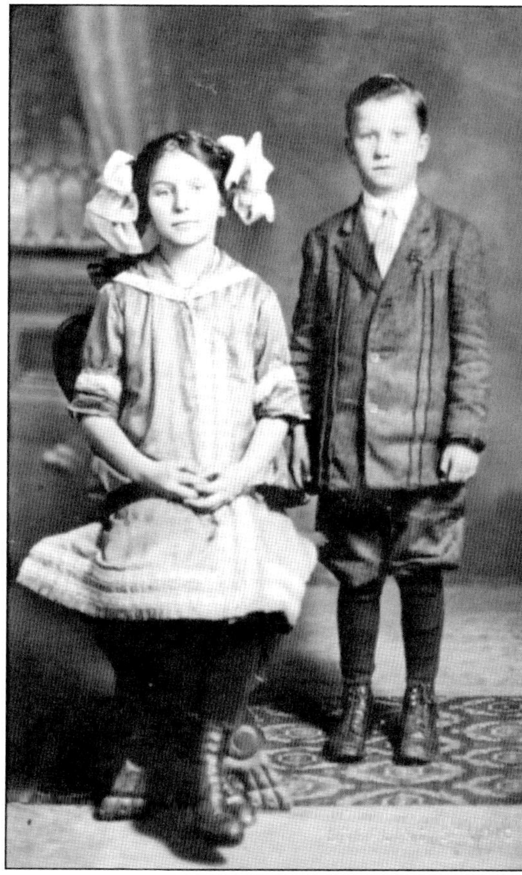

Early residents of Regents Park included Elsie and Charlie Mason, at right, in 1910. They were the children of Cap'n Mason, one of the park's early builders. Below, Francis Marion Stephens stands in front of his store. The Stephens Store, located on University (Nineteenth Street) and Berkeley Avenues, was the only store in the area at the time. It carried hardware items, groceries, meat, and vegetables. In the summer, Francis Stephens opened a "tent" store in present-day University Place. He gave control of his Regents Park store to his son. By 1912, business had diminished to the point that the store could no longer afford to operate. (Both courtesy of the City of Fircrest.)

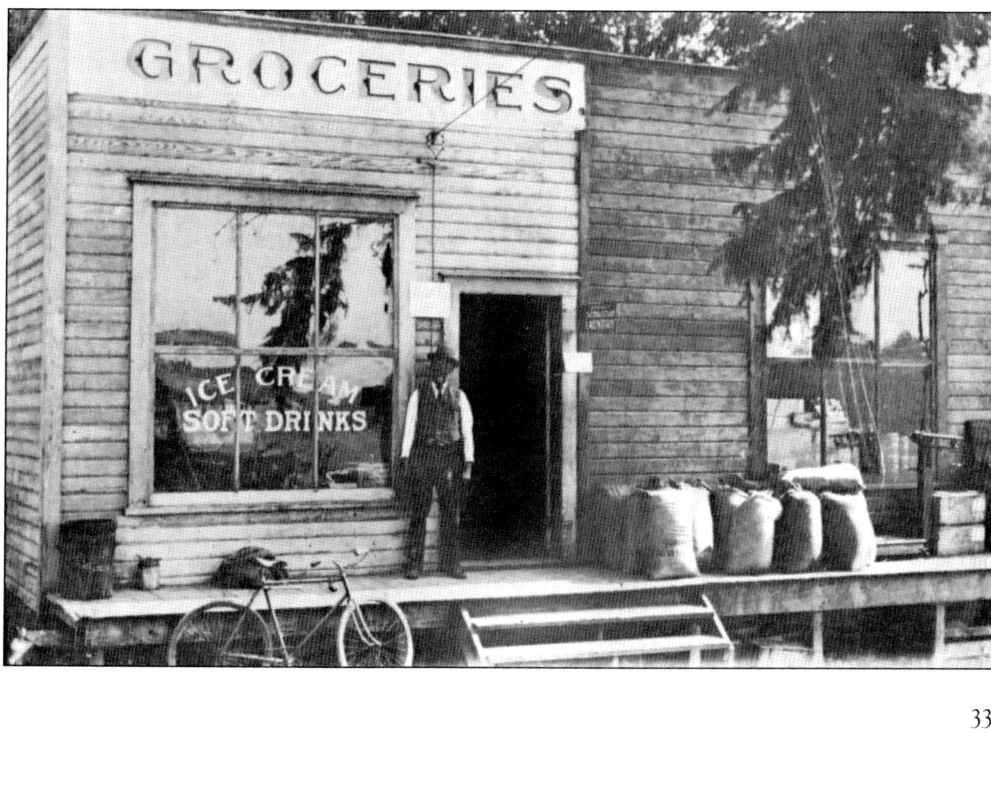

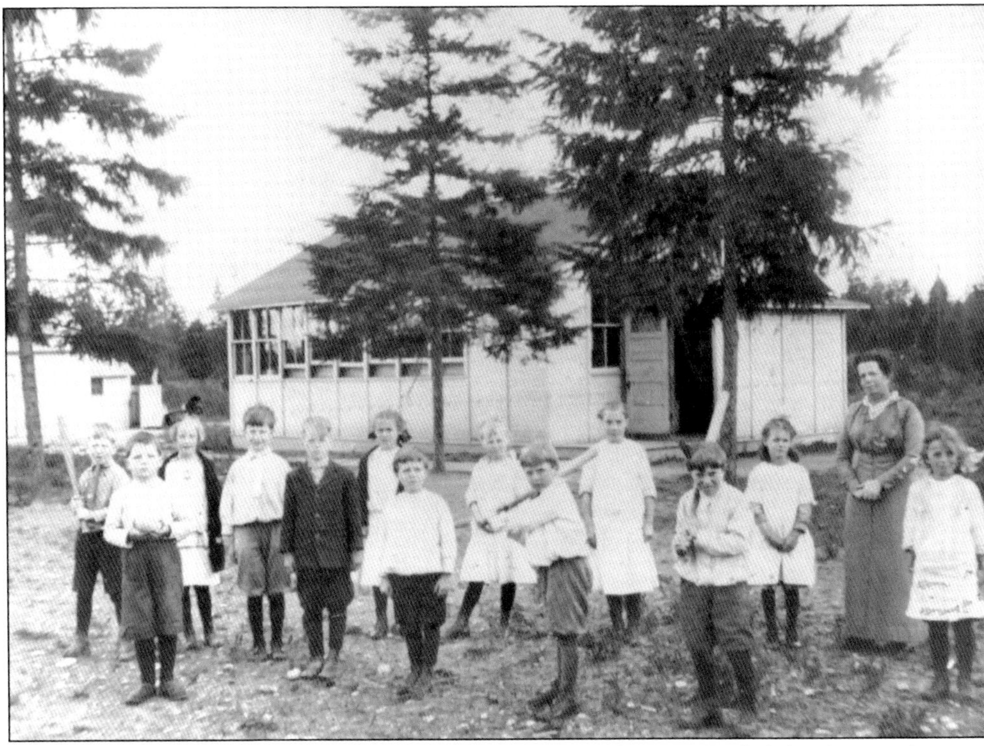

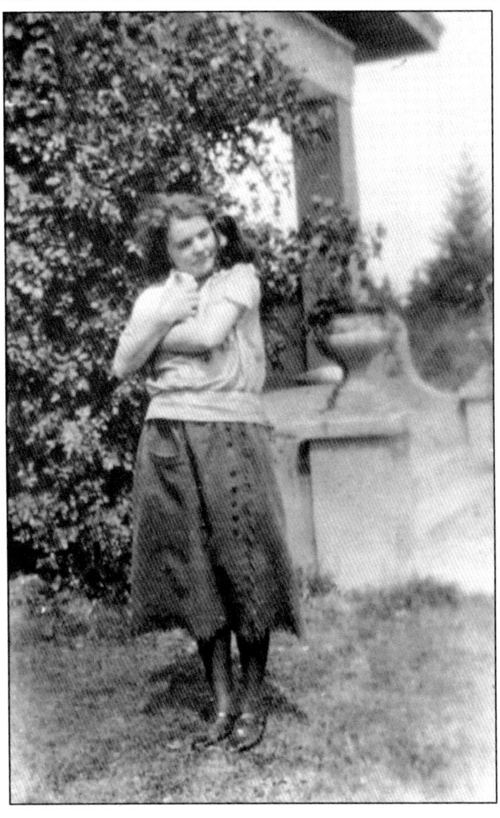

In 1911, Regents Park School, seen above, opened on the grounds of what is now Wainwright Elementary. It was a small, portable building with a potbellied stove and outdoor restroom facilities. Children in grades one through three attended this school, which was operated by one teacher. Upon completion of third grade, students had to commute to other schools far beyond the boundaries of Regents Park. This school remained in use until 1924, when the Tacoma School District voted to build a new school on the property. The new brick building boasted three rooms, one for primary instruction, one for intermediate classes, and one dedicated as the lunchroom/kitchen. The children pictured are, from left to right, John Pierce, Ted Frace, Mildred Beal, Charles Mason, Clifford Frace, Florence Wiley, Joe Baker, Carmen Rogers, Oren Peers, Ellen Washburn, Arthur Bunny Gammon, Arnie McDougal, Mrs. Bell (teacher), and W. Moore. At left, Margaret Wight poses in 1923 with a couple of kittens in front of her family home on Contra Costa Avenue and Spring Street. (Both courtesy of the City of Fircrest.)

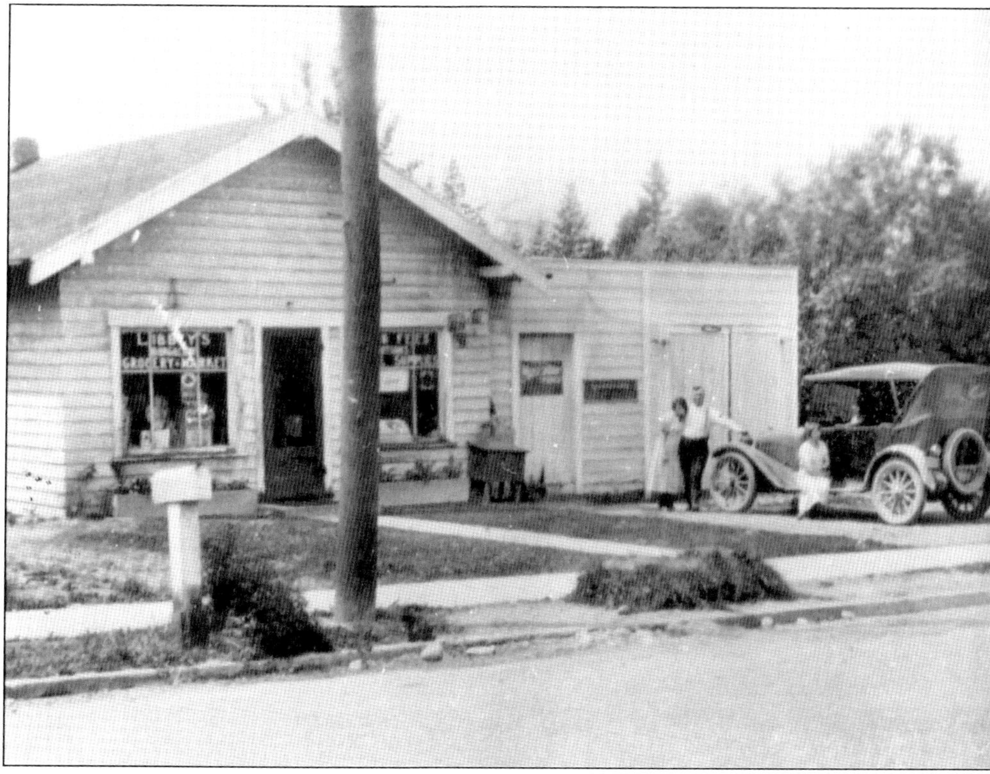

This store, at 220 Farallone Avenue, was originally established by Mr. Hodahi. At the time of this 1924 photograph, however, it was run by the Earl Libbey family and was known as the Libbey Store. Other shopping options included the old Stephens Grocery, which had been reopened by the McLean family. (Courtesy of the City of Fircrest.)

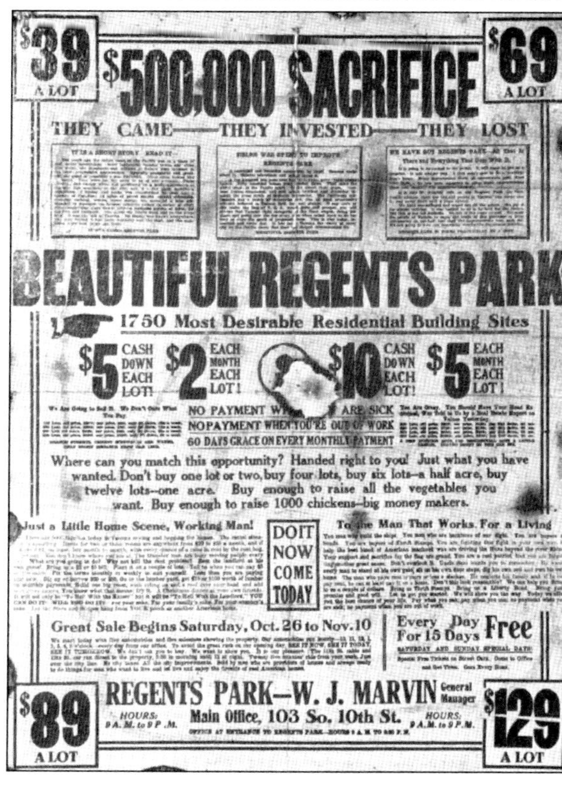

With the end of World War I, there was renewed interest in real estate and land development. Advertisements hit the newspapers and trade papers, professing the glories of buying property in "Beautiful Regents Park." The small print reads, "Where can you match this opportunity? Handed right to you? Just what you have wanted. Don't buy one lot or two, buy four lots, buy six lots." (Courtesy of the City of Fircrest.)

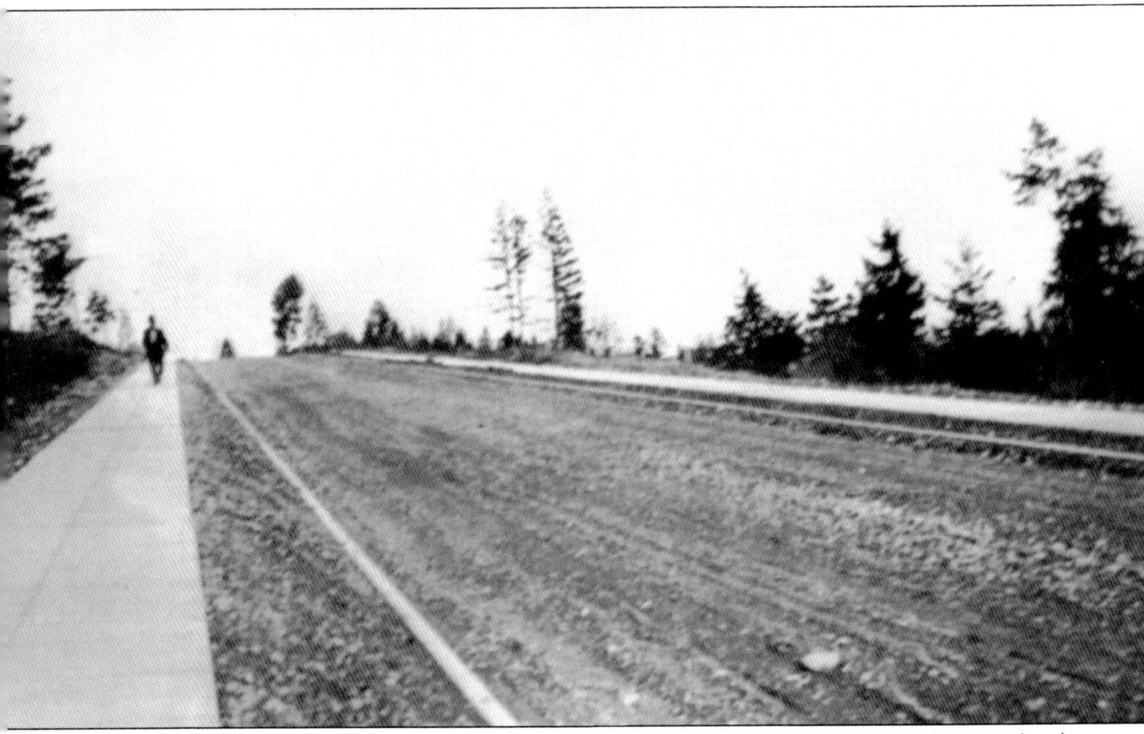

A solitary figure walks north along Farallone Avenue toward University Way (now Columbia Avenue). At the time of this photograph, the developer had laid sewers and waterlines, graded the streets, and poured concrete curbs and sidewalks, but the asphalt road had not yet been laid. It would be the lot owner's responsibility to plant grass. (Courtesy of the City of Fircrest.)

Two

A Round of Golf

From the beginning, Edward Bowes's vision for Regents Park included a golf course, and he set aside land on the development's west side for this purpose. Even though Bowes divested himself of any interest long before, the land he set aside was still available when residents, led by Sydney "Syd" Anderson, formed Fircrest Golf Club in 1922. Its initial members were Anderson, Earl C. Reynolds, Frank C. Neal, W.B. Stephens, J.A. McLeod, Russell Barlow, and Harry Mathews. The club incorporated in May 1923, and the first nine holes opened for play on July 26, 1924. At 1:00 p.m. on a beautiful Saturday, the first ball was struck. The first foursome to tee off was made up of Anderson (club president), Reynolds (vice president), McLeod (secretary), and Stephens (chairman of the building committee).

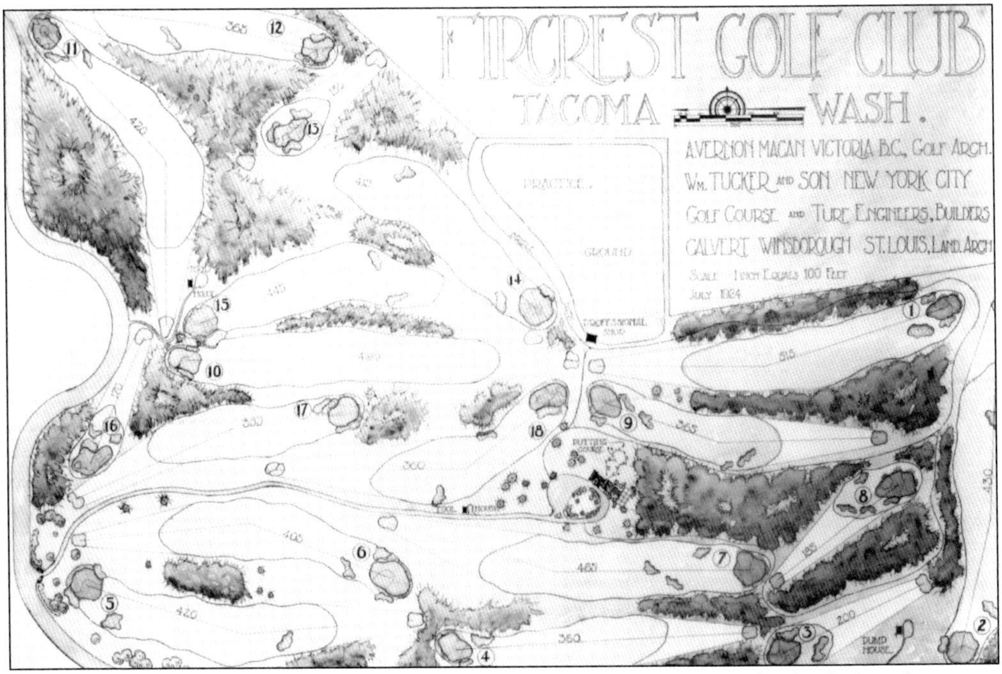

The map of Fircrest Golf Club seen above was on display on July 25, 1924, the day before the course opened for the first time. It includes hole lengths and the locations of the clubhouse, practice field, and pro shop. Although this rendering of the 165-acre site shows 18 holes, the course would open with only nine holes completed. Designed by A. Vernon Macan of Victoria, British Columbia, the course measured 6,455 yards with a par of 70. Below, four golfers, accompanied by their caddies, play a round of golf in August 1925. By that year, these golfers were able to play a full 18 holes. Sand traps and rolling ground made the course a challenge for the members. (Both courtesy of the Tacoma Public Library: above, Boland-B10566; below, Boland-B13197.)

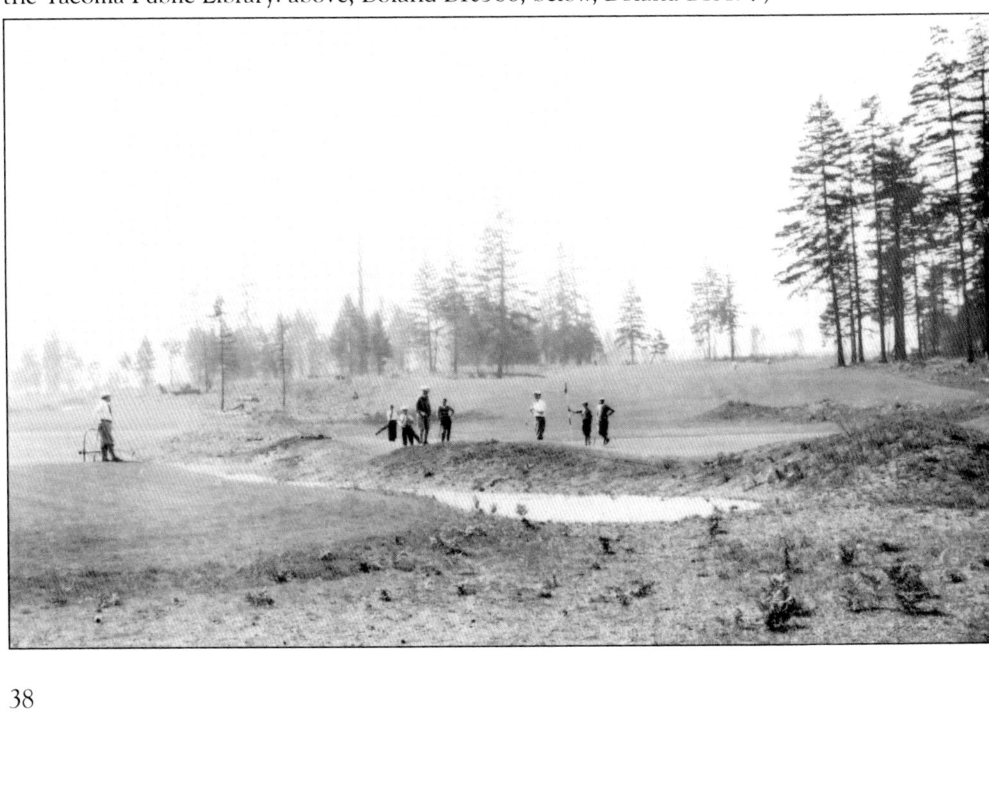

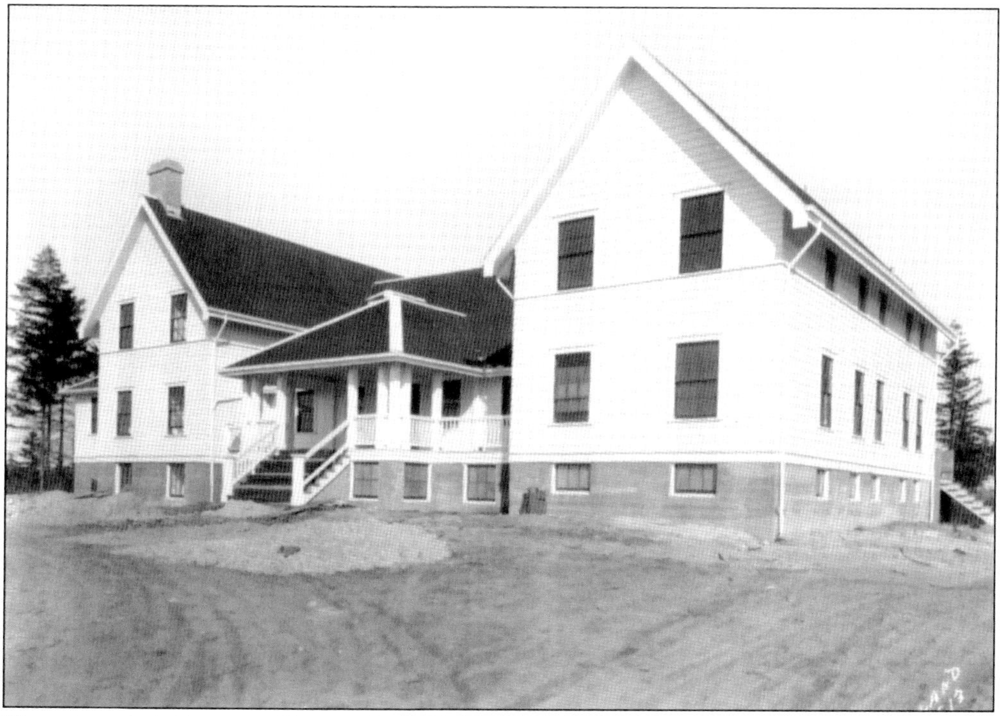

The original clubhouse at Fircrest Golf Club was nearly complete when the above photograph was taken six days before the first nine holes opened on July 26, 1924. Regents Park resident George Turnbull, who had learned golf in Scotland, was named the institution's first club pro. Even though the clubhouse was yet to open, there were 100 lockers ready and waiting for those who wanted them. Tacoma lumberman Leonard Howarth generously donated $30,000 for the construction of the clubhouse and other improvements. (Both courtesy of the Tacoma Public Library: above, Boland-B10513; below, Boland-A7137.)

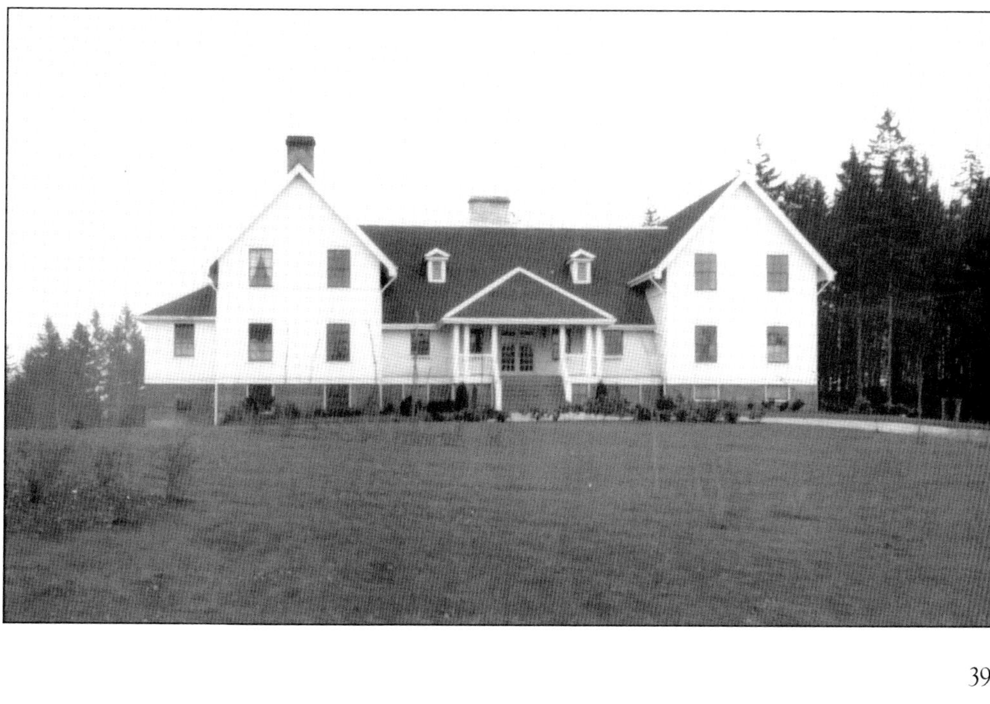

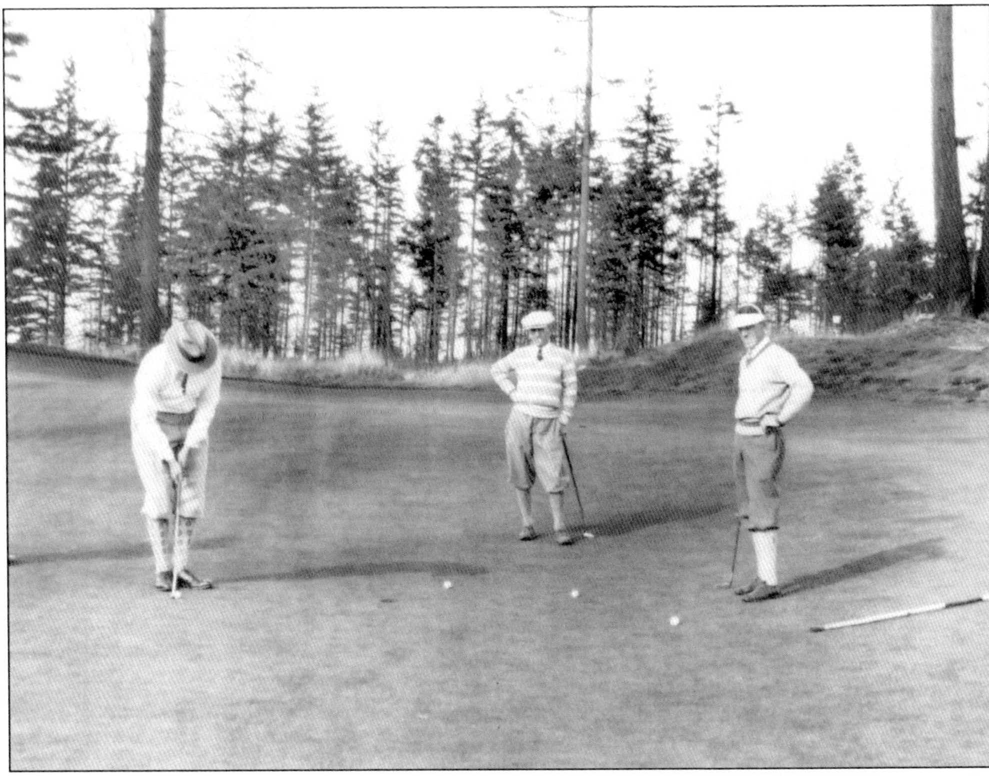

The back nine holes of Fircrest Golf Club opened in the summer of 1925. Here, on the 10th hole in the fall of 1926, a golfer addresses the ball as his playing partners quietly wait for the putt. (Courtesy of the Tacoma Public Library, Boland-B15729.)

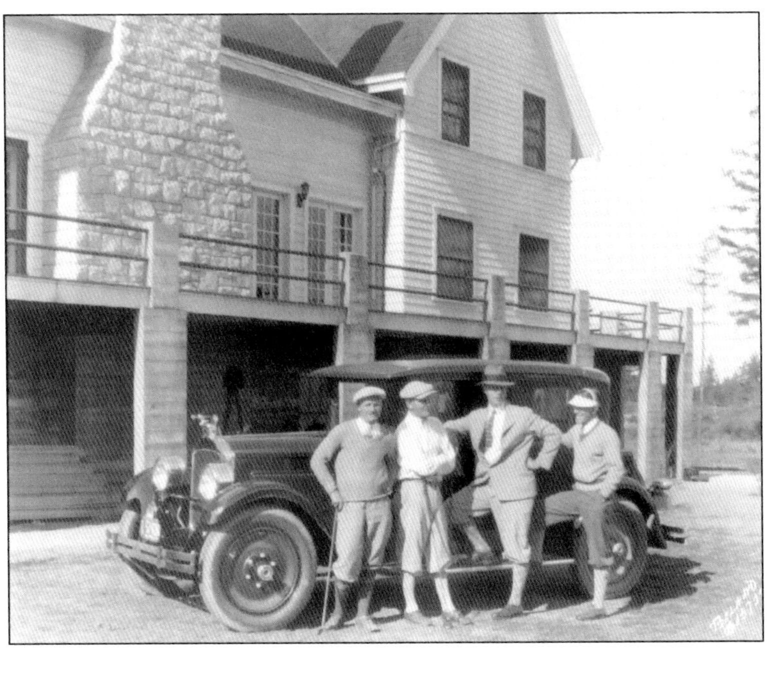

Behind the clubhouse, four unidentified golfers pose with a late-model automobile. At the time of this photograph, the golf course had been open for only two years. Note the golf attire of the day. (Courtesy of the Tacoma Public Library, Boland-B15729.)

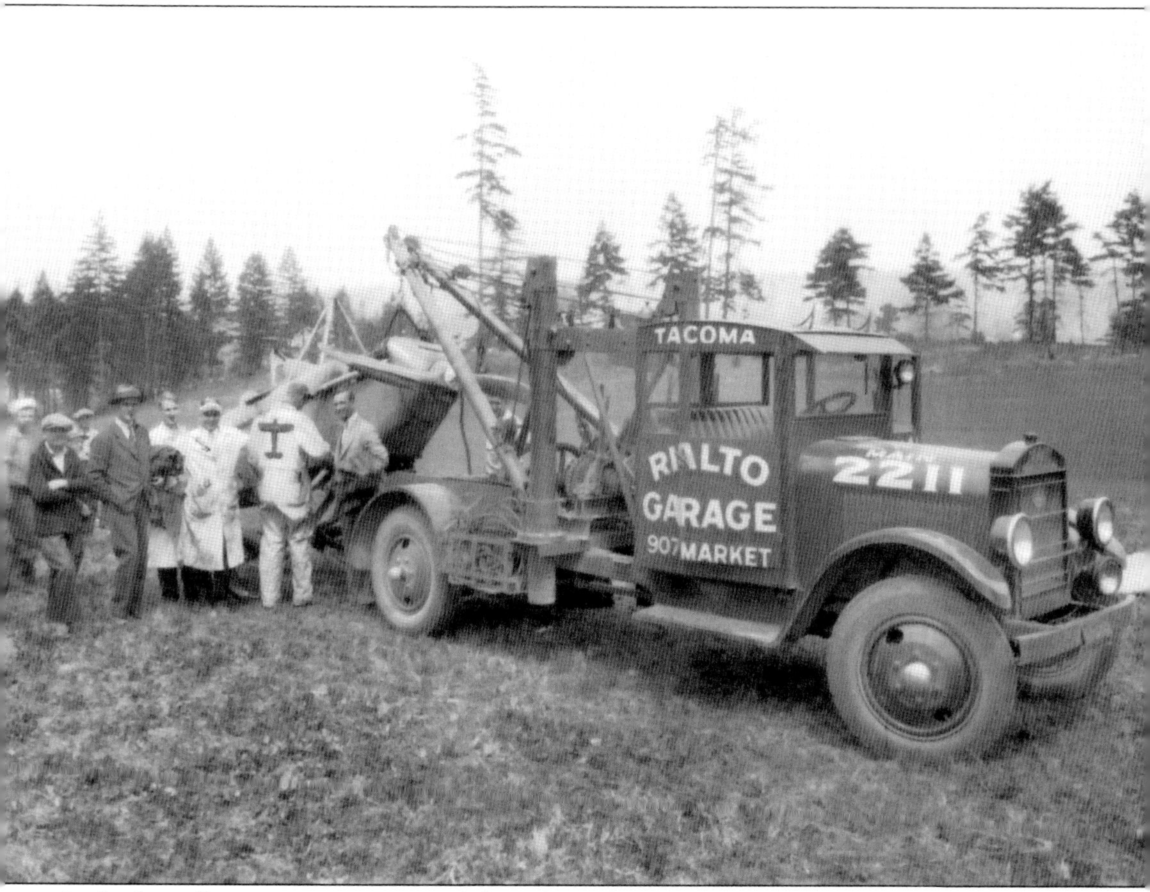

In the days of barnstorming, a tow truck from the Rialto Garage gets ready to haul away a biplane from Fircrest Golf Club on July 19, 1928. Apparently, this is the first time a crashed airplane was transported by a local wrecking truck. The plane was returning to Victoria, British Columbia, when it made a forced landing on the golf course. The plane's pilot, A.H. Wilson, was accompanied by Ernest Eve, president of British Columbia Airway, Ltd. It is unknown how badly the airplane was damaged. (Courtesy of the Tacoma Public Library, Boland-B18962.)

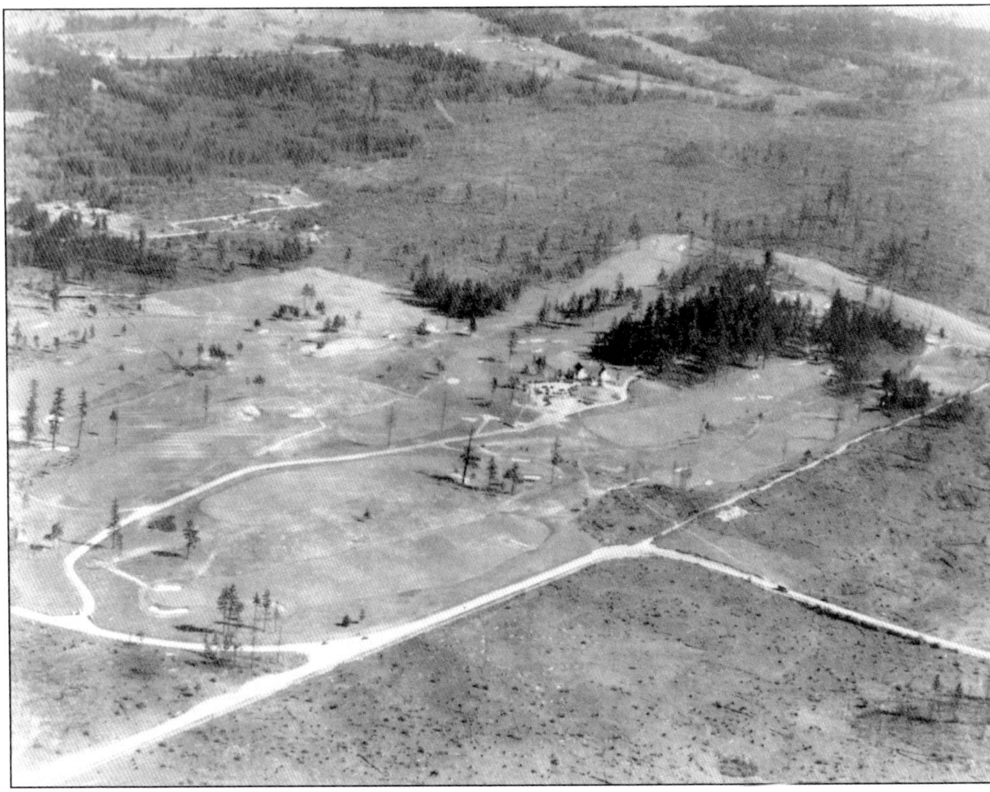

The 165 acres of Fircrest Golf Club are seen from the air in this 1930 image. At lower left is the course's fifth hole. The intersection in the bottom left corner is the entrance to Fircrest Golf Club and Regents Boulevard. The photographer is looking east. Most of the homes in Fircrest are just out of the frame to the left. (Courtesy of the Tacoma Public Library, G54.1-035.)

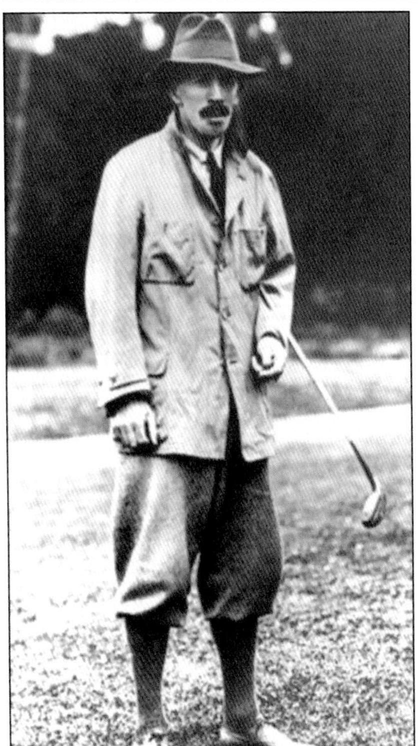

The Fircrest Golf Club course was designed by Arthur Vernon Macan of Victoria, British Columbia. The Irishman moved to Victoria in 1912 and played in tournaments around the Pacific Northwest. An excellent competitive golfer, Macan's tournament days ended with the outbreak of World War I. While serving with the Canadian army in France, Macan lost his left foot at the Battle of Vimy Ridge. Amazingly, his handicap only went from a four to a six. (Courtesy of PNGA.)

Every year, the Co-Ed Club hosted a party for all of its younger members. Held nine months after the attack on Pearl Harbor, the Back to School Dance had a patriotic theme, which included a war bond as a door prize. The Co-Ed Club members seen here were heading off to college for the first time. (Courtesy of the Tacoma Public Library, D13252-2.)

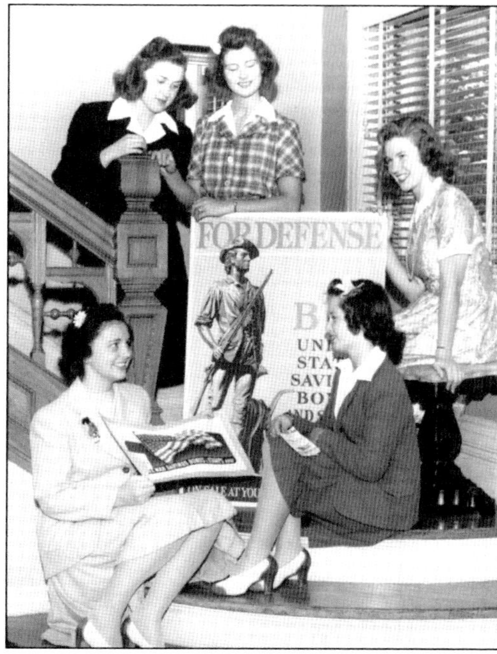

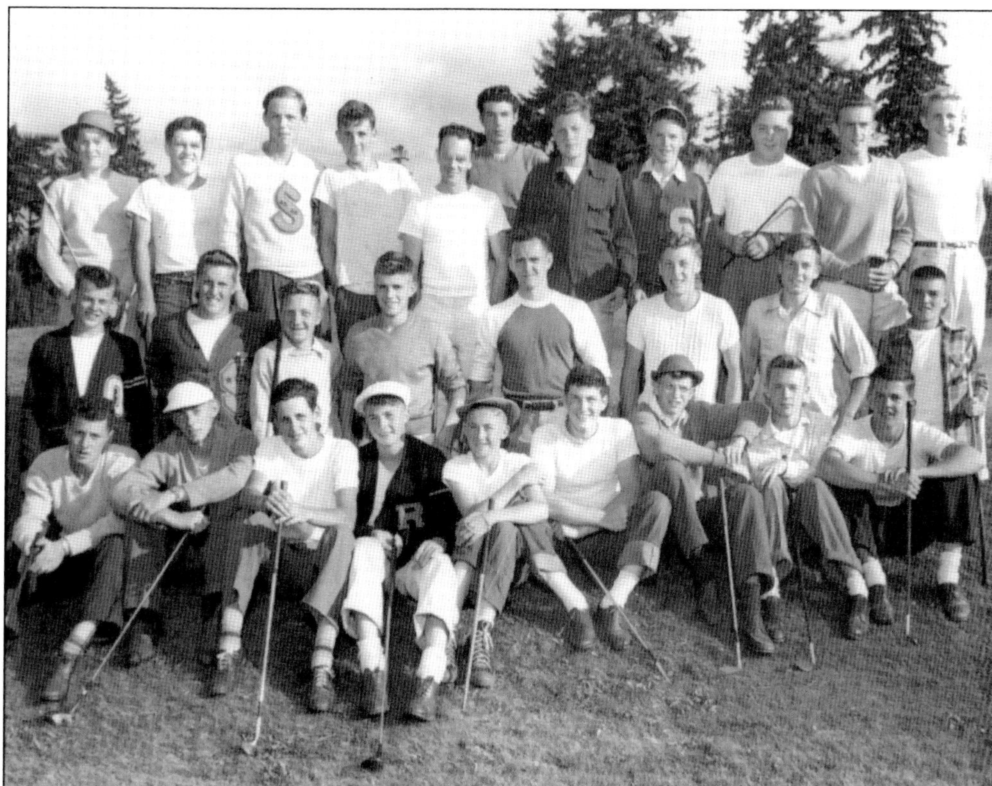

The call went out in 1946 for young men interested in being caddies for the upcoming Pacific Northwest Golf Association Championship Tournament. These 28 young golfers would man three caddy stations set up around the course. (Courtesy of the Tacoma Public Library, D22790-1.)

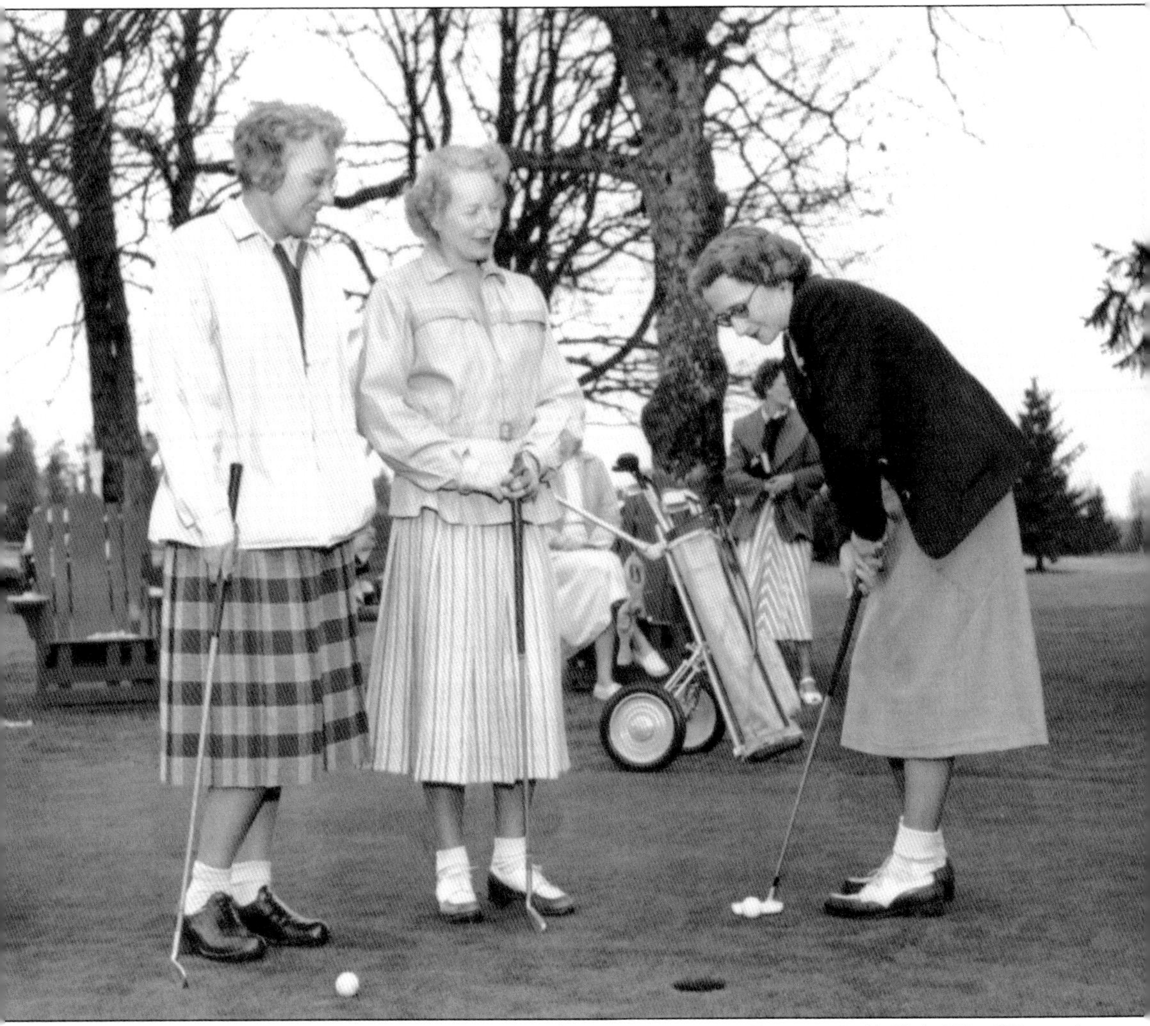

The summer golf season officially opened with Women's Day at Fircrest Golf Club. The Women's Club president, Mrs. Percy J. Quam (not pictured), welcomed new members and beginning golfers in 1948. After introductions and greetings, members were sent on their way for a competitive round of golf. The summer season began in May, so jackets were often part of the wardrobe. These three unidentified female golfers are completing their final putts of the day. (Courtesy of the Tacoma Public Library, 0d33157-8.)

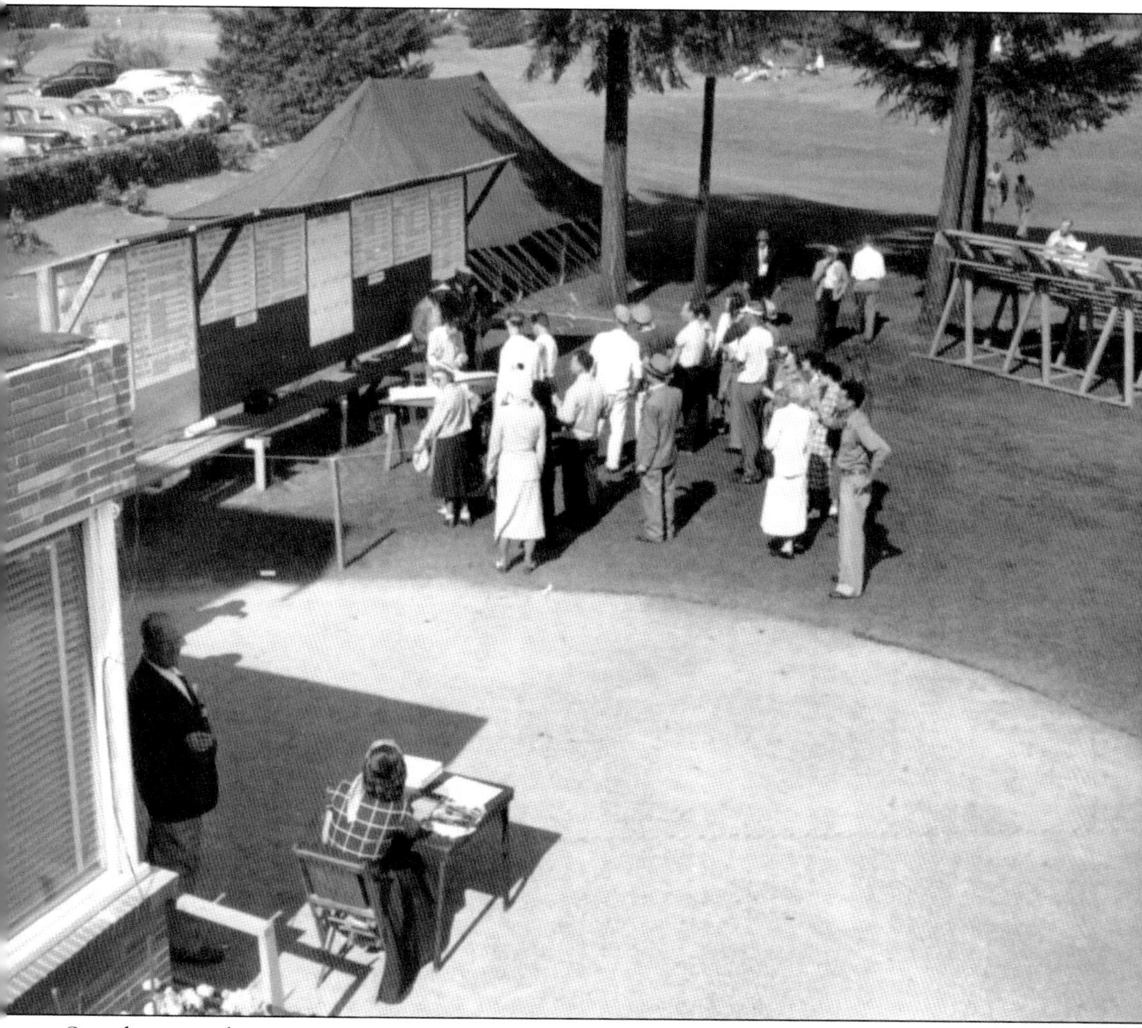

Seen here are the registration point and leaderboard for the Tacoma Open Golf Tournament, held at Fircrest Golf Club in September 1948. A total of 112 golfers entered the tournament. After two days of golf, 41 professionals and 10 amateurs had made the cut, with scores of 150 or better. (Courtesy of the Tacoma Public Library, D35320-7.)

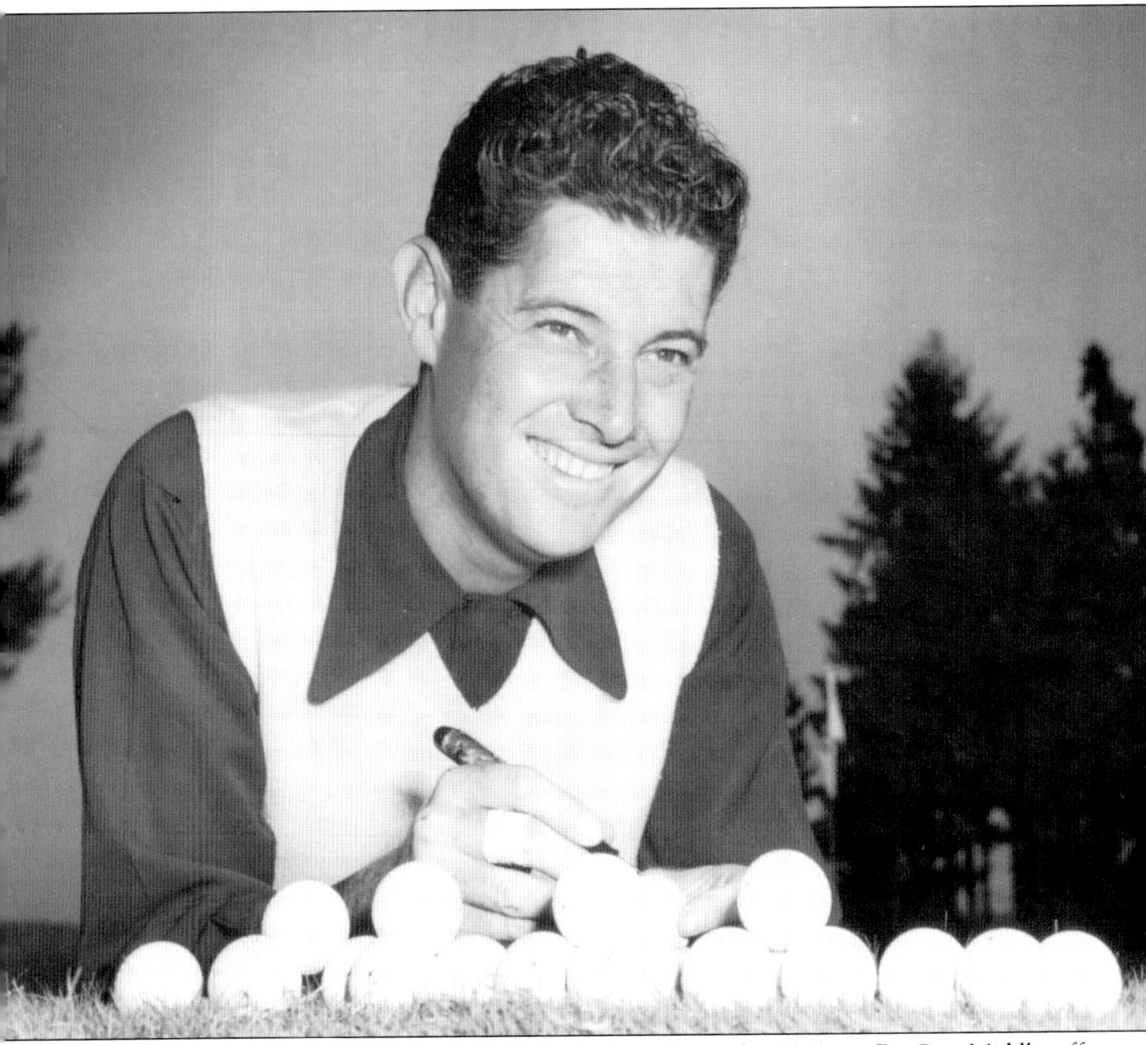

Among the professional golfers at the Tacoma Open in September 1948 was Dr. Cary Middlecoff, seen here autographing golf balls. Golf history was made when Middlecoff and four others were tied after 72 holes, with 274 strokes each. After 18 holes on Monday with still no winner, they went into sudden death. Ed "Porky" Oliver claimed the championship, beating Middlecoff by a single stroke. Middlecoff, a dentist, would go on to win two US Opens and one Masters. (Courtesy of the Tacoma Public Library, D35320-3.)

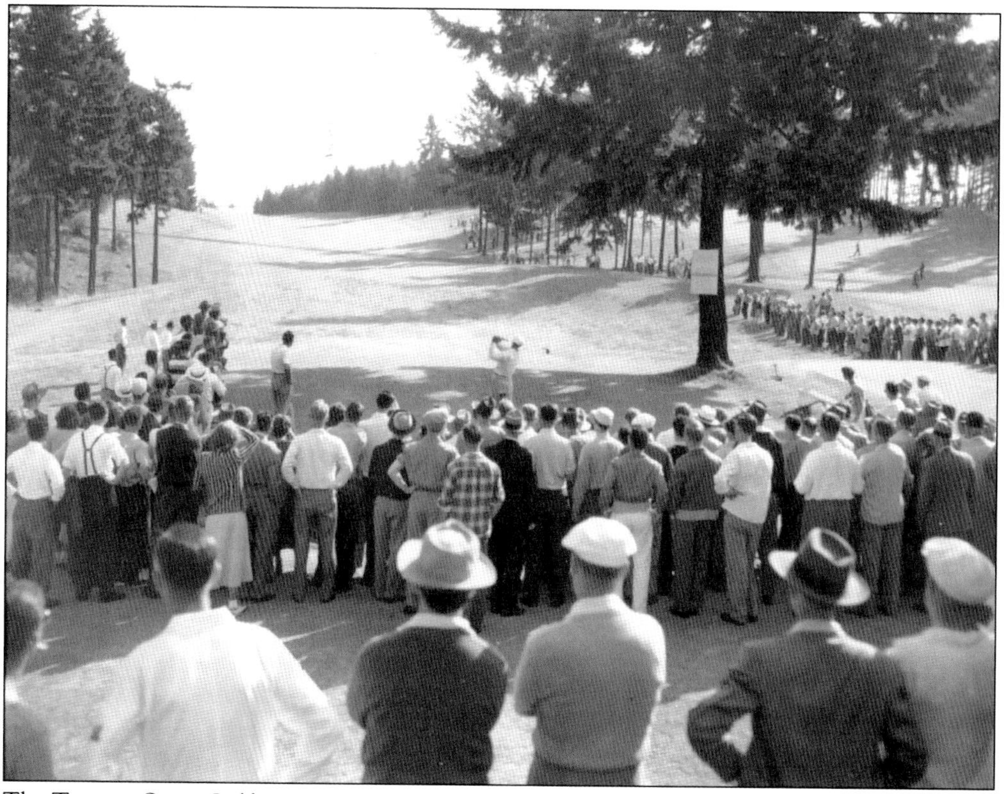

The Tacoma Open Golf Tournament at Fircrest Golf Club was scheduled to be a four-day event, starting Thursday, September 17, 1948. The tournament was sponsored by the Tacoma Athletic Commission and attracted a large gallery. Each day, 18 holes were played, and because of a five-way tie on Sunday, another 18 holes were played, along with a 19th hole of sudden death on Monday, September 21. (Both courtesy of the Tacoma Public Library: above, D35320-16; below, D35320-5.)

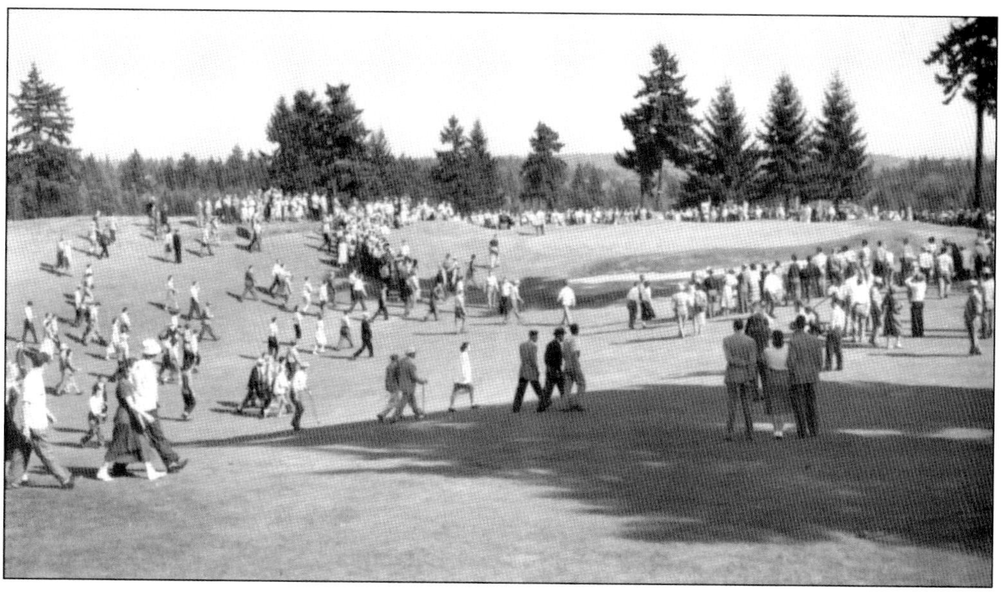

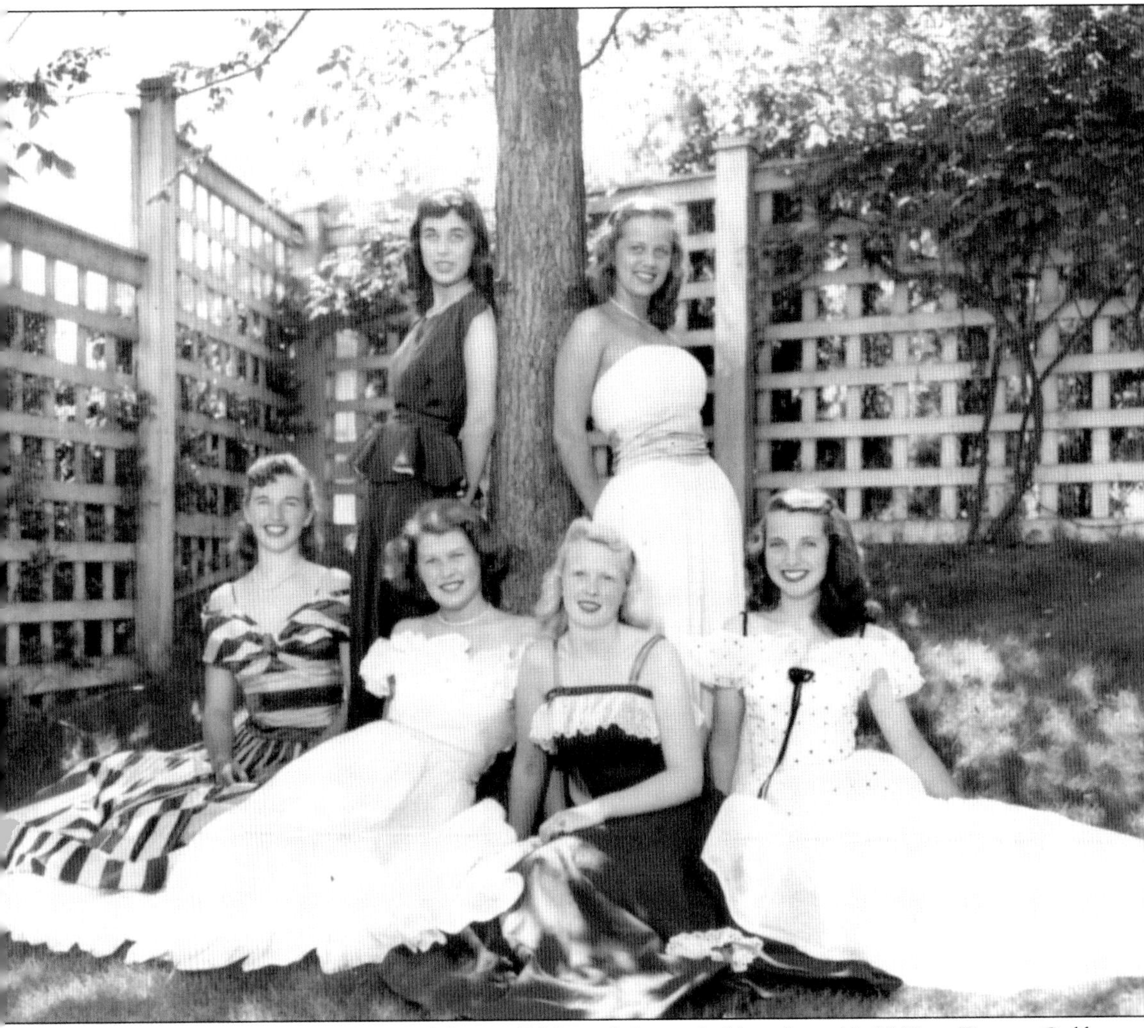

"Summertime" was the theme of the Co-Ed formal dance, held on June 19, 1948, at Fircrest Golf Club. Virginia Allen was the dance chairwoman, and the other committee members were Jane Magnuson, Rosemary Matheson, Nancy Bartles, Joan Estey, and Nancy Creswell. The dance, customarily held in June each year to welcome home returning college students, served as a final social event for the school year. (Courtesy of the Tacoma Public Library, D33789.)

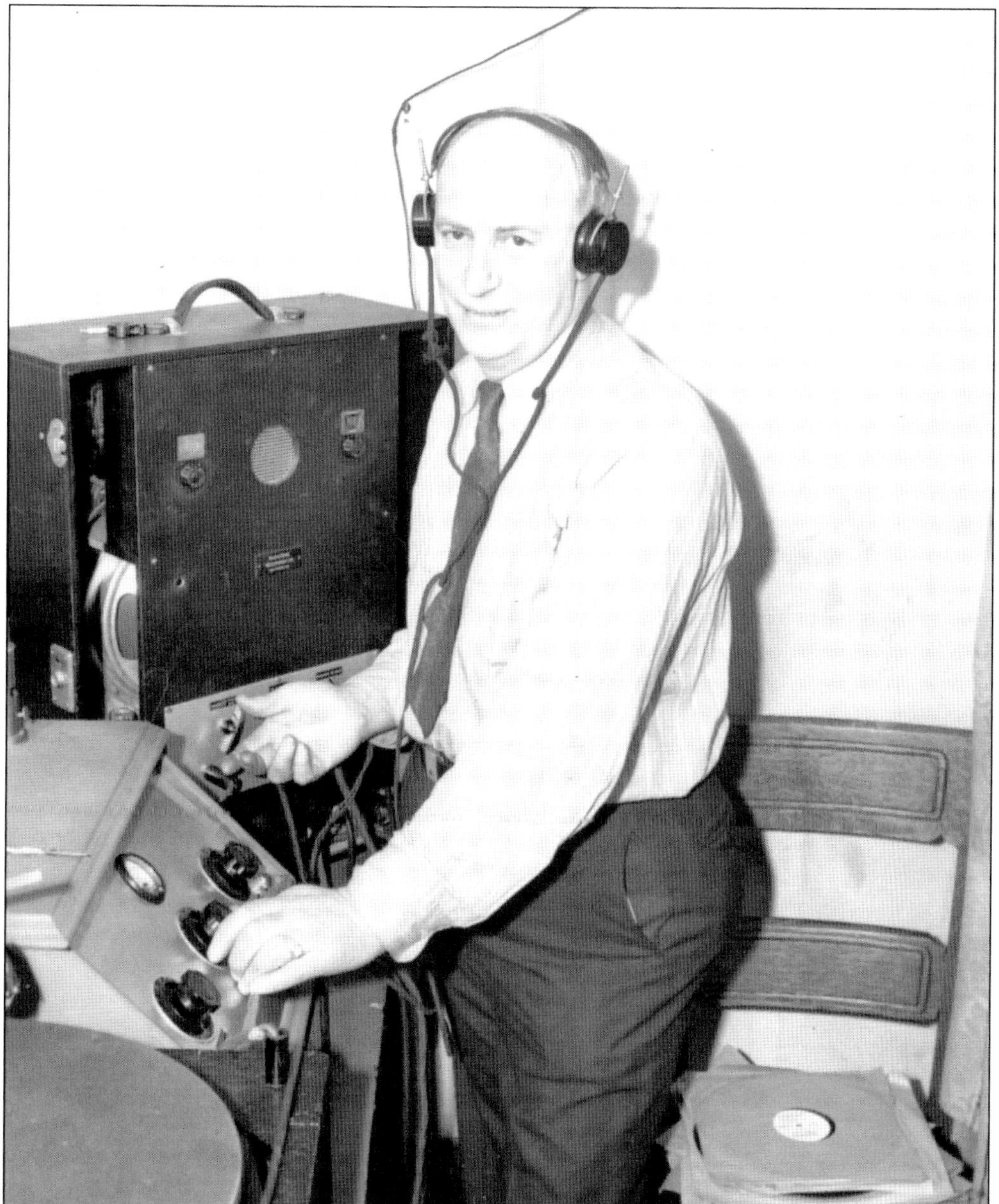

Inventor, real estate developer, entrepreneur, and avid golfer Oscar B. Clow is seen here in his recording studio in Tacoma, Washington. Clow was a modern-day renaissance man. The amazing Mr. Clow patented several inventions and was a prolific composer. In 1940, the newly formed Broadcast Music Inc. (BMI) optioned 4,000 of his tunes. Clow also owned the Clow Milling Company, which made and distributed Clow Waffle Flour. At one point, Clow owned as many as 52 restaurants, including Clow Waffle Shop and Clow's Grill. In July 1942, after a great day of golf at Fircrest Golf Club, Oscar B. Clow passed away of an apparent heart attack. He was 56 years old. (Courtesy of the Tacoma Public Library, D1066-7.)

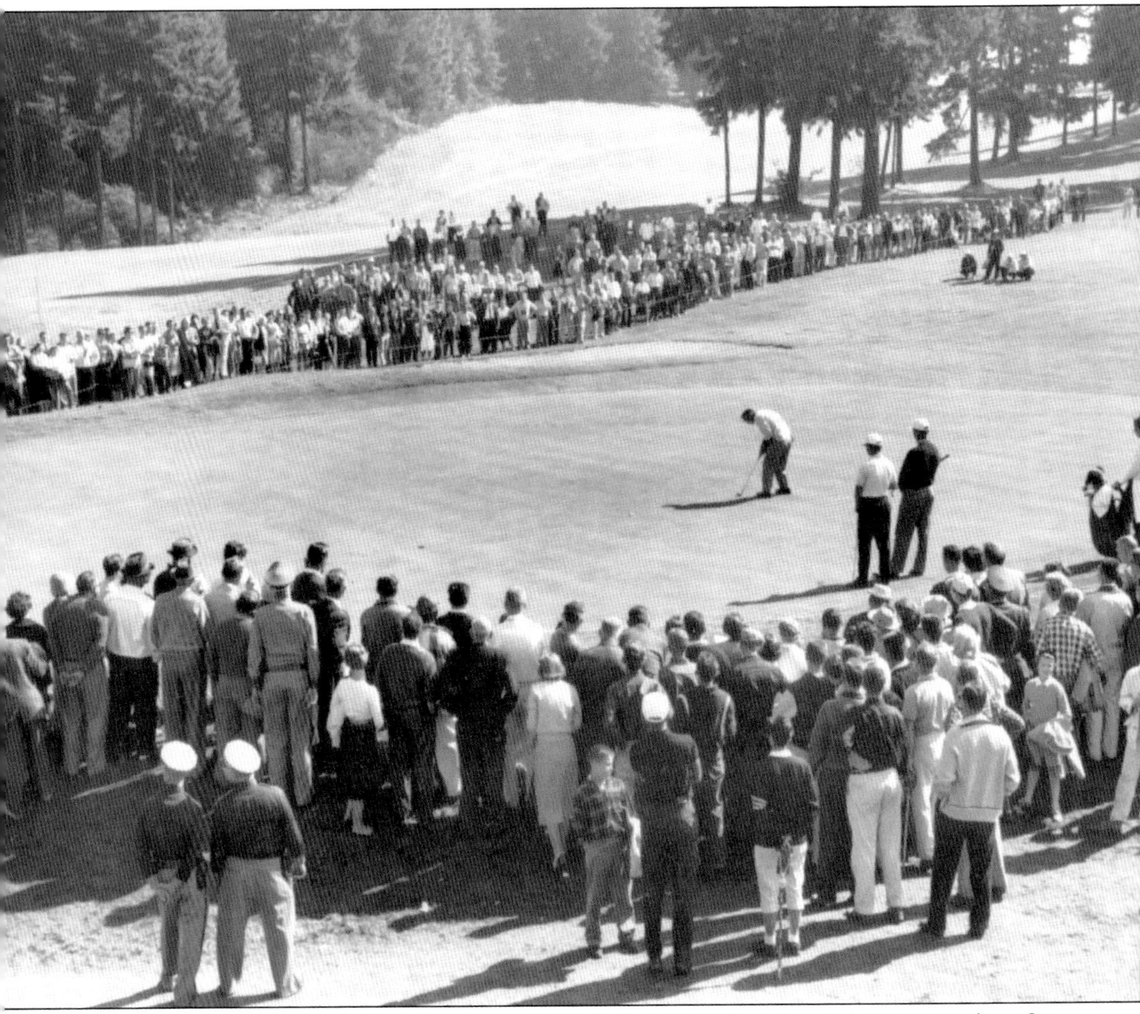

Arnold Palmer watches his ball head toward the hole on the final day of the 1960 Carling Open, held in September of that year at Fircrest Golf Club. His playing partners and caddy, along with hundreds of spectators, watch intently as Palmer, at the top of his game, looked to add $3,500 in prize money to his earnings. Palmer finished a disappointing nine strokes behind Ernie Vossler, from Midland, Texas, who won the tournament by one stroke over Paul Harney. (Courtesy of the Tacoma Public Library, D128236-4.)

Three

A City Called Fircrest

Regents Park's fortune rose and fell with the fluctuating economy of the times. On average, lot prices and sales declined until by the Great Depression they could be gotten for what was owed in back taxes. An advertisement of the Regents Park Land Company proclaimed: "We ask only one quarter of the former price. Your luck—the other man's loss." By 1925, the 306 residents of Regents Park felt that their community needed a fresh start and a new outlook. After a vote in September 1925, the community incorporated as the new city of Fircrest. The incorporation allowed them financial stability and control over repairs, development of infrastructure, and services.

During the lean years of the Great Depression, the new town of Fircrest showed its resolve by working together to support one another. Men, women, and children took extra jobs to make ends meet. Volunteers maintained the lake and roads, dug ditches, and cleaned up the empty lots. The town leaders tried to provide a job for anyone who could not pay their water and light bills. Women came together to plant flowers and beautify the Fircrest landscape, and they provided meals for hungry schoolchildren. Even so, many prominent citizens lost the rights to their Fircrest homes and were forced to "begin again."

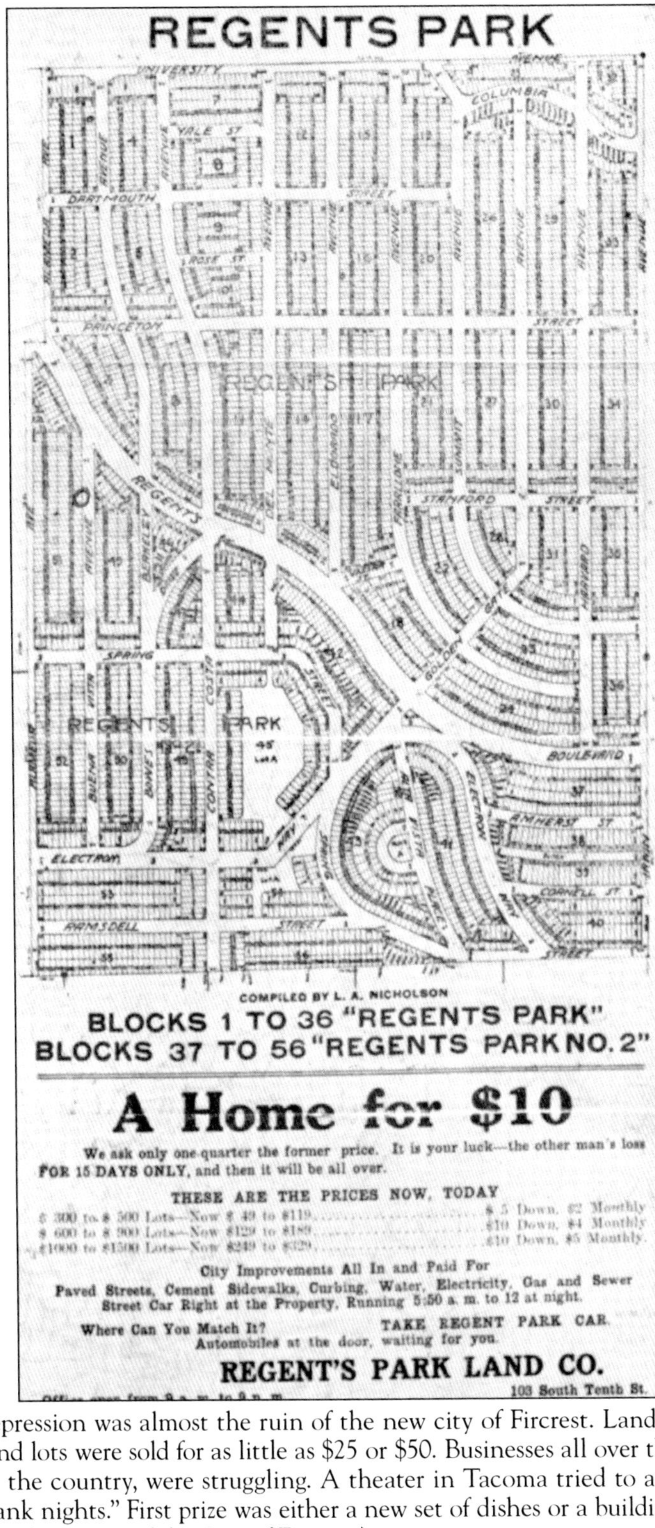

The Great Depression was almost the ruin of the new city of Fircrest. Land prices continued to plummet, and lots were sold for as little as $25 or $50. Businesses all over the county, as well as throughout the country, were struggling. A theater in Tacoma tried to attract business by sponsoring "bank nights." First prize was either a new set of dishes or a building site in Fircrest, winner's choice. (Courtesy of the City of Fircrest.)

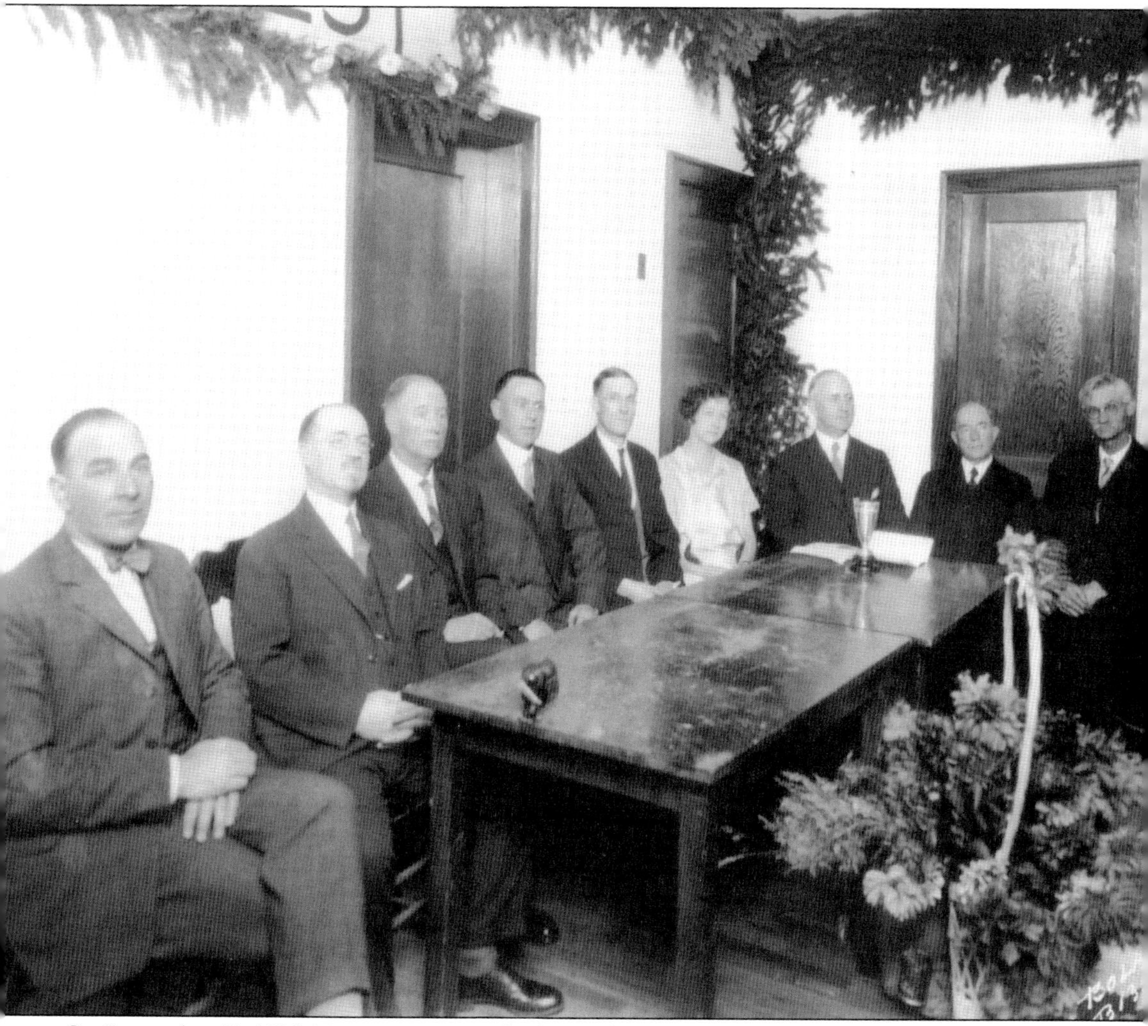

On September 21, 1925, Mayor W.A. Woodkirk presided over the first city council meeting of the city of Fircrest. Woodkirk had been unanimously elected mayor on September 8. Garlands and bouquets decorated Fircrest School (later Wainwright Elementary), where a swearing-in ceremony preceded a public meeting. At the ceremony, an effigy of Regents Park was symbolically laid to rest, and the new city of Fircrest was christened. Ernie Fox intoned, "Although you are only an infant, you have made yourself heard, and with that ability and the constant need of attention you will thrive and soon become a healthy young city." Shown here are, from left to right, councilmen Clarence M. Brown, Dr. J.A. Caswell, D.R. Rogers, C.H. Renschler, E.H. Fox, Irene B. Edwards (treasurer), Judge E.M. Card, J. Van Fossen (city clerk), and Mayor Woodkirk. Card administered the oaths of office. (Courtesy of the Tacoma Public Library, Boland-B13436.)

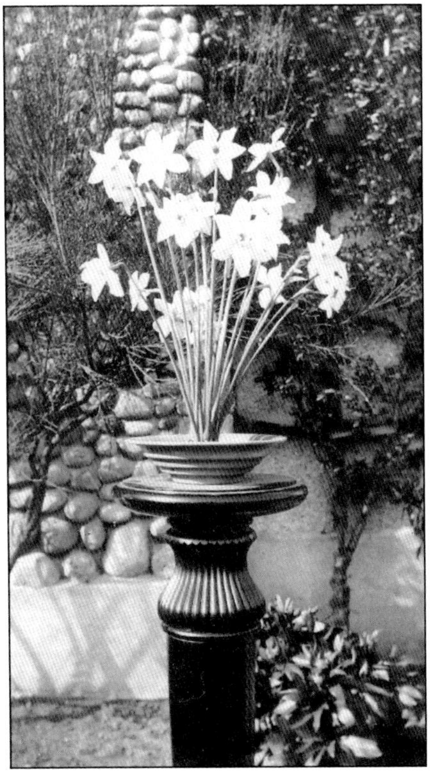

During the Great Depression, there was no extra money for land improvements, and Fircrest quickly began to look unkempt and bedraggled. Volunteer labor was recruited, and crews began to clean the grass from the sidewalk cracks, repair sewer lines, and rehabilitate Spring Lake. The women of the community started their own beautification project in the form of the Fircrest Garden Club. The club met biweekly and invited the public to many events to promote interest in their projects. The club's motto was "You're nearer God's heart in a garden than anywhere else on earth" from the poem "God's Garden" by Dorothy Francis Gurney. This was the first of many garden clubs in and around Fircrest. They were even responsible for planting the flowering cherry trees along Regents Boulevard. The clubs put much effort into living up to a comment made in a 1908 article from the Tacoma newspaper that read, "Fircrest is one of the most beautiful residence subdivisions in the United States." (Both courtesy of the City of Fircrest.)

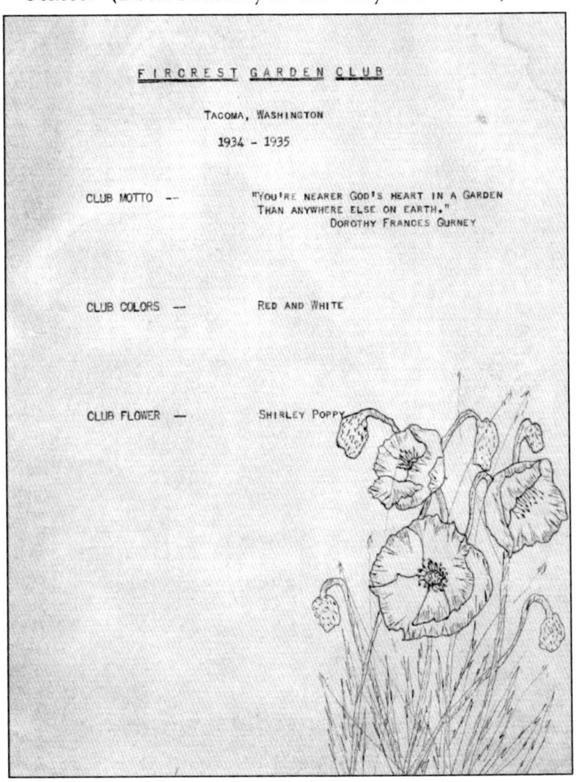

FIRCREST GARDEN CLUB

TACOMA, WASHINGTON

1934 - 1935

CLUB MOTTO -- "YOU'RE NEARER GOD'S HEART IN A GARDEN THAN ANYWHERE ELSE ON EARTH."
DOROTHY FRANCES GURNEY

CLUB COLORS -- RED AND WHITE

CLUB FLOWER -- SHIRLEY POPPY

The photograph at right reportedly shows an entrance to a "Chinese tunnel." The term refers to the tunnels or caves used to hide undocumented workers and opium smuggled into Puget Sound by sailing ships. There is a great deal of debate as to whether the tunnels were ever used for smuggling. Around Puget Sound, any man-made hole might be labeled a "Chinese tunnel" if the origin was unknown or forgotten. This one was located near the corner of Columbia and Eldorado Avenues. Just north of this intersection is China Lake Park, seen below. The area was leased in the 1880s by Chinese immigrants, as it was illegal at the time for the Chinese to own property. The tunnel was most likely dug by these farmers for the purpose of draining the marshy ground around the lake. (At right, courtesy of the Tacoma Public Library Boland-B13415; below, photograph by R.R. Colyer.)

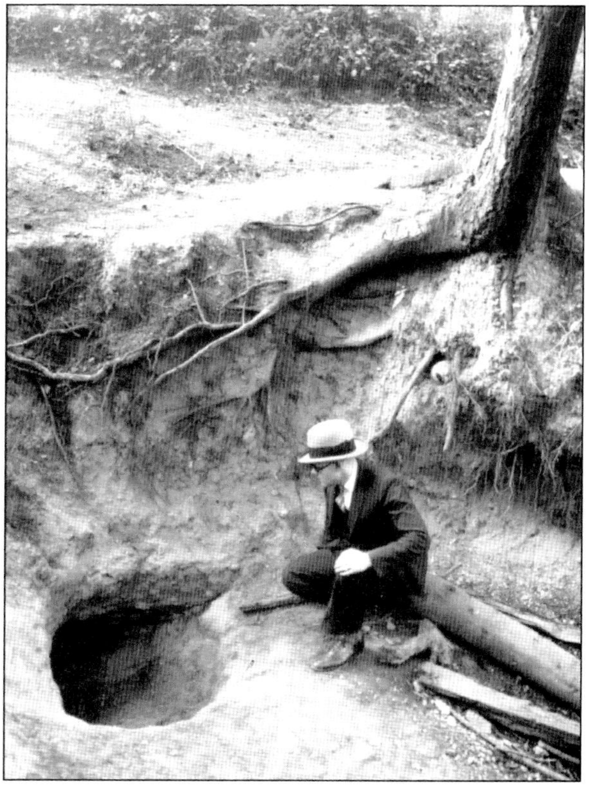

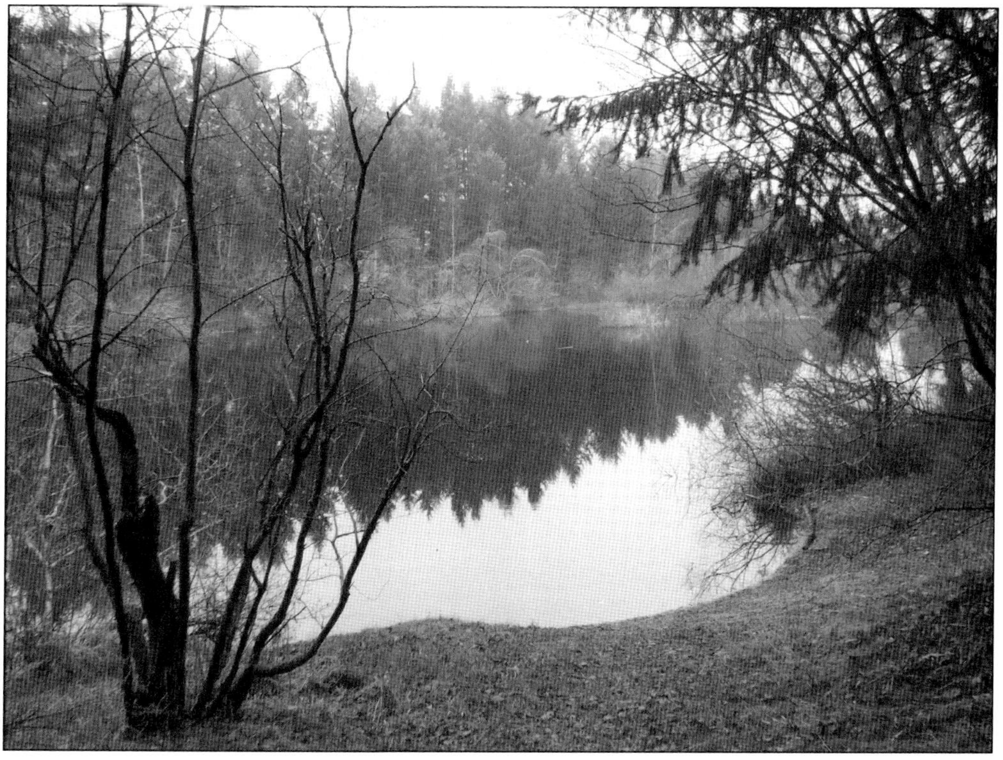

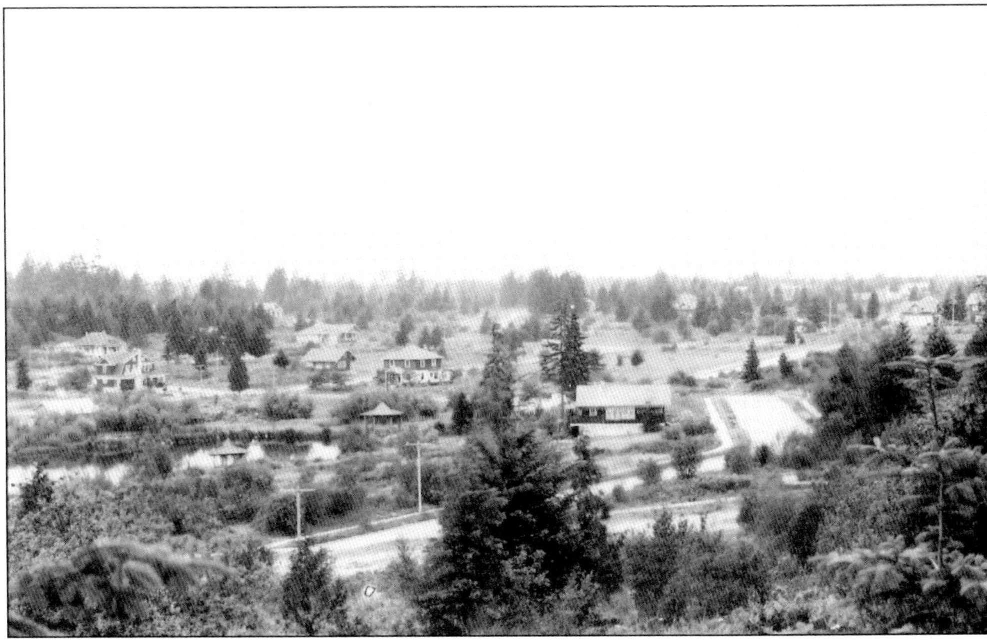

The photograph above shows Regents Park in the summer of 1919. Spring Lake, named for one of the original Regents Park financiers, John H. Spring, is visible just beyond Regents Boulevard. Spring Lake was the town's recreational and social center. At one time, there was even a small zoo housed near the lake consisting of monkeys, parrots, and a kangaroo. The surrounding area also had picnic facilities and gazebos, walking trails, playgrounds, boats, and swimming holes. Spring Lake actually consisted of one larger lake and two smaller bodies of water connected by a walkway across Electron Way. (Above, courtesy of the Tacoma Public Library, G72.1-108, below, the City of Fircrest.)

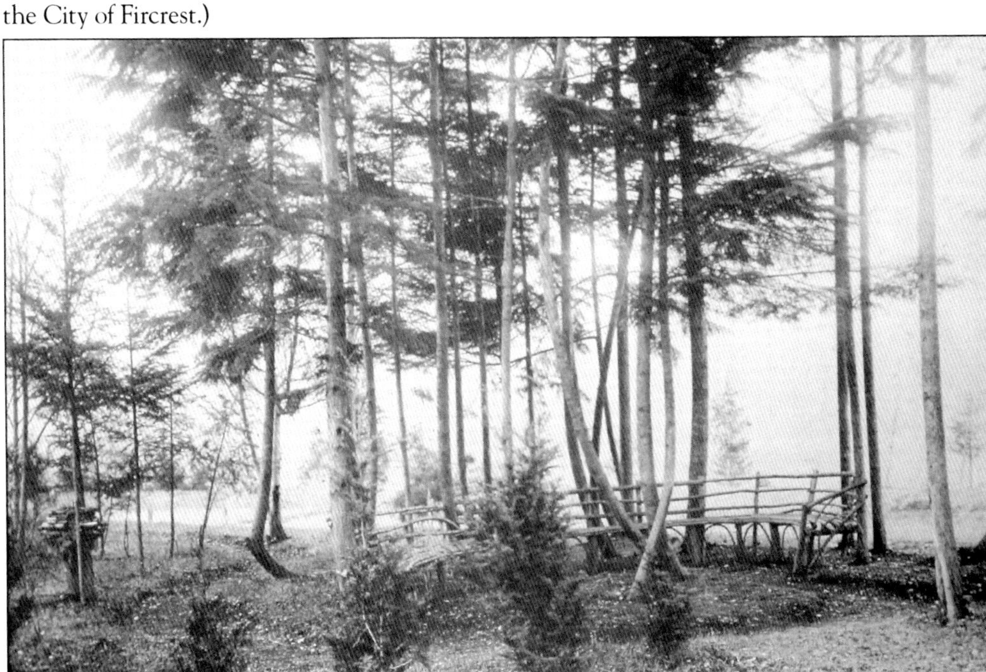

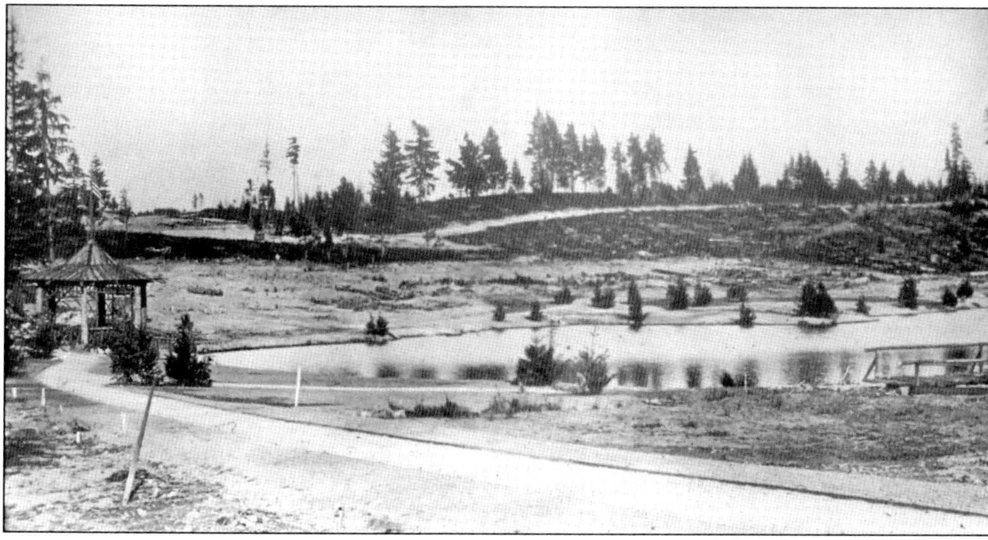

Spring Lake was a man-made, spring-fed lake located in the heart of Regents Park. By the spring of 1925, the lake and surrounding area were showing signs of neglect. A group of Regents Park residents, armed with tools of beautification, spent a day clearing out brush and planting flowers and shrubbery. The photograph below was taken at the intersection of Spring Street and Del Monte Avenue. The cement base in the background had been the pedestal for one of Fircrest's lion statues. Among the people in the photograph are, in no particular order, Earl Libby, Norma Pickering, Mr. and Mrs. Ernie Fox, Jack Pickering, Oscar Ellison, Joe Baker, Owen Ellison, H.D. Baker, Bob Rasmussen, Dr. Caswell, Ernie and Harold White, Robert Freeman, Grady Hume, Bruce Hume, Mr. Glen, John and Bob Van De Mark, Lewis Ellison, Mayor Woodkirk, Bill Brock, Irene Edwards, and Mr. and Mrs. Frank Boyd. (Both courtesy of the City of Fircrest.)

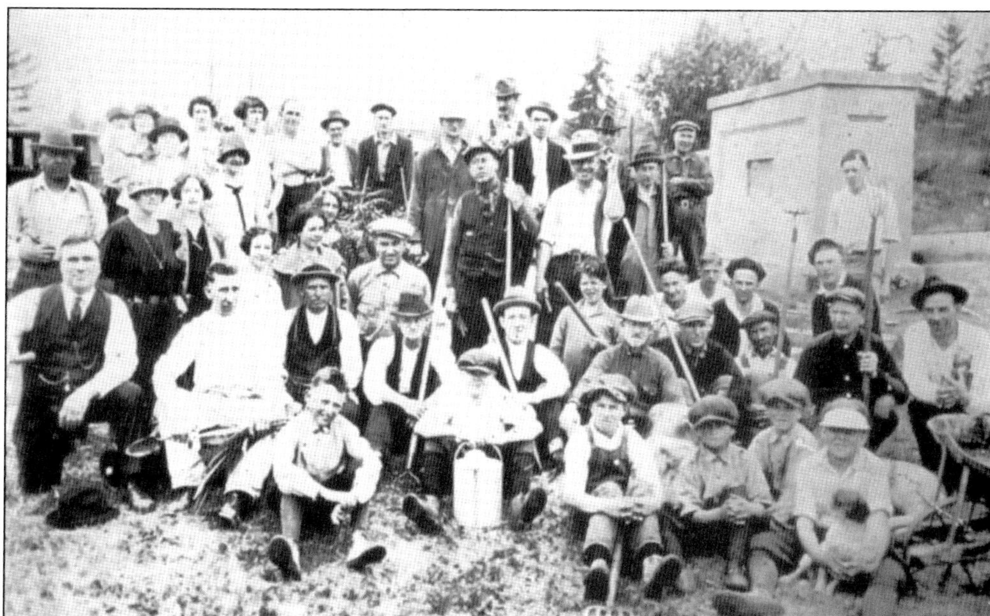

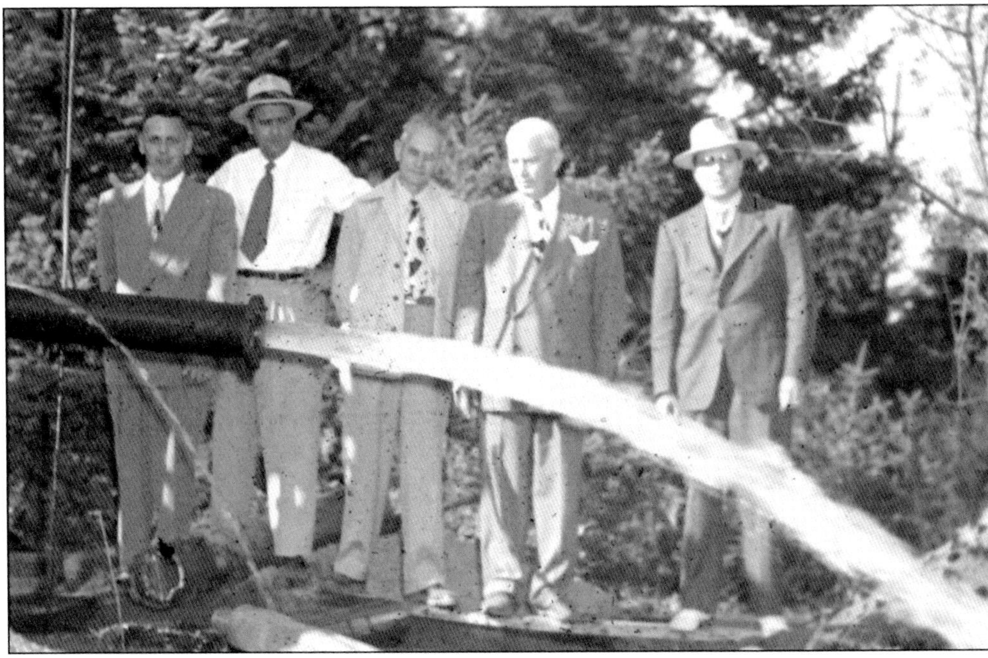

By the 1940s, Fircrest's original water system needed updating. To give the town an adequate water supply, two artesian wells were drilled. The wells hit water at 170 feet and produced 1,500 gallons per minute, enough to fill a 35,000-gallon reservoir. The project included replacing leaky water mains with new pipe and installing new pumps and fittings. The infrastructure improvements cost the City of Fircrest $77,000. (Courtesy of the City of Fircrest.)

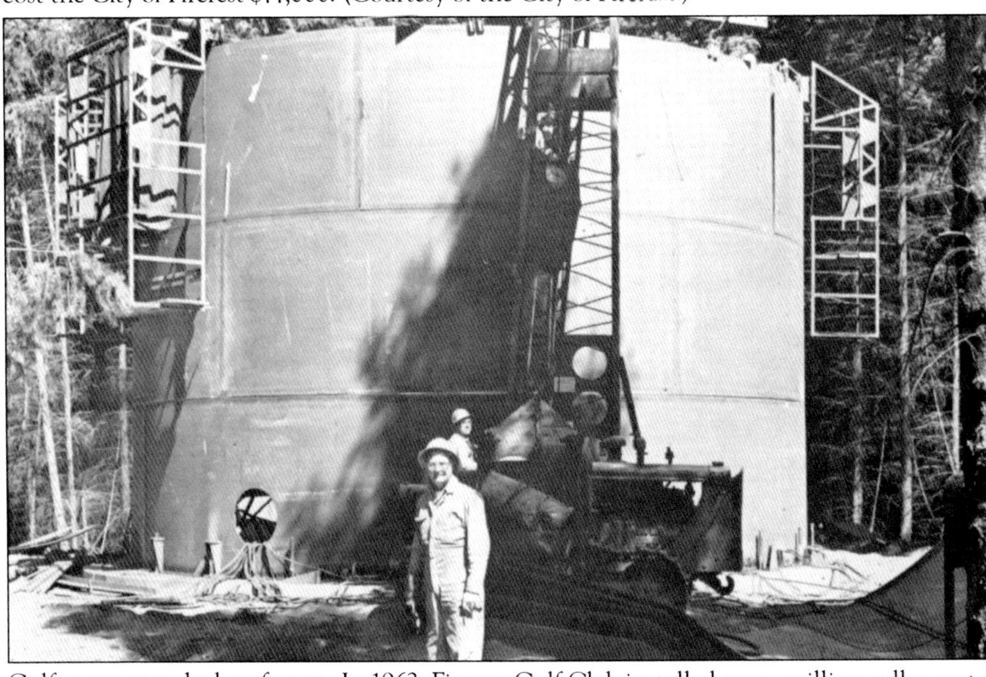

Golf courses need a lot of water. In 1962, Fircrest Golf Club installed a one-million-gallon water tank. Here, the crew builds the massive tank on the grounds of the golf course. (Courtesy of the City of Fircrest.)

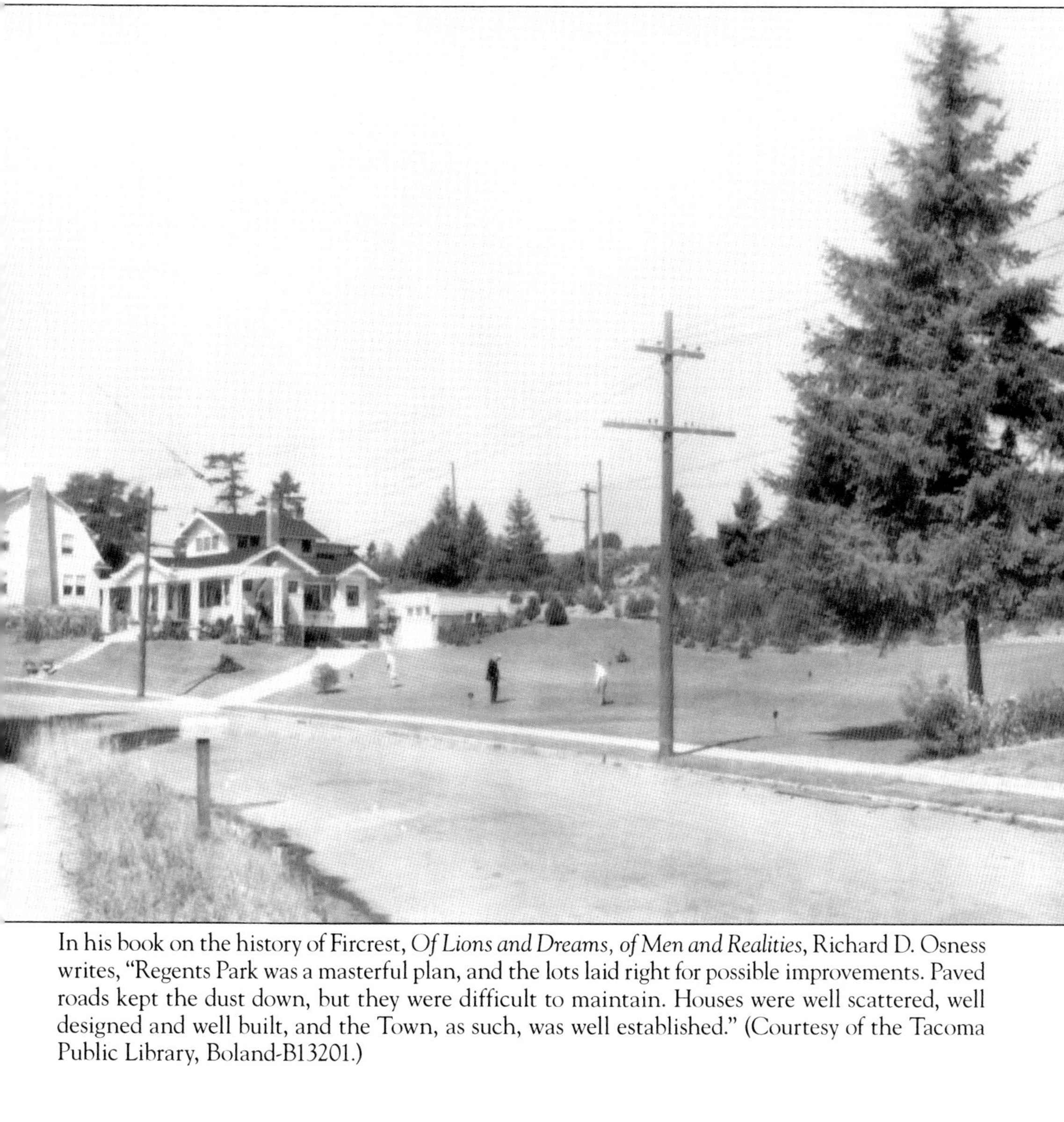

In his book on the history of Fircrest, *Of Lions and Dreams, of Men and Realities*, Richard D. Osness writes, "Regents Park was a masterful plan, and the lots laid right for possible improvements. Paved roads kept the dust down, but they were difficult to maintain. Houses were well scattered, well designed and well built, and the Town, as such, was well established." (Courtesy of the Tacoma Public Library, Boland-B13201.)

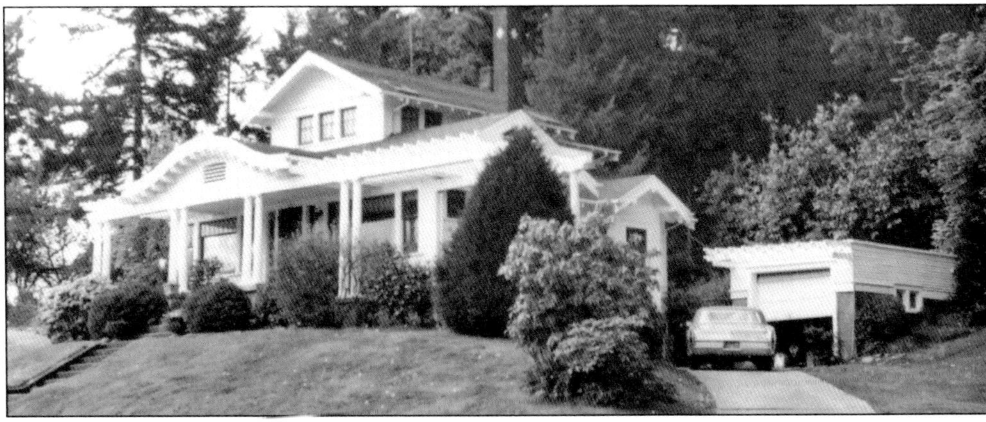

This house on Columbia Avenue, built in 1925, was the residence of Dr. and Mrs. J.A. Caswell, owners of Caswell Optical. Note the interesting details on the front porch. Dr. Caswell, a civic leader, served on several committees during his years in Fircrest. The home was later bought by the Oscar Lundberg family. The Lundbergs were also very civic-minded, and their names can be seen on the rosters of many early Fircrest committees and organizations. (Courtesy of the Tacoma Public Library.)

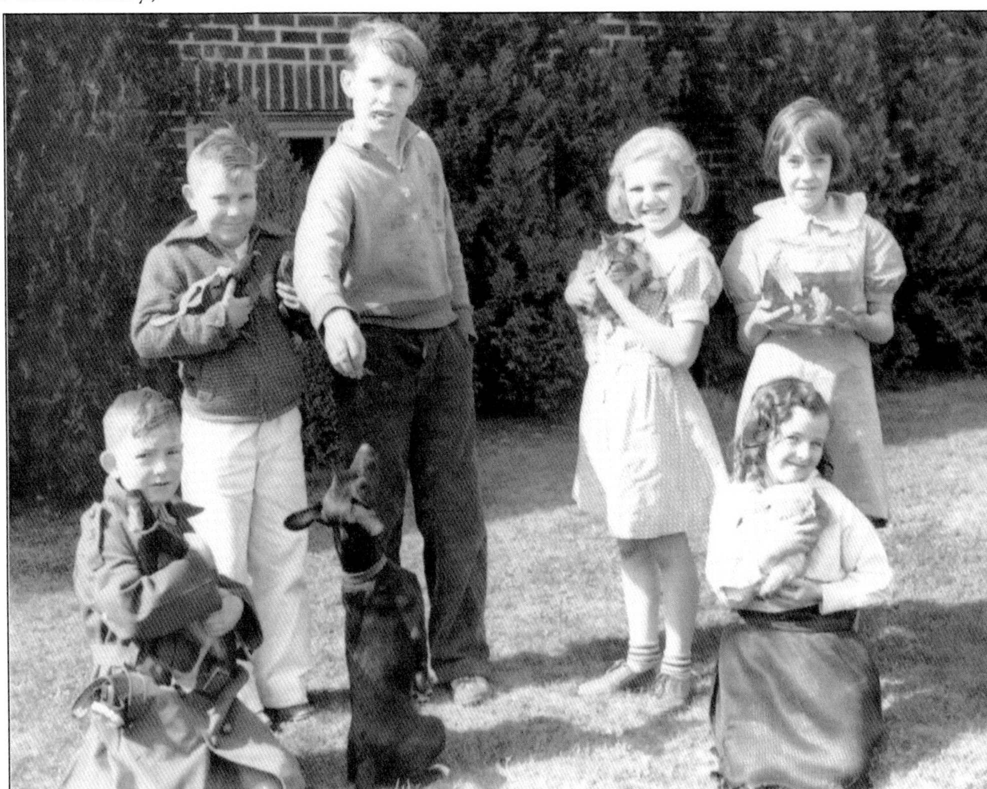

In this photograph, six students from Fircrest School exhibit their prize-winning pets. The pet show was held as part of Be Kind to Animals Week. The six owners pose on the lawn next to the school. Shown are chickens, a duck, a dog, a cat, and a bowl of fish. The students are, from left to right, Donald Masco, Jerry Baker, Bill Dunsmore, Joyce Wheeler, Helen Gansen, and Tynne Smith. (Courtesy of the Tacoma Public Library, D776-2.)

In March 1937, Fircrest School (later Wainwright Elementary) sponsored a Be Kind to Animals Week. Marilyn White brought her puppy, and Douglas Shacklett shared his pet rabbit with his classmates. Among the other pets shown here are goldfish, chickens, ducks, and other birds. (Courtesy of the Tacoma Public Library, D776-1.)

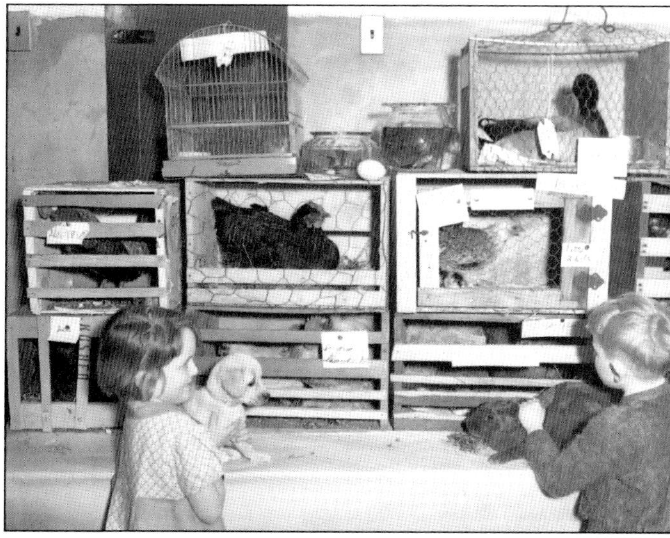

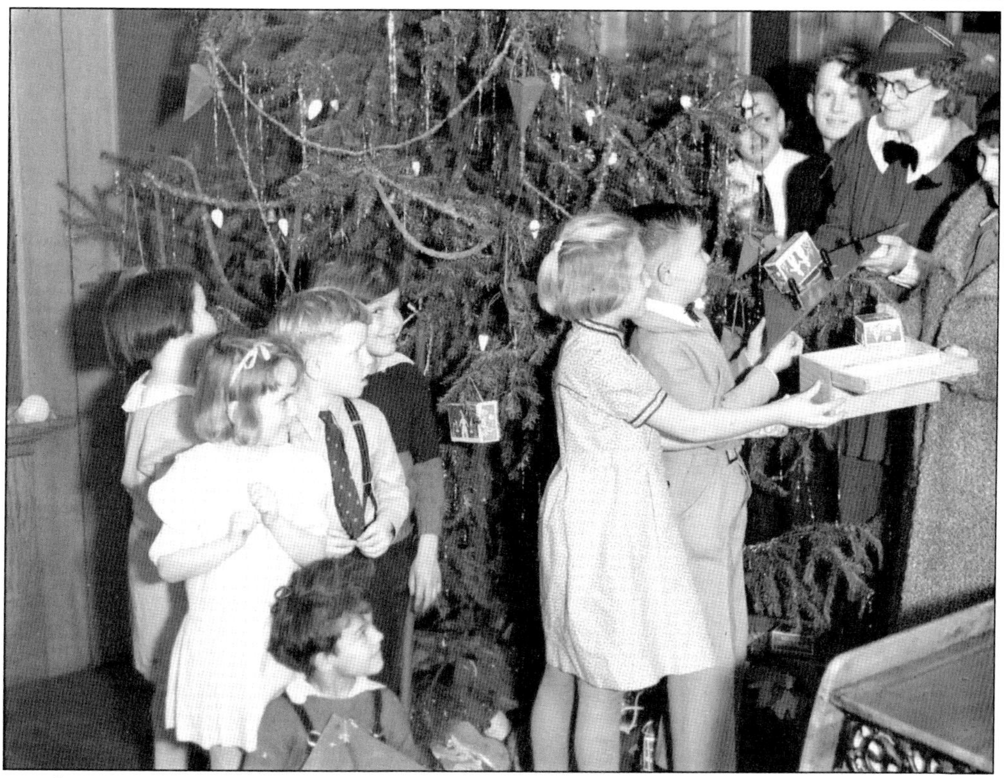

"Made in Fircrest" was a PTA and Preschool Women project that took place in the fall of 1936 during the Great Depression. The goal was for every child in Fircrest, from the sixth grade down, to receive a handmade toy and some yuletide candy. The town received donations from local businesses. At a cost of just $10, they were able to create $100 worth of toys. When all was said and done, the committee, working for 10 straight days far into the nights, created 30 rocking horses, 30 hobbyhorses, 30 ring-toss games, 25 candles, and 12 plywood chests. These children are receiving gifts from Mrs. Lynn Baker and Mrs. Oscar Lundberg. (Courtesy of the Tacoma Public Library, D736-1.)

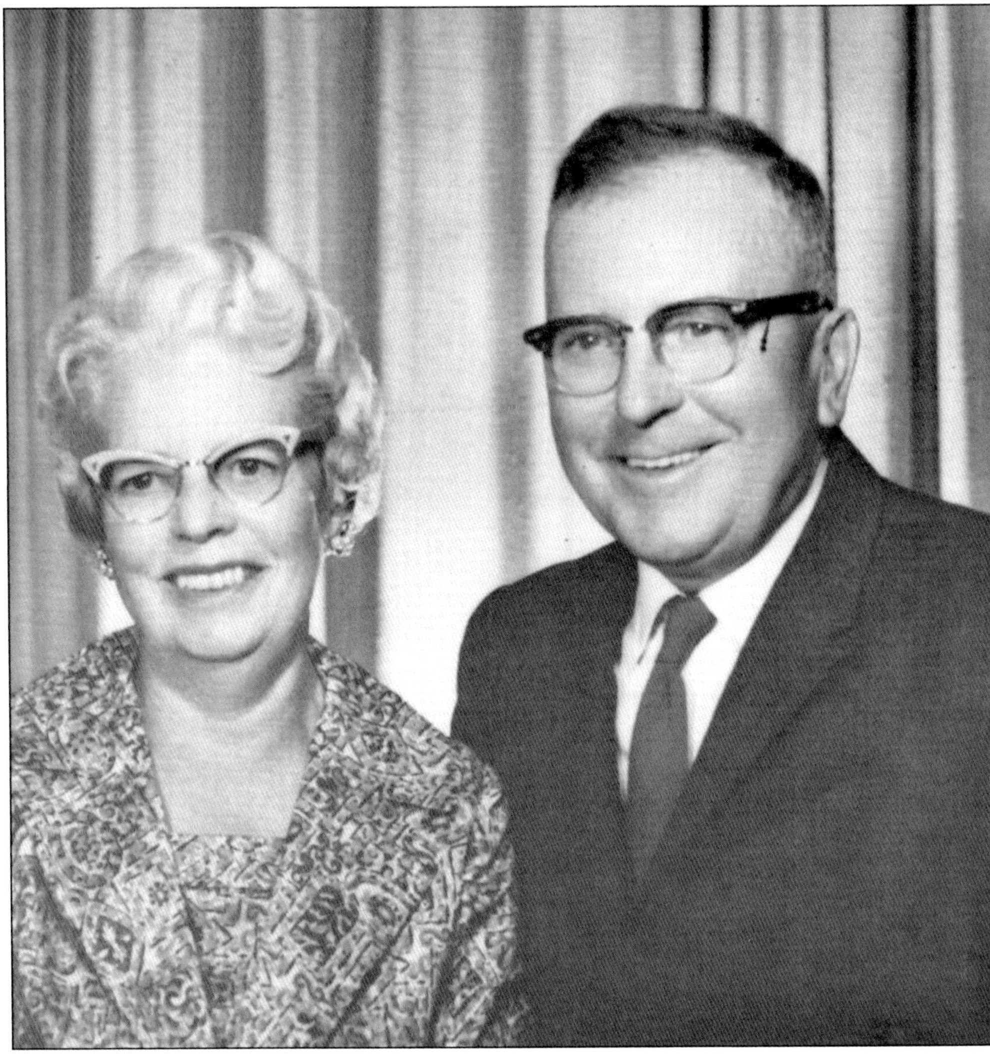

Clay Curtiss and his wife, Arliene, moved to Fircrest in 1939. Clay began working for the town in the building and utility sector (with George Masko) and also as a town marshal. Like many in the community, he wore many hats and was truly a "jack of all trades." He supervised the drilling of five new wells for the town and was instrumental in the installation of the town's water pumps. After his retirement in 1969, Curtiss continued to serve his community as volunteer historian; many of the photographs in the Fircrest archives are credited to him. (Courtesy of the City of Fircrest.)

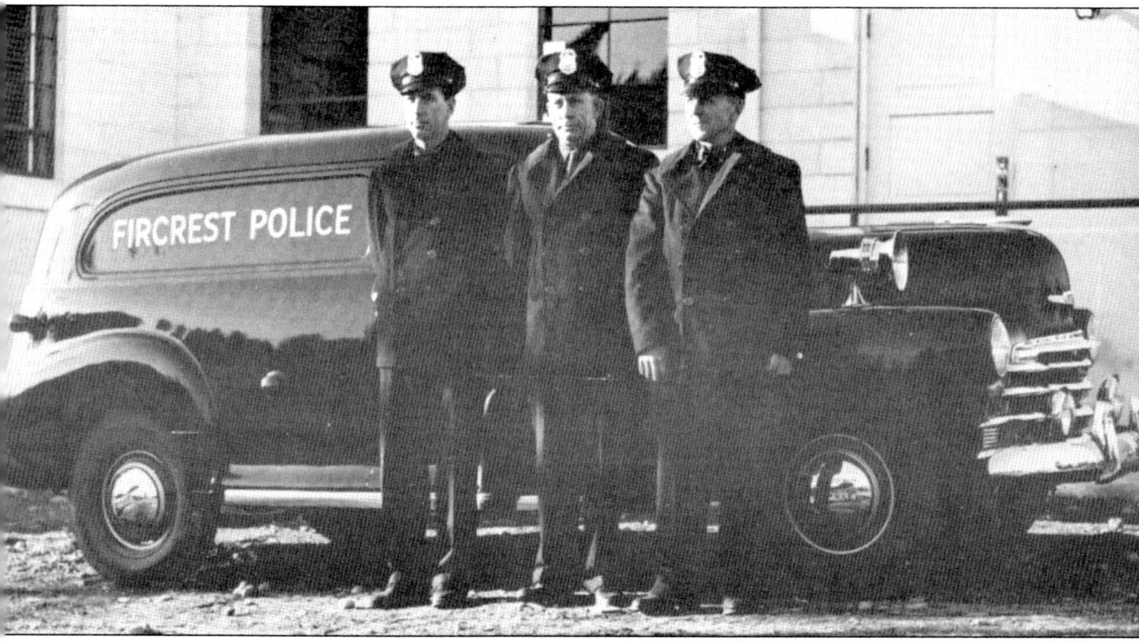

Originally, Fircrest police officers (marshals) used their own vehicles to go out on calls. The officers had phones at their residences but no radios for communication, therefore they improvised. If out on patrol, they could look toward their homes. If a certain light was on, it meant that their wives had received a call and they were needed. The officers would speed home, pick up the "message," and answer the call for help. In 1947, a truck was purchased and converted to a paddy wagon, complete with first-aid equipment, lights, sirens, and a radio. (Courtesy of the City of Fircrest.)

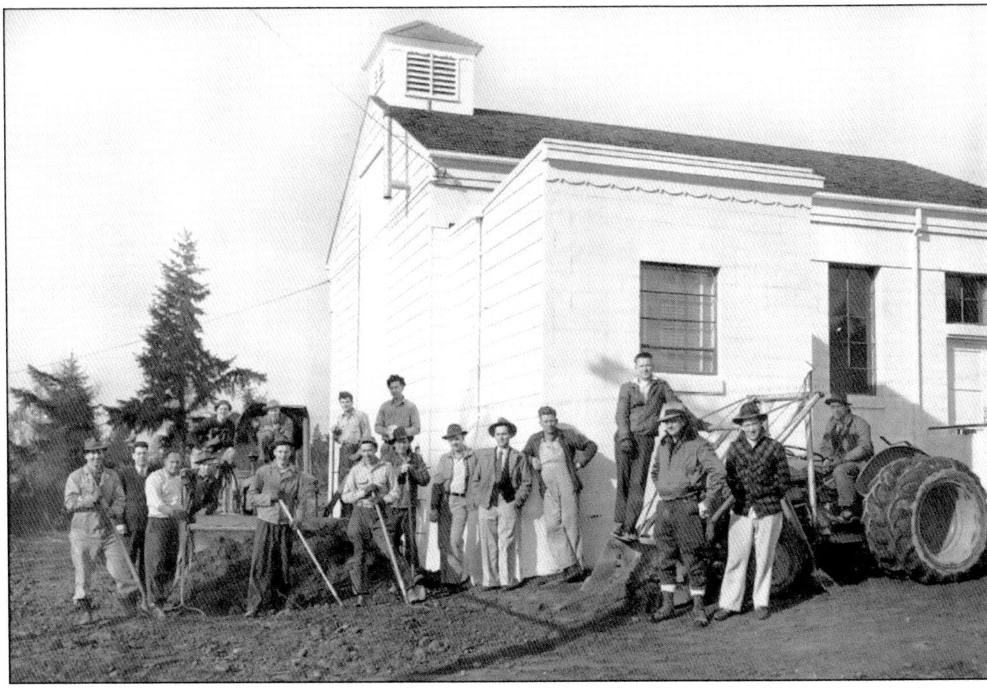

The Fircrest Volunteer Fire Department was organized in 1943. In 1946, the town council passed an ordinance to construct a fire hall. It would be erected on the corner of Electron Way and Regents Boulevard and house a squad of 25 volunteers. Fire hydrants were also installed during this period. This facility would allow Fircrest to do a more efficient job of protecting its citizenry. Above, volunteers prepare the sod and add finishing touches to the grounds. The image below shows the rainy dedication ceremony. (Above, courtesy of the City of Fircrest; below, the Tacoma Public Library, D42698-6.)

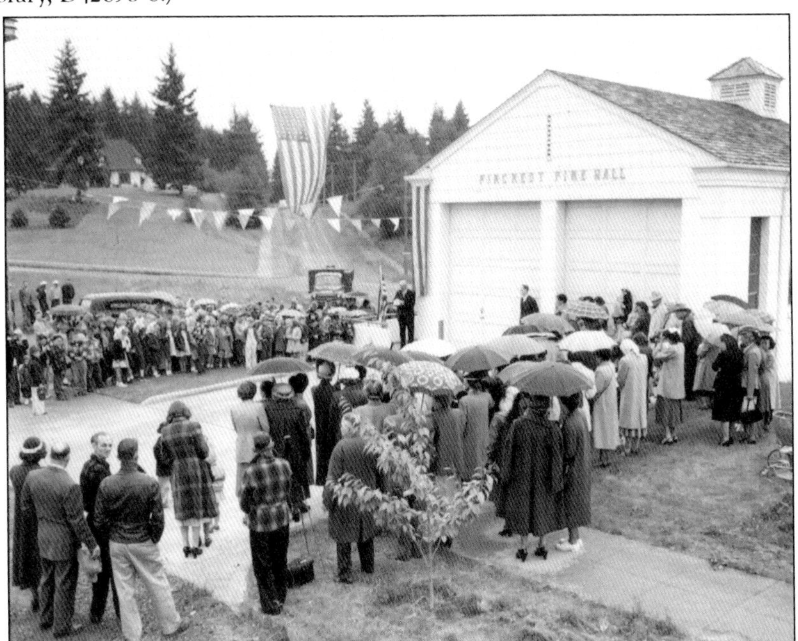

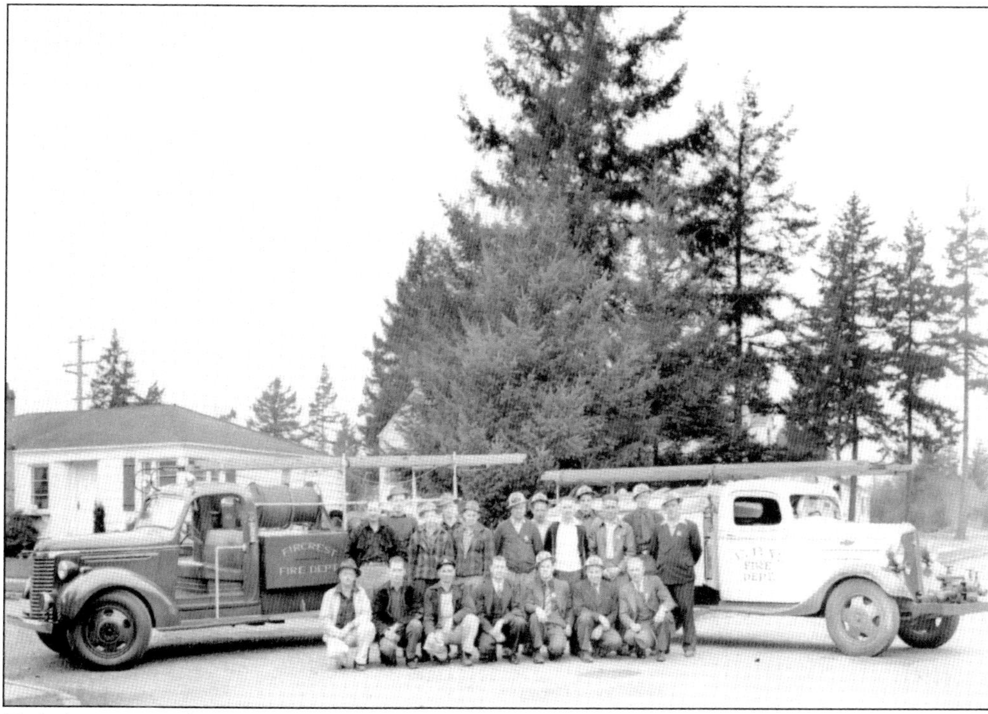

To help support the war effort, Mayor Maxwell Laken created the Fircrest Home Defense in 1942. The purpose of the organization, as outlined by the president of the United States, was "the cooperation and assistance of all municipalities in carrying out the Civilian Defense program." A voluntary subscription was approved for the amount of $10 from each Fircrest family. One of the first purchases was a fire hose. It was also recommended that a fire truck be fabricated to maneuver the often winding and narrow Fircrest streets. This also led to the establishment of the volunteer fire department. (Above, courtesy of the Tacoma Public Library, D12303-B; below, the City of Fircrest.)

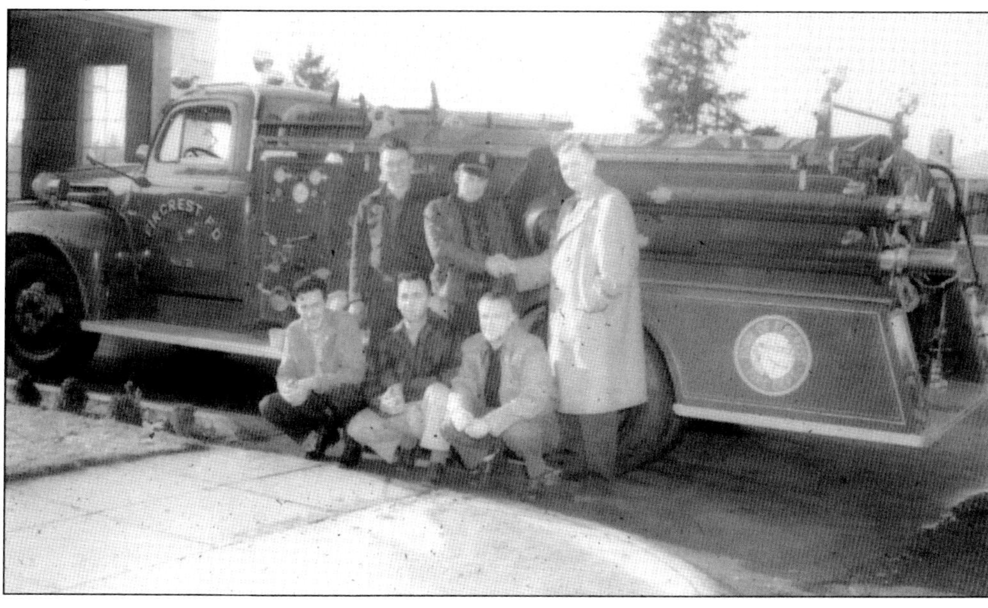

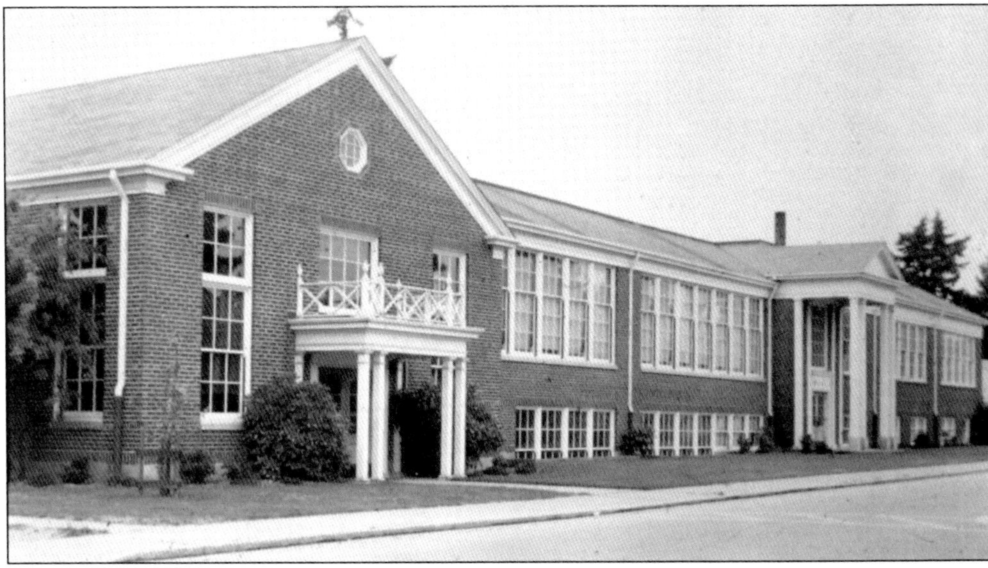

After World War II, Fircrest had grown to a population of nearly 1,200. The people of the city, along with the Tacoma School District, ran a levy to build a much-needed addition to Regents School, Fircrest's only elementary school. The levy passed, and construction began in 1949. As was the custom at the time, it was decided that the new school would bear the name of an American hero, in this case Gen. Jonathan Wainwright, a hero of World War II. The general agreed to attend the opening ceremonies. (Courtesy of the City of Fircrest.)

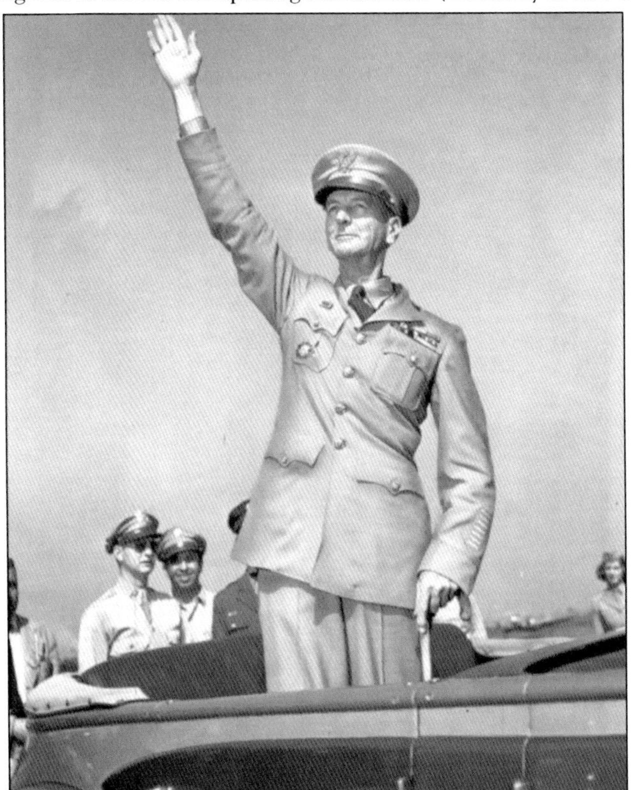

The streets leading to Wainwright School were lined with military personnel as well as most of the citizens of Fircrest. Jonathan "Skinny" Wainwright IV was an officer in the US Army. During the early stages of World War II, Wainwright was the commander of Allied forces in the Philippines at the time of their surrender to the Empire of Japan. He was a prisoner of war for three years. This time of deprivation earned him the nickname "Skinny." He was the recipient of the Medal of Honor for his courageous leadership. (Courtesy of the Library of Congress.)

Four

Mid-Century Modern

Like America in general, Fircrest experienced an explosion in population and building following World War II. People found in Fircrest shovel-ready building sites and in-place infrastructure. These were plum sites for builders eager to meet the demands for housing. Businesses quickly followed the populace. Besides the advantages of the developed infrastructure, Fircrest still offered what Regents Park first promised: meandering streets, parks, activities for families, and a "Mayberry-like" lifestyle. The streets were well designed, the houses were well built, and the town was well established. It was impossible for the mid-century population to ignore the allure of a town so aligned with the American dream. Realtors, such as Hawkins-Poe, builders, like Swanstrom, and entrepreneurs, such as the Manley family, recognized the value of locating in Fircrest.

As houses and businesses were established, the City of Fircrest recognized that it needed to meet the demands of its growing population. Pipes were laid and updated, surface roads were replaced, and amenities, such as parks and pools, were created. City government became more formalized, with specific jobs and responsibilities.

The people who moved to Fircrest tended toward affluence and were civic-minded and socially involved. Sometimes referred to as the "cocktail culture," Fircrest reflected the characteristics of classic mid-century America. These citizens built bars in their dens and bomb shelters in their backyards. The rambler was the preferred residential architectural style, and American Modern was the interior style of choice. There were parades, pool parties, and dancing at the community center.

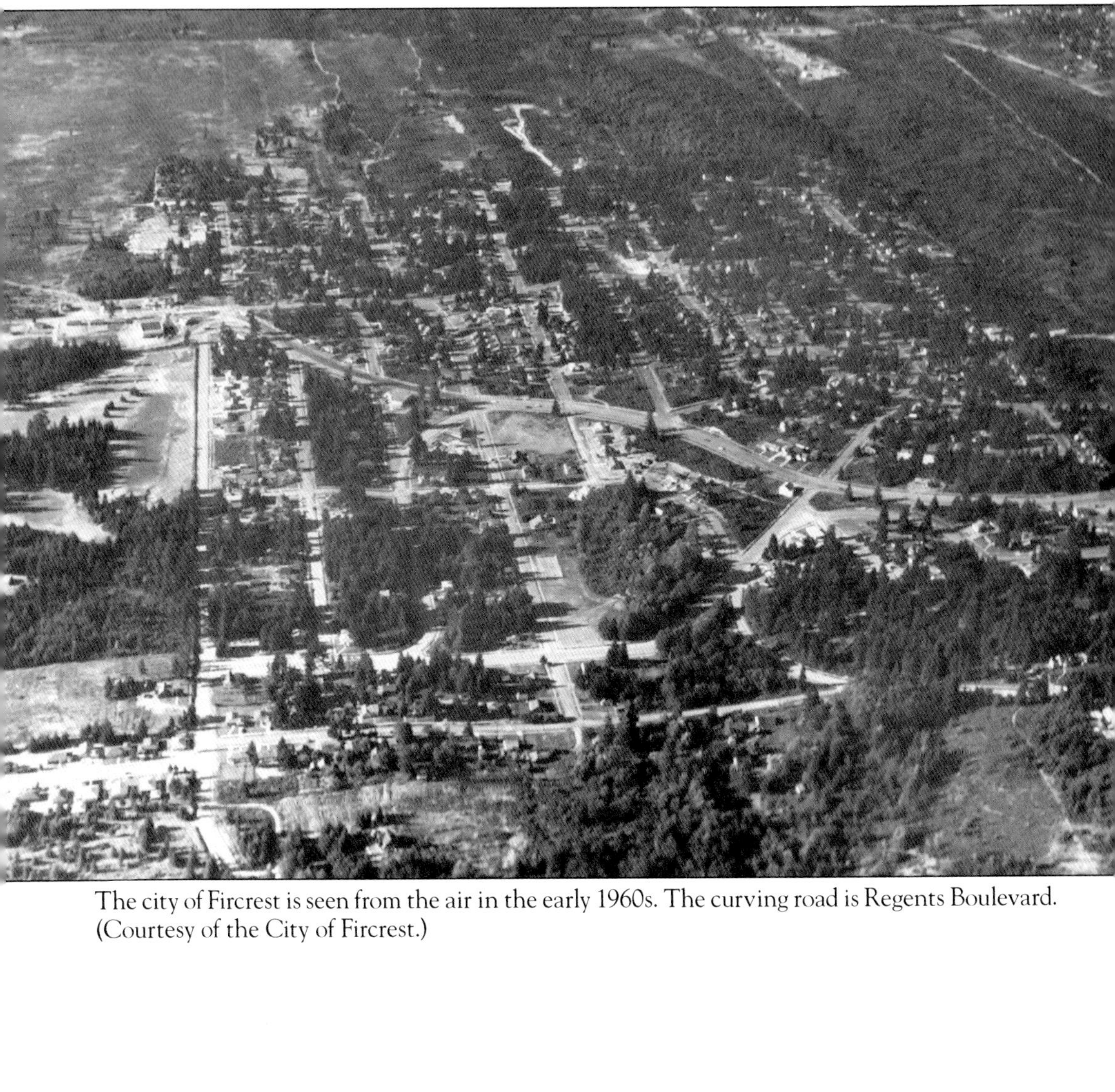

The city of Fircrest is seen from the air in the early 1960s. The curving road is Regents Boulevard. (Courtesy of the City of Fircrest.)

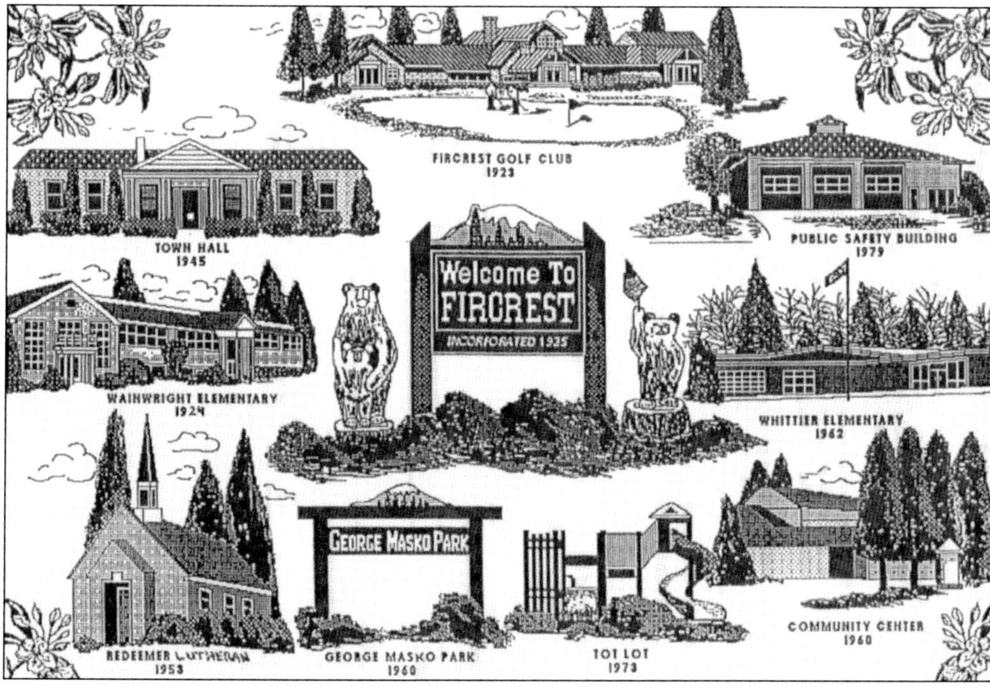

In 1946, Jack Hawkins started a real estate company in Fircrest. Burns Poe joined the company in 1952, and Hawkins-Poe Realty was formed. For many years, the firm's offices were located on Regents Boulevard. The company was responsible for purchasing land and developing commercial and residential sites. This Hawkins-Poe advertisement shows local attractions. (Courtesy of the City of Fircrest.)

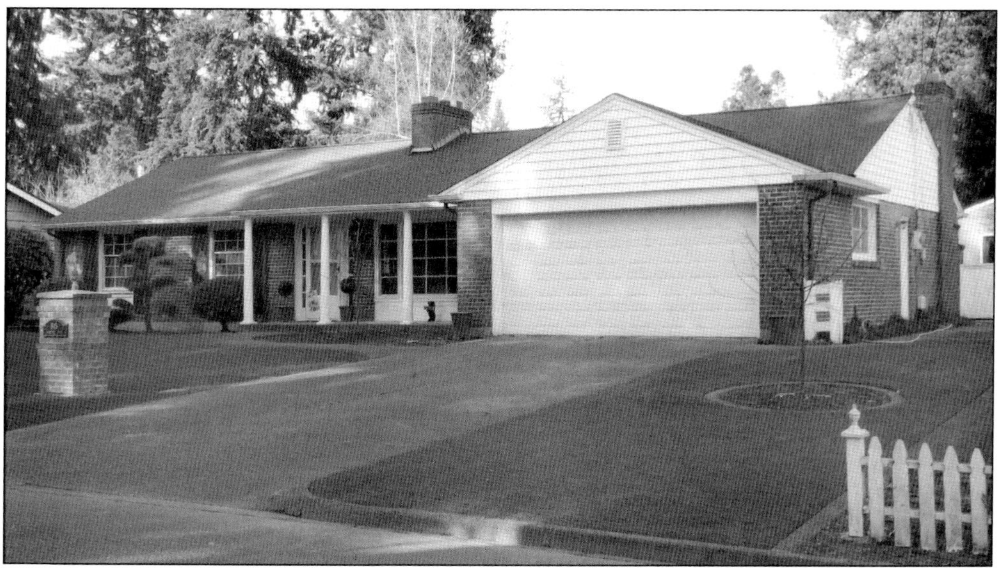

Alfred Swanstrom was a well-known builder in the Fircrest/Tacoma area in the 1950s and 1960s. Many of his iconic homes can still be seen in Fircrest today. Pictured here is a typical example of the high-quality homes that Swanstrom built. The "Swanstrom's Addition" to Fircrest was incorporated into the city in 1954. This section, west of Alameda Avenue and south and east of Fircrest Golf Club, is centered on Fairway Drive. (Photograph by R.R. Colyer.)

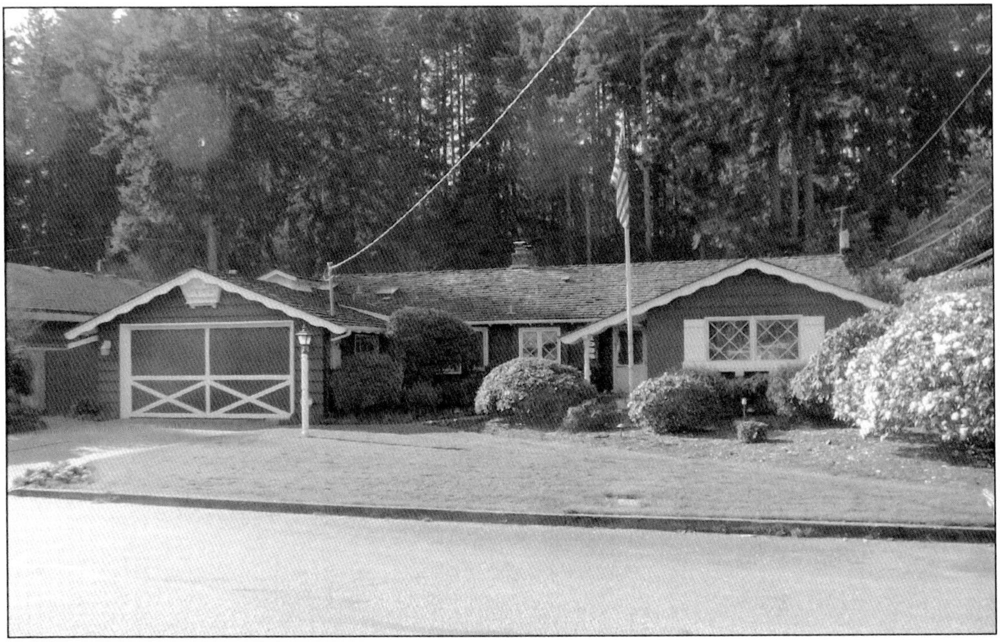

Swanstrom homes were built with design features that identified their style to passersby in an early example of branding. A typical Swanstrom home was an American rambler with shuttered windows of diamond glass, wide porches, dormers, and gingerbread eaves with multifamily birdhouses. Alfred Swanstrom's iconic homes, coveted in Fircrest, bring premium prices in the local real estate market. (Both photographs by R.R. Colyer.)

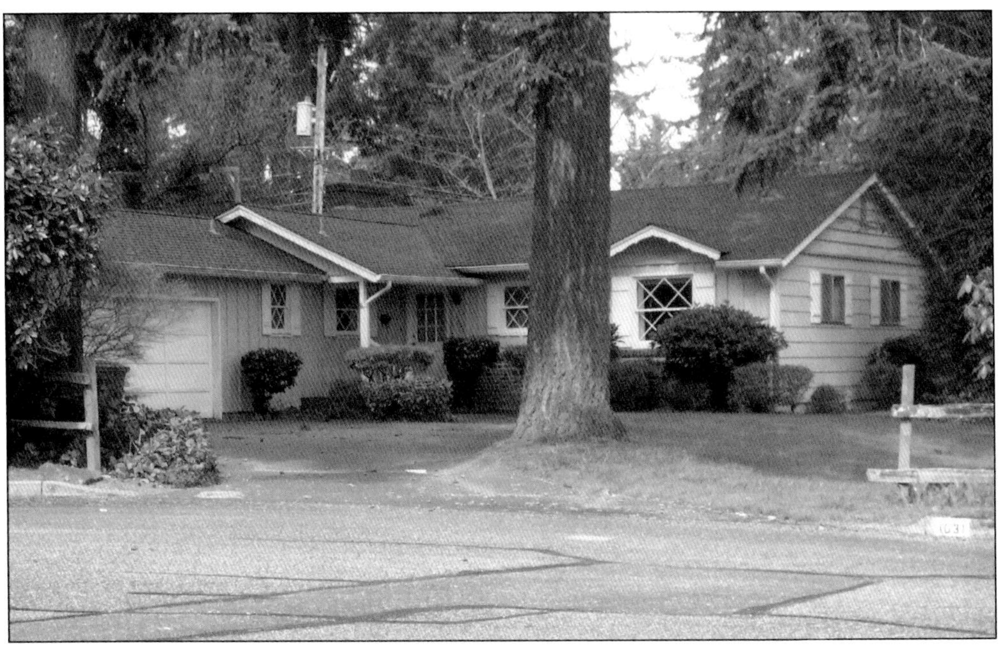

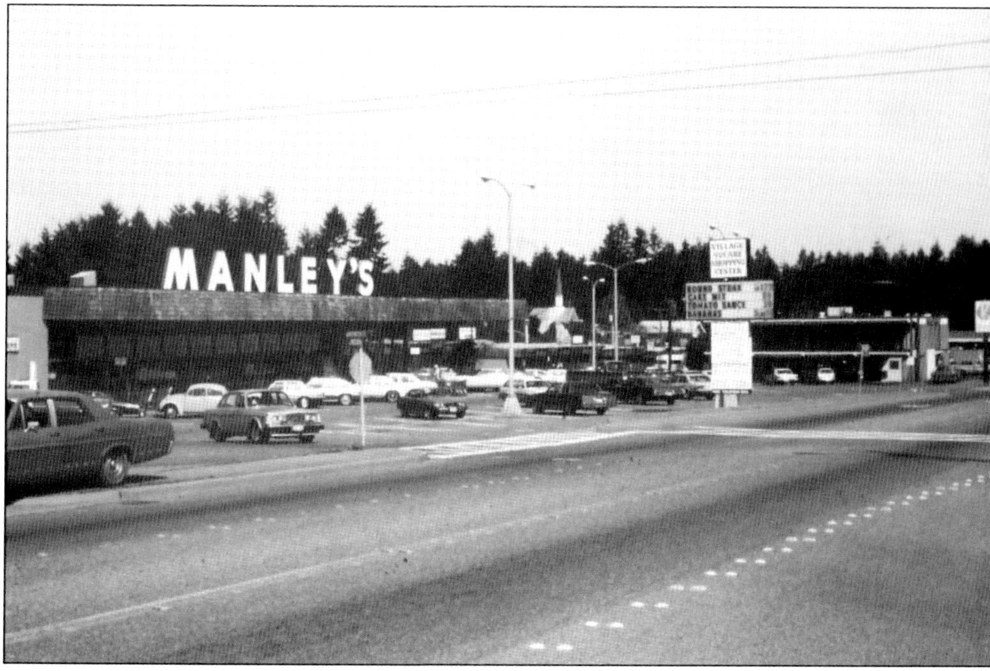

On March 16, 1945, Manley-Davis Market (above) opened on Regents Boulevard, down the street from the original business district in Fircrest. Manley-Davis was strategically located next to Birchler's Cold Storage (below). This was very handy for the many hunters in the area; Manley-Davis cut and wrapped their meats, which were then stored next door at Birchler's. (Both courtesy of the City of Fircrest.)

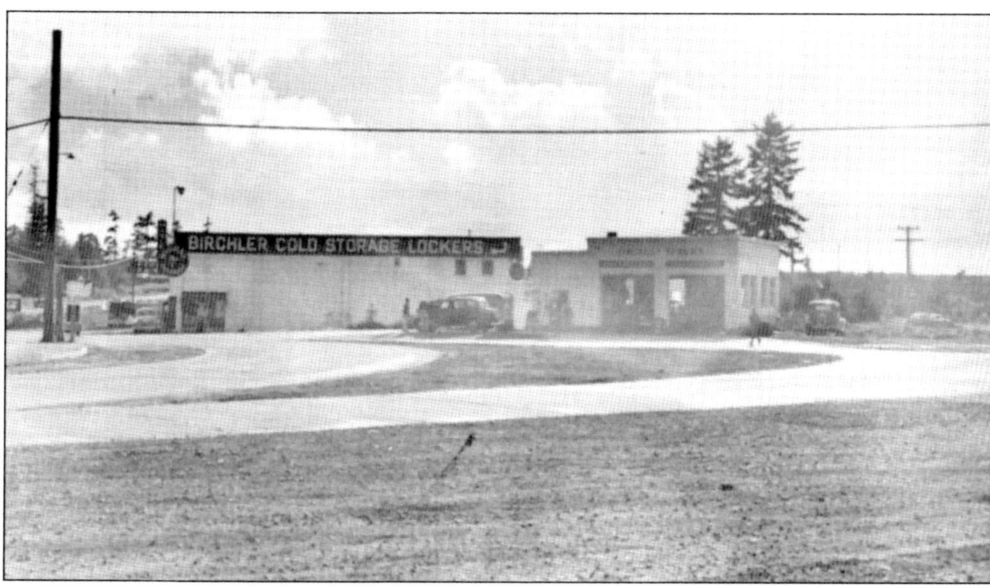

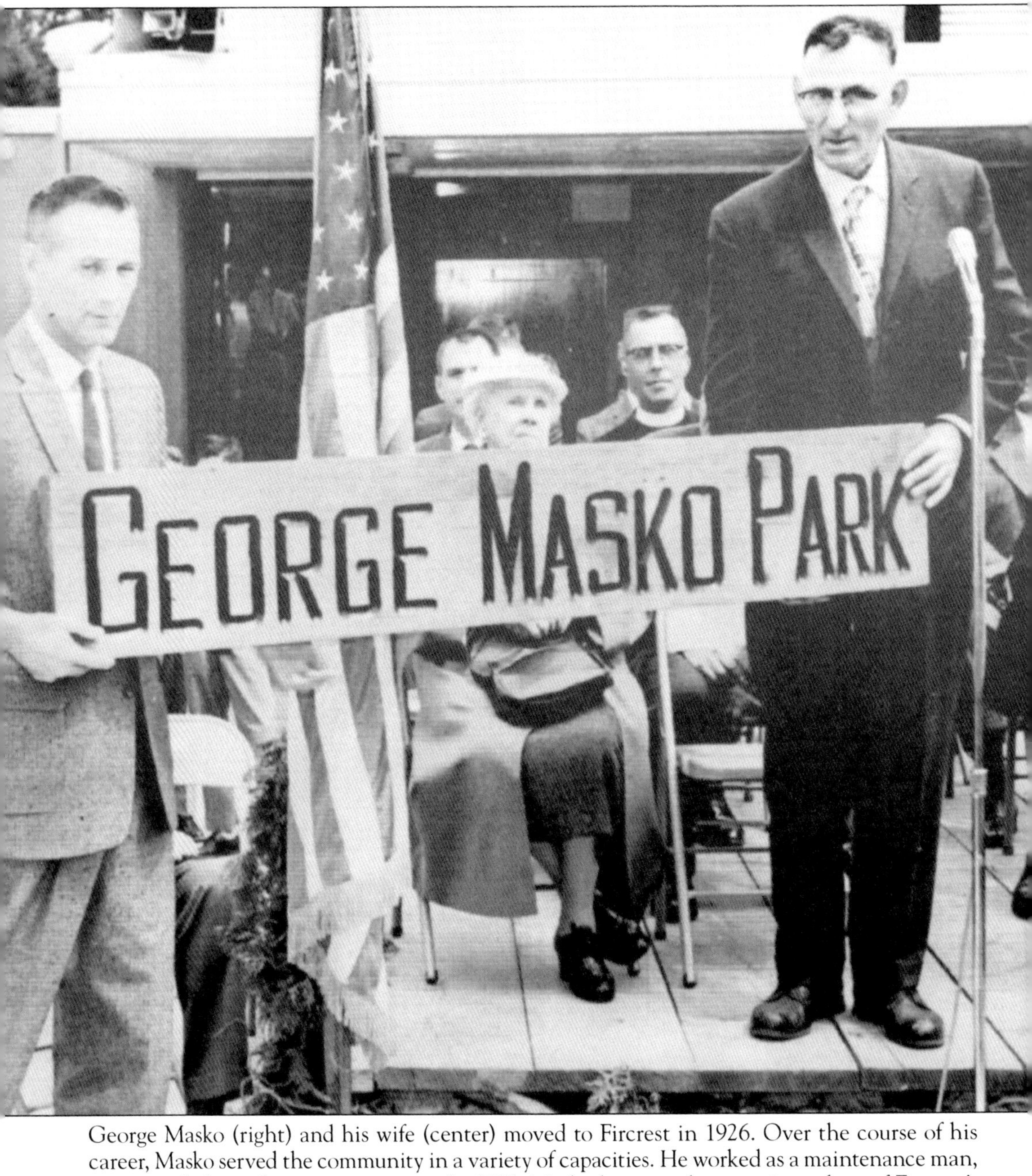

George Masko (right) and his wife (center) moved to Fircrest in 1926. Over the course of his career, Masko served the community in a variety of capacities. He worked as a maintenance man, repairing light and water equipment. In 1935, Masko became the superintendent of Fircrest's maintenance and utility department. As such, he personally mapped out the town's entire sewer, electrical, water, and street systems. His maps were an invaluable source of information for years to come. In 1960, Masko Park was dedicated in his honor. The park was really three parks in one: a rhododendron garden, a war memorial, and a memorial garden for music composers, authors, and artists. (Courtesy of the City of Fircrest.)

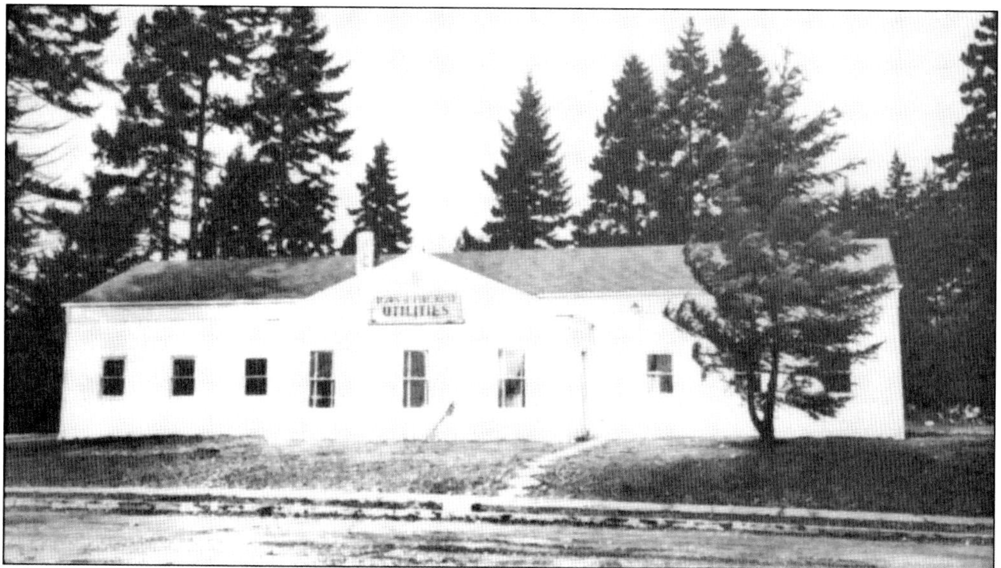

The town's utility building was constructed in 1945 at 115 Ramsdell Street. This allowed the City of Fircrest to purchase much-needed equipment to help maintain grounds, utilities, and infrastructure. The building also contained meeting space for the town council. Later, the building was devoted entirely to the government of Fircrest, and new utility facilities were built. (Courtesy of the City of Fircrest.)

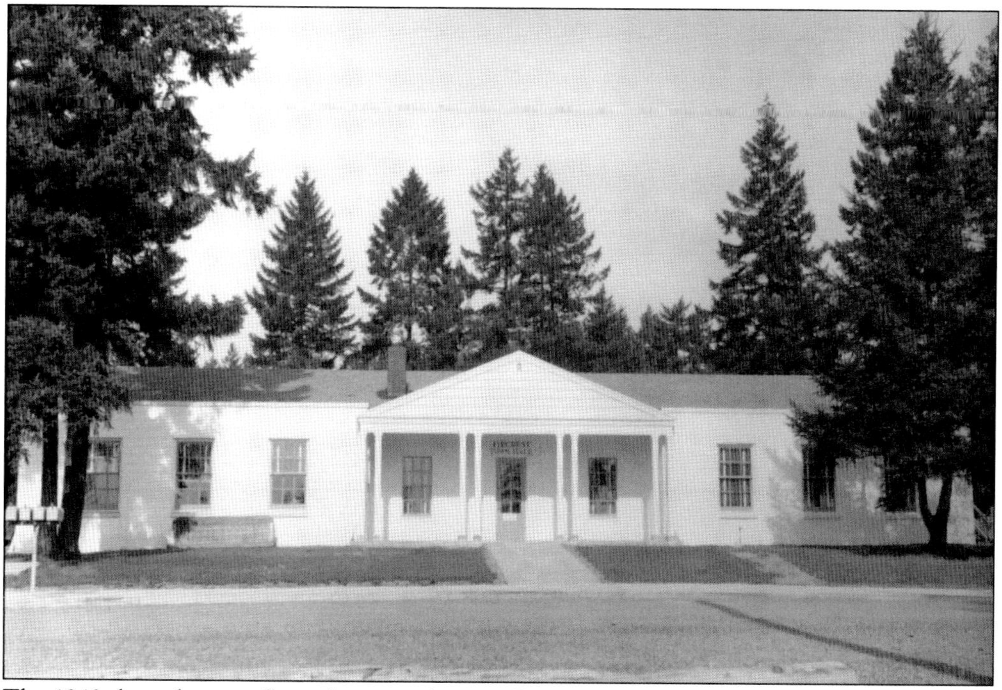

The 1940s brought an influx of new residents to Fircrest. Because of housing shortages, officers from Fort Lewis were allowed to live farther from the base; several settled in the Fircrest area. Following World War II, towns and cities throughout Washington experienced rapid growth. In 1953, the town hall (formally the Utility Building) was remodeled to accommodate the growing community. (Courtesy of the City of Fircrest.)

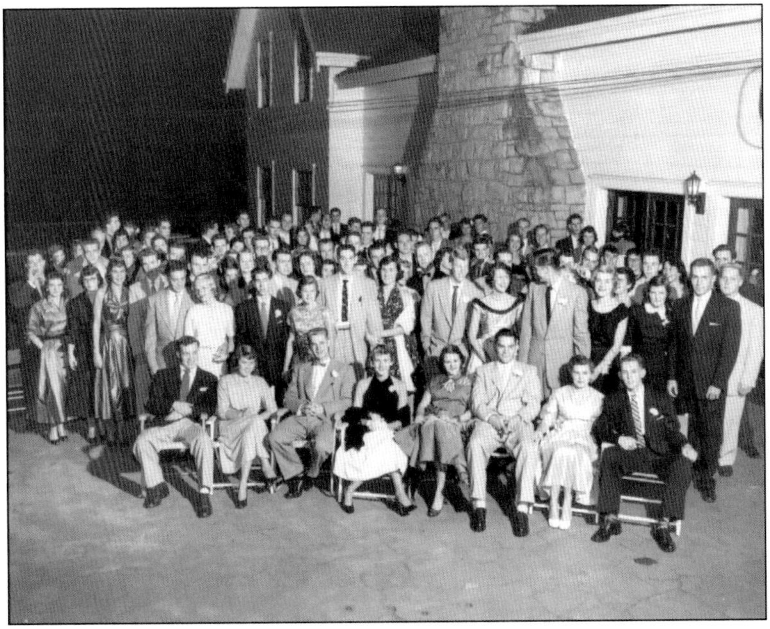

On a beautiful evening in August 1952, the Delta Theta Sorority held its summer dance at Fircrest Golf Club. The theme for the evening soiree was "A Night in Monte Carlo." The summer dance was held each year to honor the members of the group who would be leaving for college in the fall. (Courtesy of the Tacoma Public Library, D68530-5.)

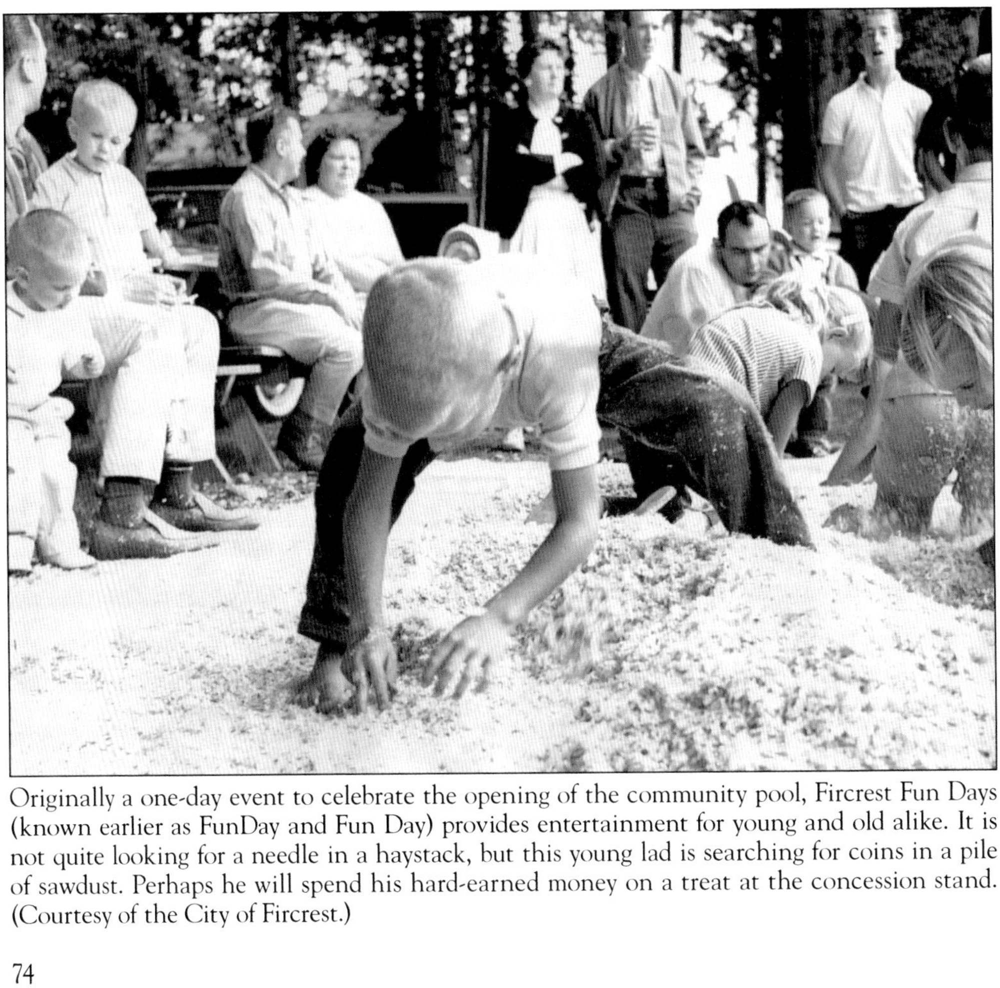

Originally a one-day event to celebrate the opening of the community pool, Fircrest Fun Days (known earlier as FunDay and Fun Day) provides entertainment for young and old alike. It is not quite looking for a needle in a haystack, but this young lad is searching for coins in a pile of sawdust. Perhaps he will spend his hard-earned money on a treat at the concession stand. (Courtesy of the City of Fircrest.)

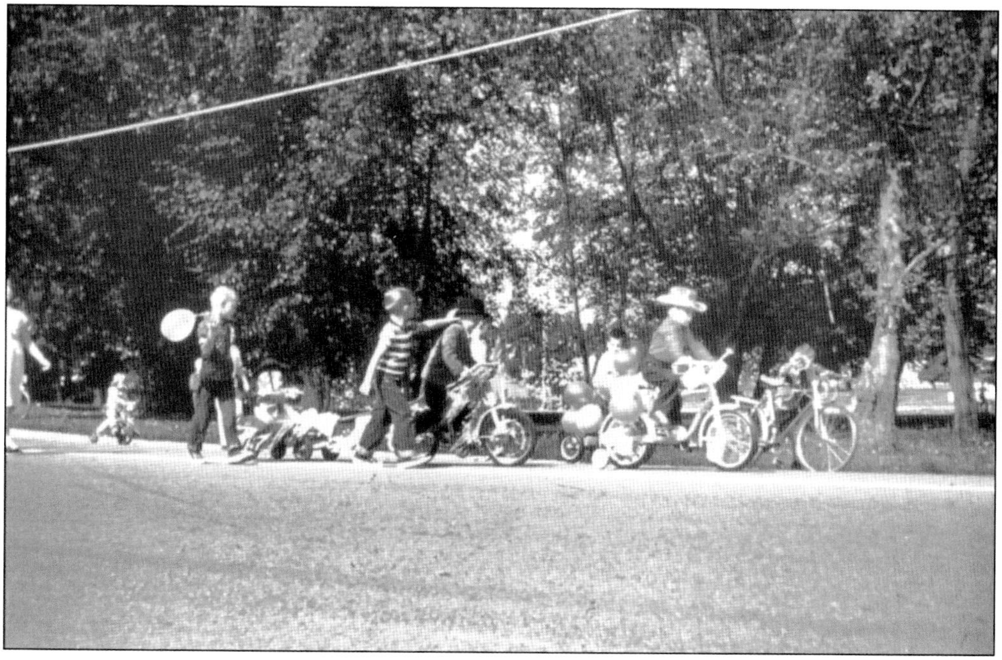

Fircrest commemorated its golden jubilee in 1957, and did so in style! A year of planning and events culminated in September with a Street-O-Rama, in which Fircrest Park was turned into a midway, with rides, booths, and ponies. There was dancing on the tennis courts, a pancake breakfast, and stage shows, among other events. Regents Boulevard was the scene of the children's bike and pet parade, as shown in these photographs. (Both courtesy of the City of Fircrest.)

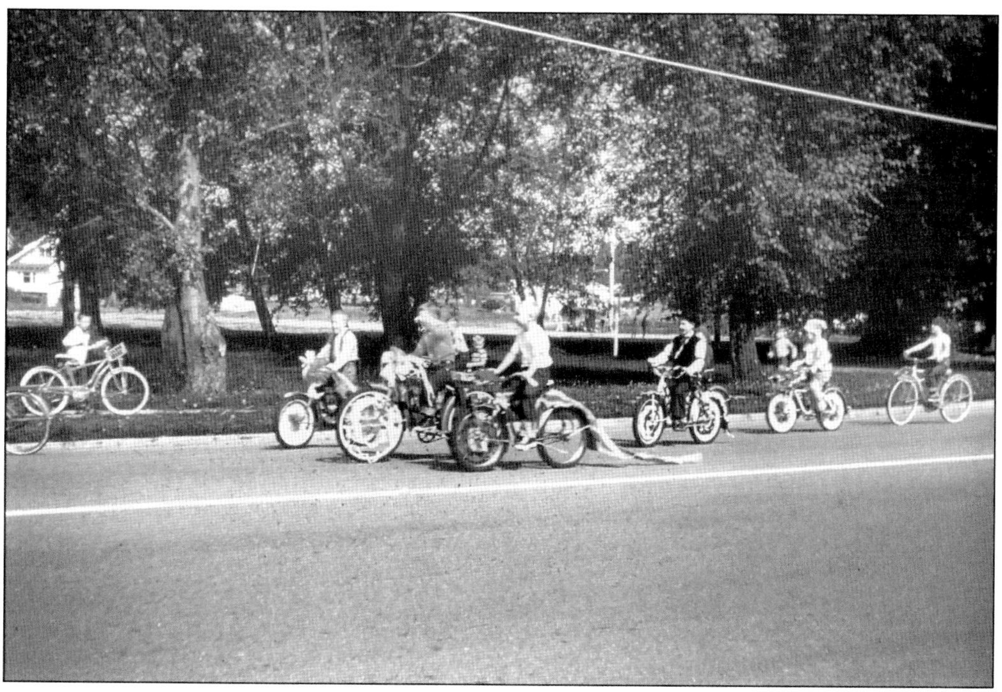

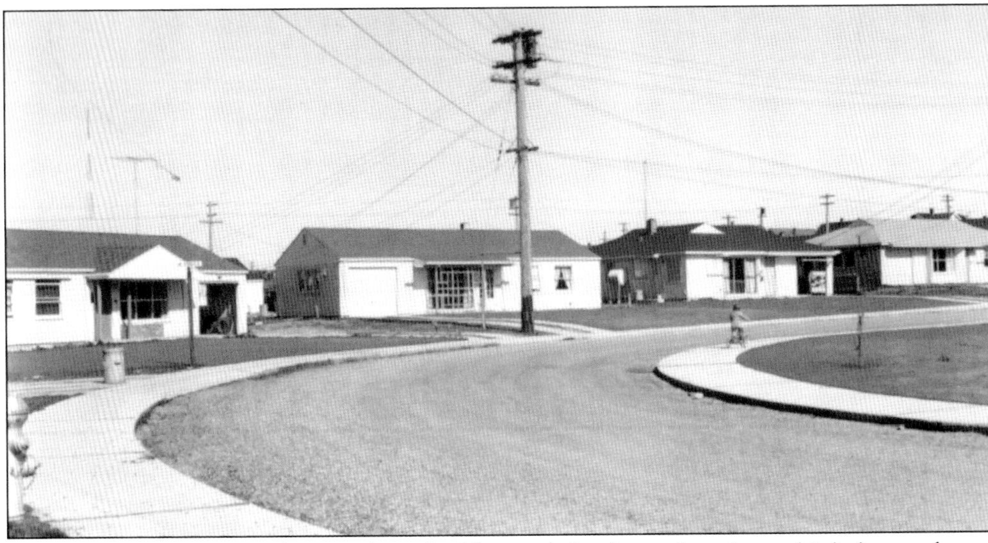

Throughout the 1950s and 1960s, homebuilders and developers bought multiple lots and even entire blocks, in order to put in multiple residences with similar floor plans. Here, houses line Spring Street, across from Fircrest Park. Note the fire hydrant in the foreground. As part of the city's infrastructure improvements, hydrants were installed in the latter half of the 1940s. (Courtesy of the Tacoma Public Library, D61271-7.)

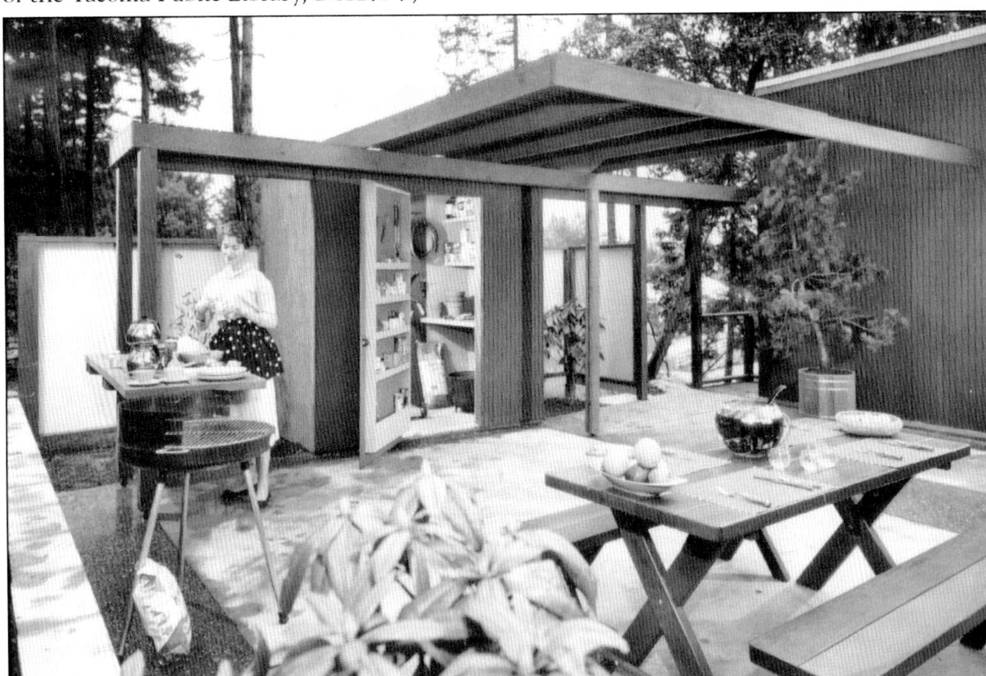

This outdoor living space and storage shed was the focus of a promotional photograph taken on behalf of the Douglas Fir Plywood Association in January 1959. The shed's interior shows garden supplies as well as storage area. Walt Widmeyer had designed the plywood storage unit for his own home in Fircrest, located at 612 Dartmouth Street. The woman in the image is a professional model and not a member of the Widmeyer family. (Courtesy of the Tacoma Public Library, A118944-6.)

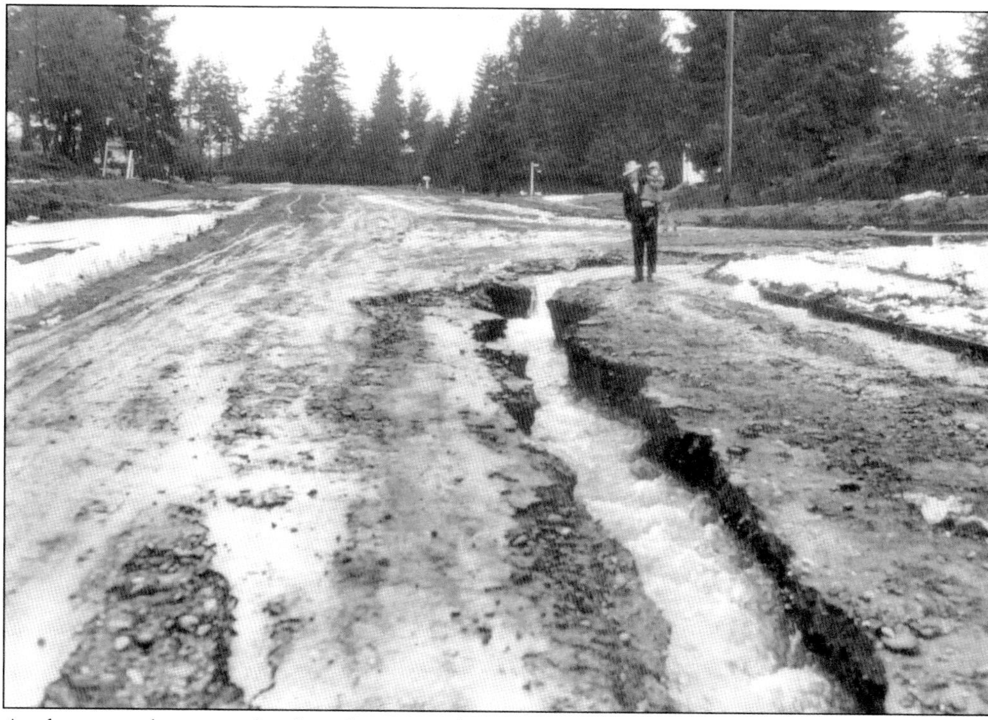

As the empty lots were developed, more and more runoff went into the aging streets of Fircrest. The roads of the city passed the 50-year mark, and it became evident nearly every time it rained that drainage was becoming a real problem. These photographs illustrate the damage from erosion due to runoff that was plaguing Fircrest at the time. (Both courtesy of the City of Fircrest.)

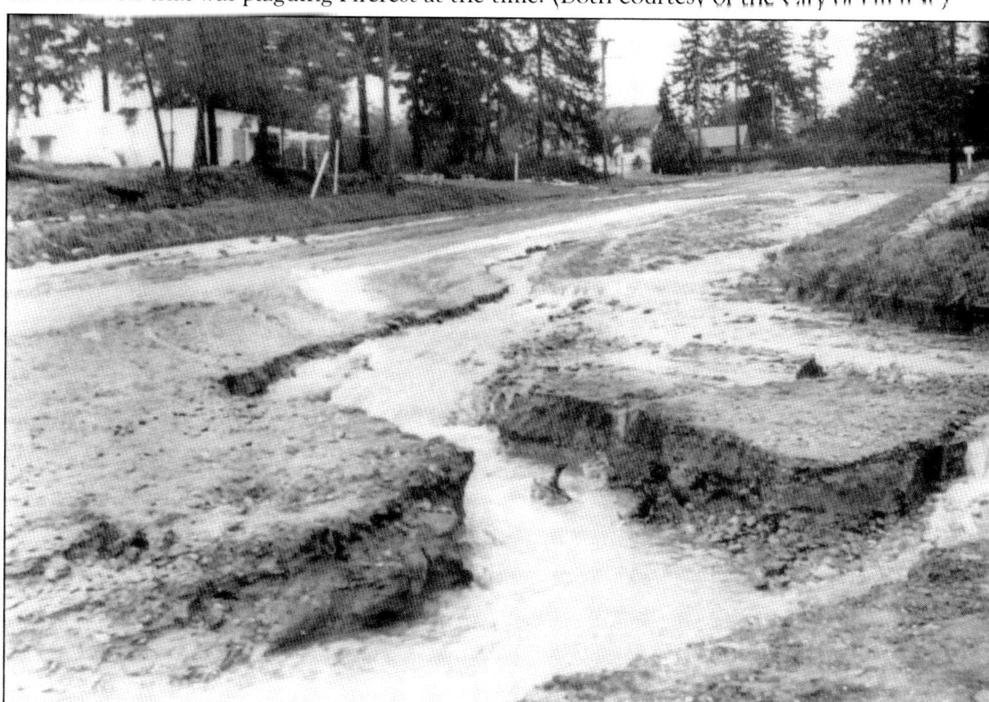

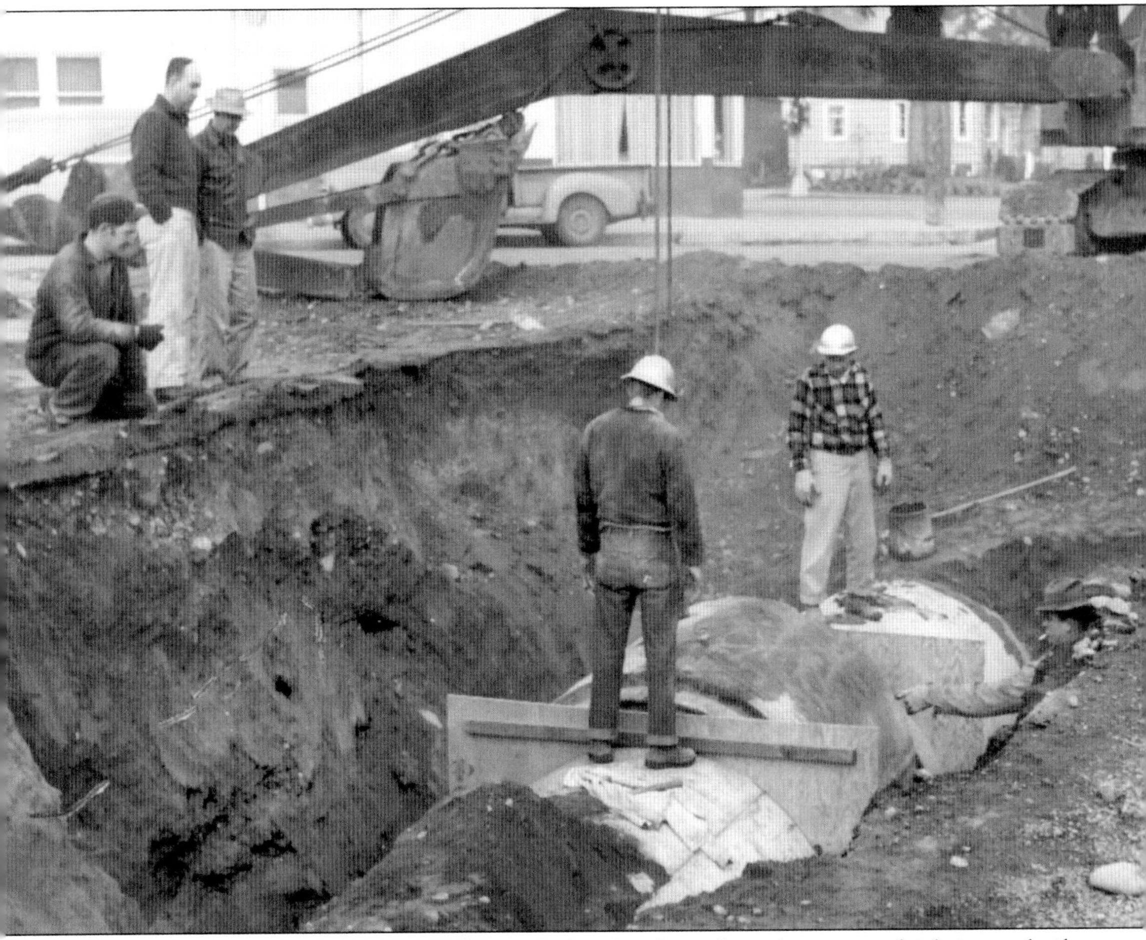

Fircrest was named for the second-growth firs that line the ridge upon which it was built. Being a western Washington community, rain and water are abundant. Fircrest was blessed and cursed with springs, streams, lakes, and wetlands. Rain only exacerbated the drainage issue. The city government tackled this nagging problem by installing storm drains and drainage systems. (Courtesy of the City of Fircrest.)

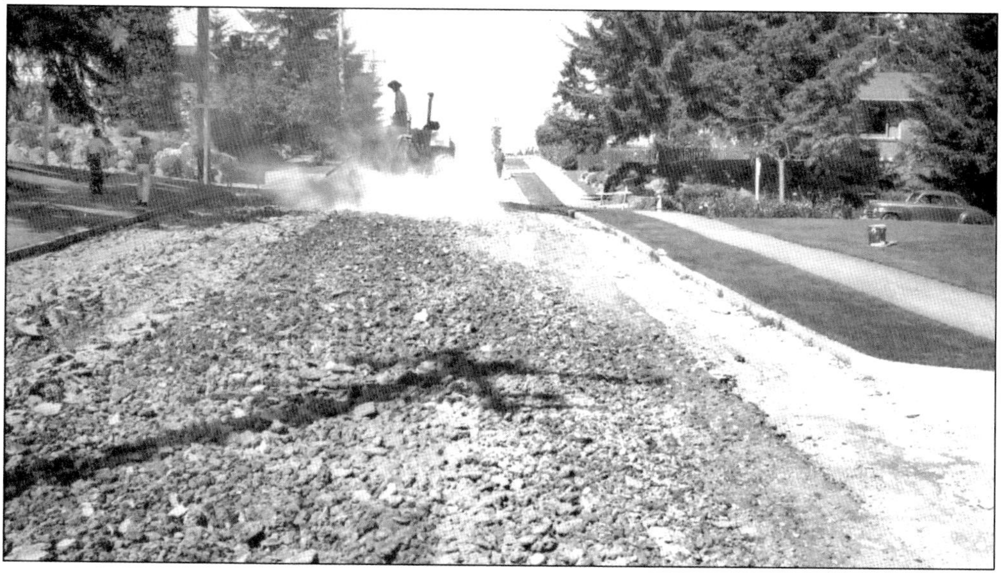

In these photographs, the original Regents Park streets, laid by men in horse-drawn wagons, are being torn up by a tractor in preparation for new paving. The original roads were asphalt, which was a new technology in 1907. After 50 years of use and disuse, the roads were ready for renewal. (Both courtesy of the City of Fircrest.)

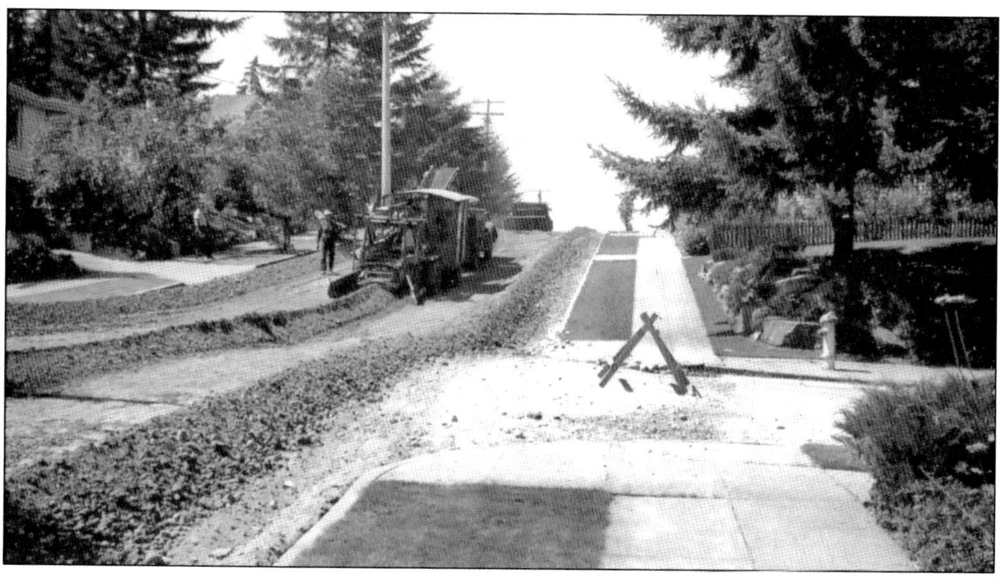

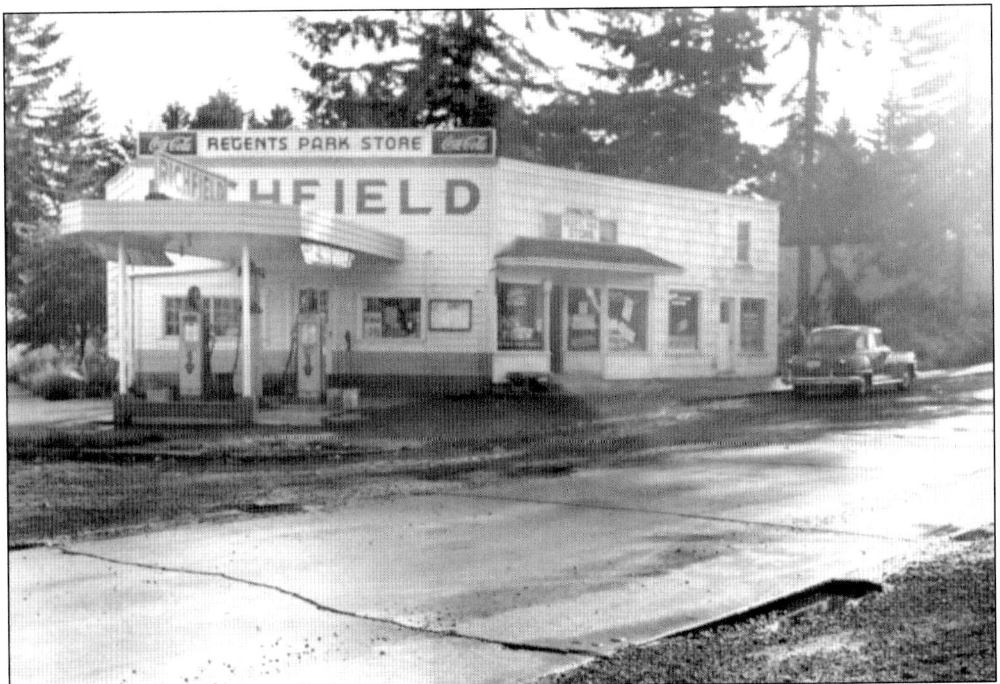

The original business district in Fircrest was located on Regents Boulevard between Berkeley Avenue and Bowes Drive. These storefronts have hosted a variety of business over the years. The photograph above shows the Regents Park Store, including a gas station. The pumps were removed in 1953, when a barbershop moved into the remodeled space. Shown below is Hagen's Grocery. Other businesses included the Crest Restaurant, Fircrest Drug Store, Twinkle Cleaners, and a beauty shop. (Both courtesy of the City of Fircrest.)

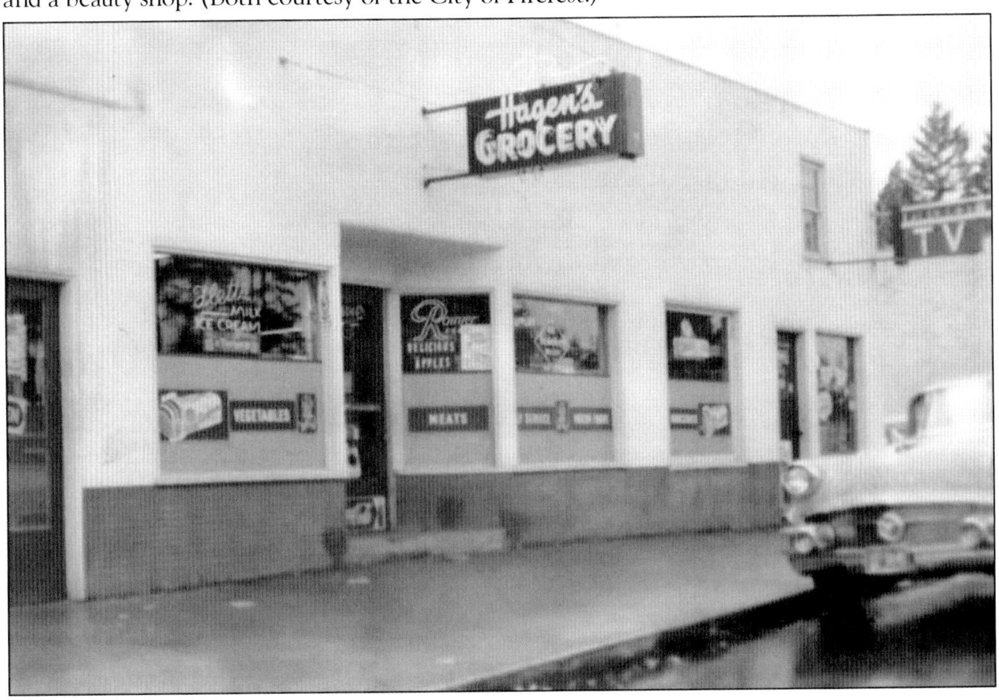

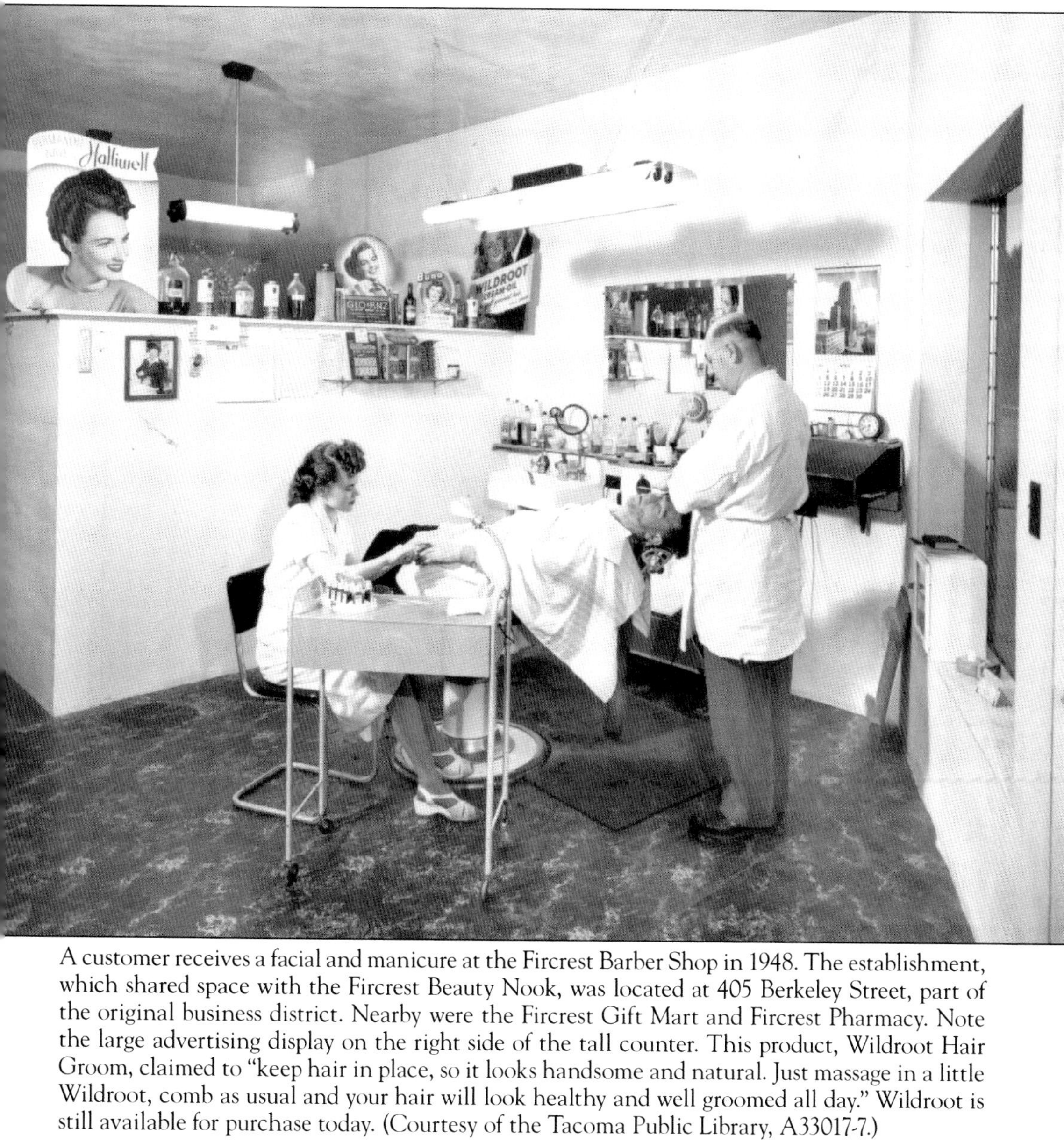

A customer receives a facial and manicure at the Fircrest Barber Shop in 1948. The establishment, which shared space with the Fircrest Beauty Nook, was located at 405 Berkeley Street, part of the original business district. Nearby were the Fircrest Gift Mart and Fircrest Pharmacy. Note the large advertising display on the right side of the tall counter. This product, Wildroot Hair Groom, claimed to "keep hair in place, so it looks handsome and natural. Just massage in a little Wildroot, comb as usual and your hair will look healthy and well groomed all day." Wildroot is still available for purchase today. (Courtesy of the Tacoma Public Library, A33017-7.)

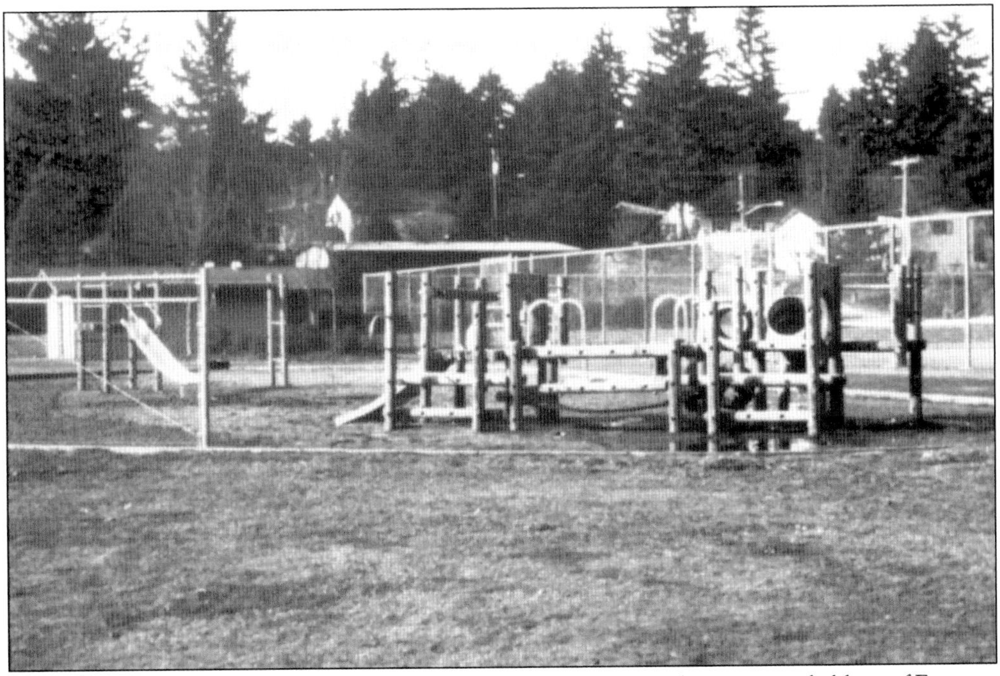

The Tot Lot was purchased in 1964 to provide a safe play area for the younger children of Fircrest. This attention to parks and recreation by the city on behalf of its citizens did not go unnoticed. An Associated Press article published by the Washington State Parks and Recreation Commission reported that residents of Fircrest were paying more financial attention to such amenities than those of any other town in the state. (Both courtesy of the City of Fircrest.)

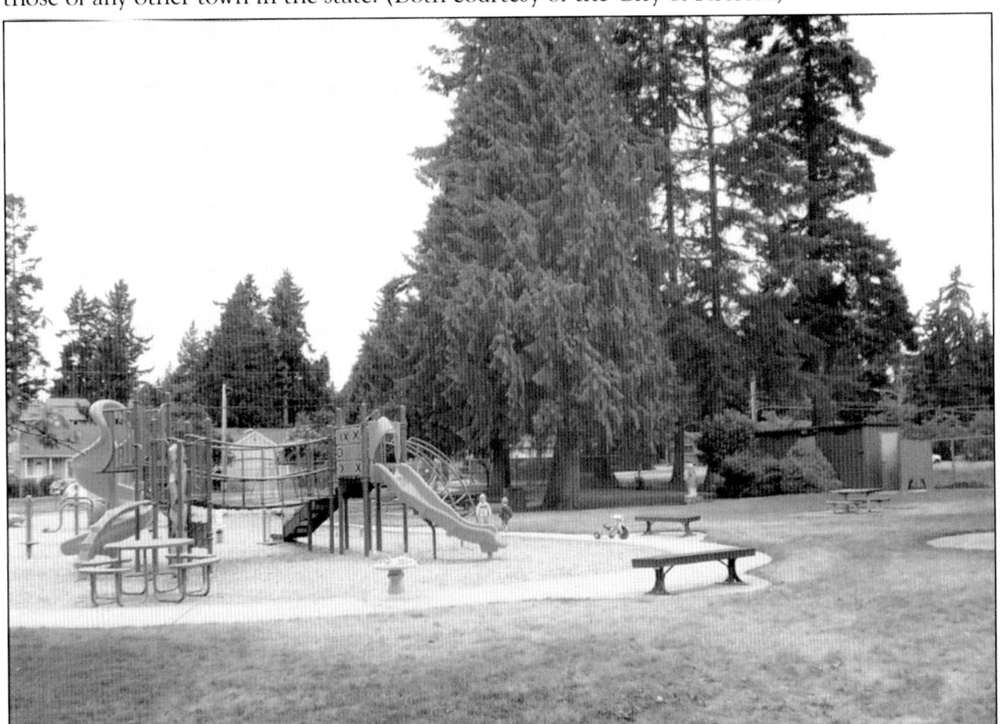

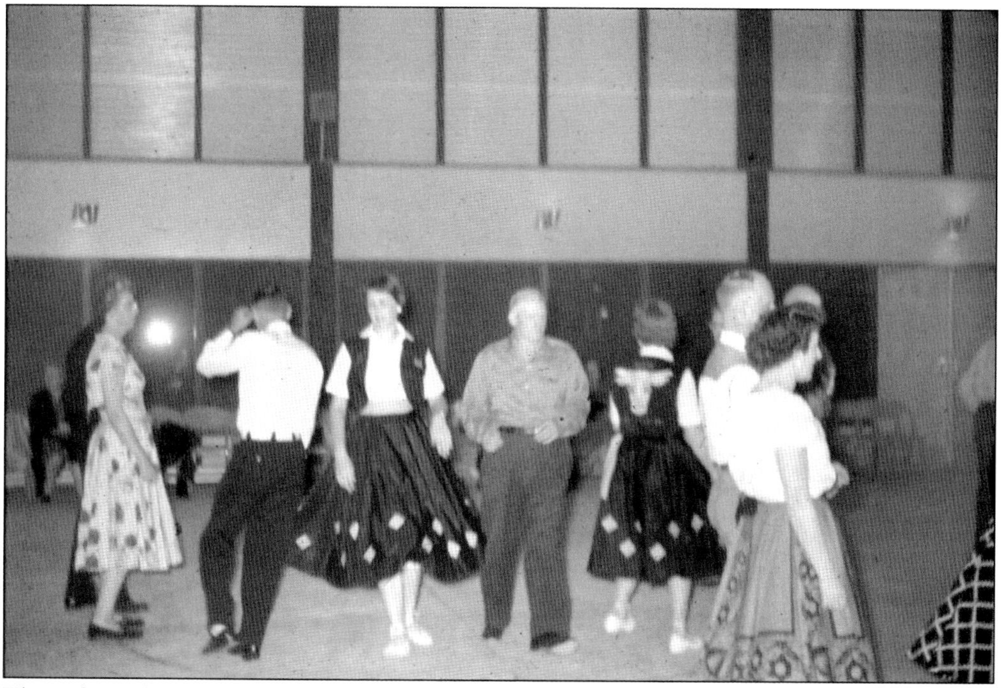

Throughout the years, the community center has hosted a variety of events. Arts-and-craft fairs, sewing classes, bingo, and photographs with Santa Claus have all been hosted in the park. Here, Fircrest residents celebrate the community's golden jubilee with a night on the town—"Turn your partner and do-si-do!" (Courtesy of the City of Fircrest.)

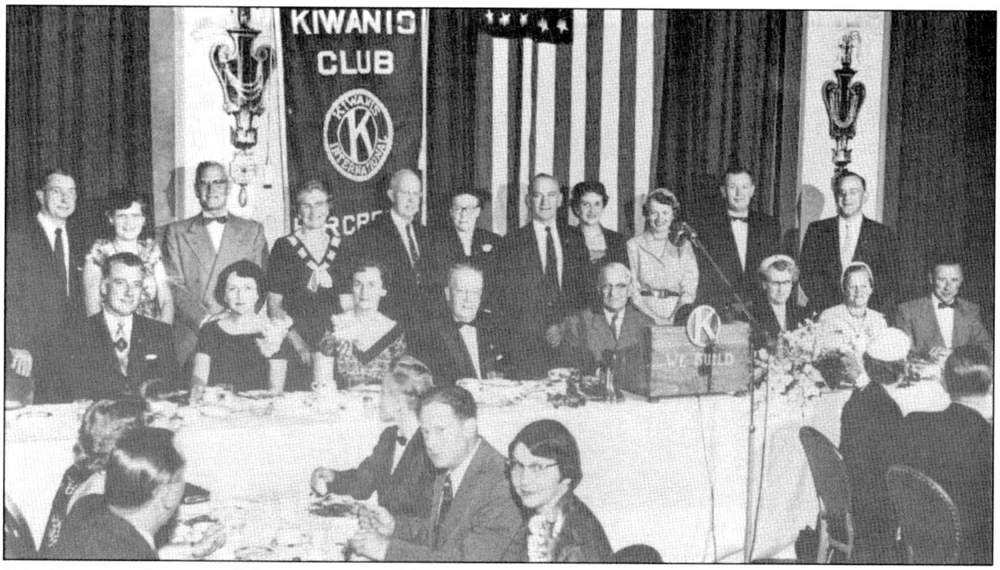

The Fircrest chapter of the Kiwanis Club was chartered in 1955. Originally a men's organization, Kiwanis is now a coeducational service club, but the goals remain the same as in 1955. Members organize volunteers to promote activities to improve health and education. They also encourage leadership and service. In Fircrest, the Kiwanis have sponsored ball teams and Scout groups, helped to establish the Tot Lot, erected a picnic structure at Whittier Park, and engaged in many other activities to improve the quality of life in Fircrest. (Courtesy of the City of Fircrest.)

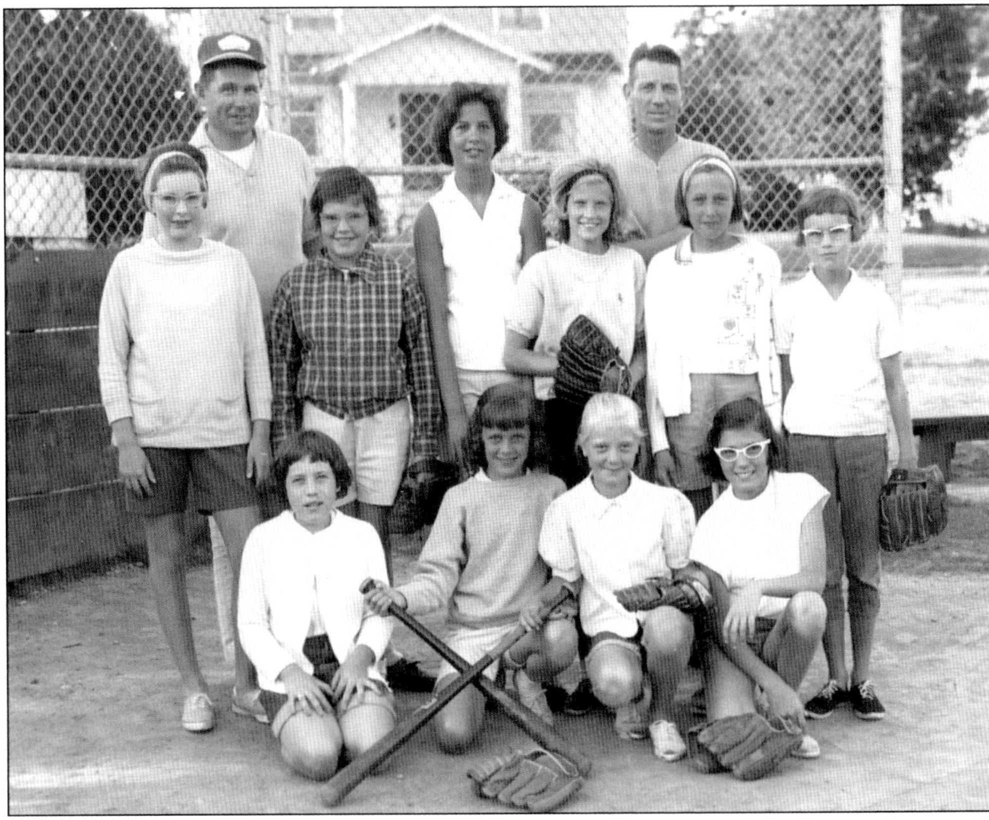

The Fircrest Kiwanis and the Fircrest Recreation Association (later renamed the Fircrest Community Club) sponsored many baseball teams and leagues, including the boys and girls teams shown on this page. (Both courtesy of the City of Fircrest.)

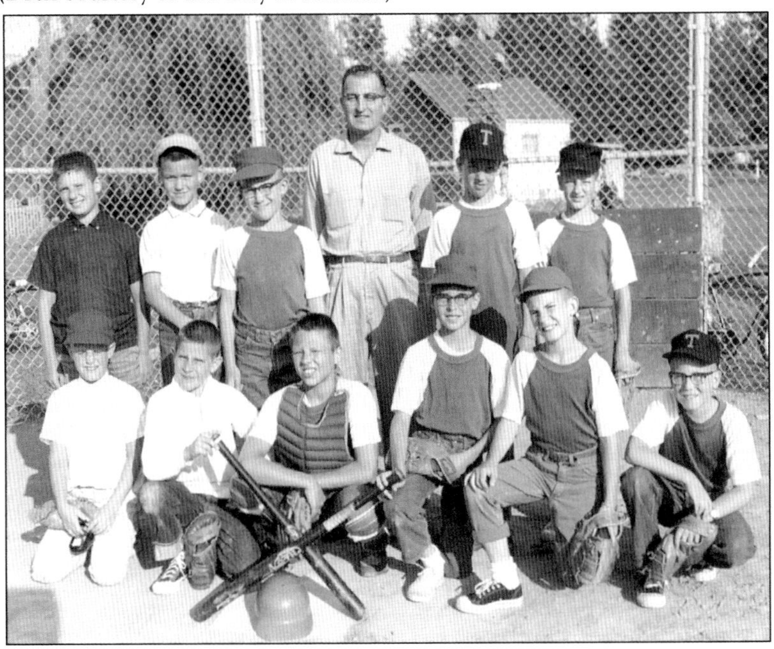

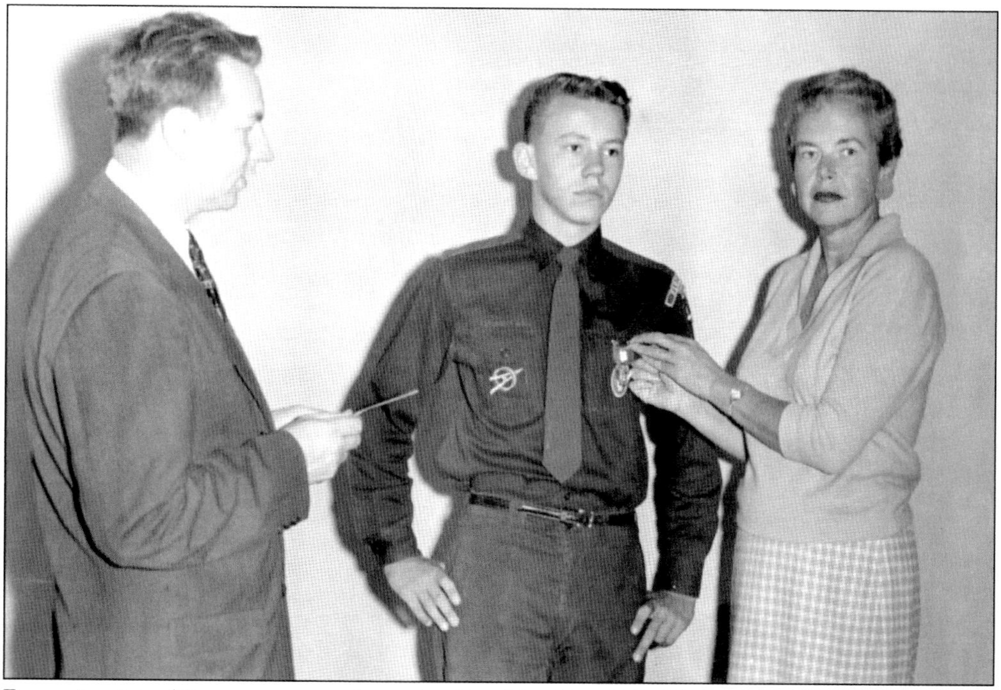

Fircrest's original Scout troop was formed as Post No. 47 in 1953. The city had its first Eagle Scout six years later. Ted Keeney was 15 years old in August 1959 when the mayor of Fircrest presented him with his award. Here, Mr. and Mrs. Al Keeney of 163 Summit Avenue in Fircrest flank their son. Ted was a Boy Scout for four years and an Explorer Scout for one year before earning his Eagle Scout. His father had been an Eagle Scout, and his mother was a Brownie troop leader in Fircrest. (Courtesy of the City of Fircrest.)

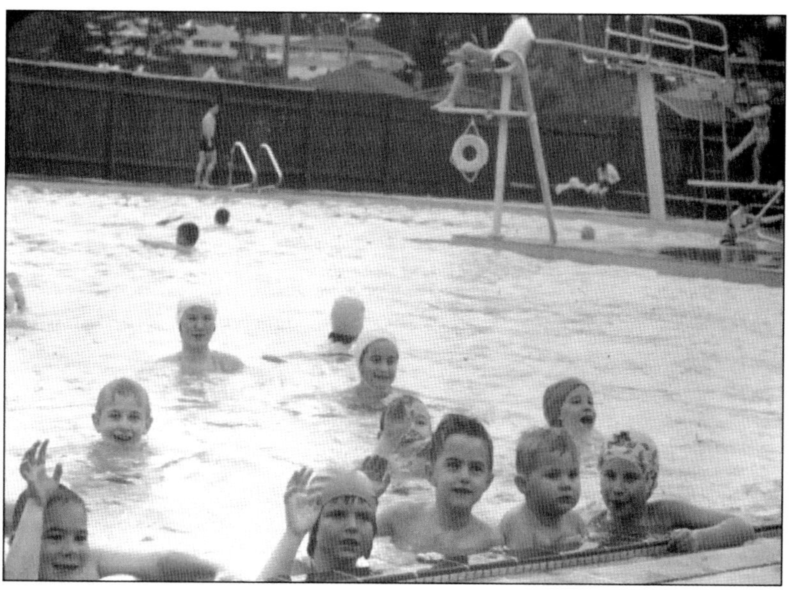

Children have had plenty of fun in the sun (or the rain) at the Fircrest Community Pool. Wading pools, swimming lanes, and diving boards provide aquatic fun for kids of all ages. (Courtesy of the City of Fircrest.)

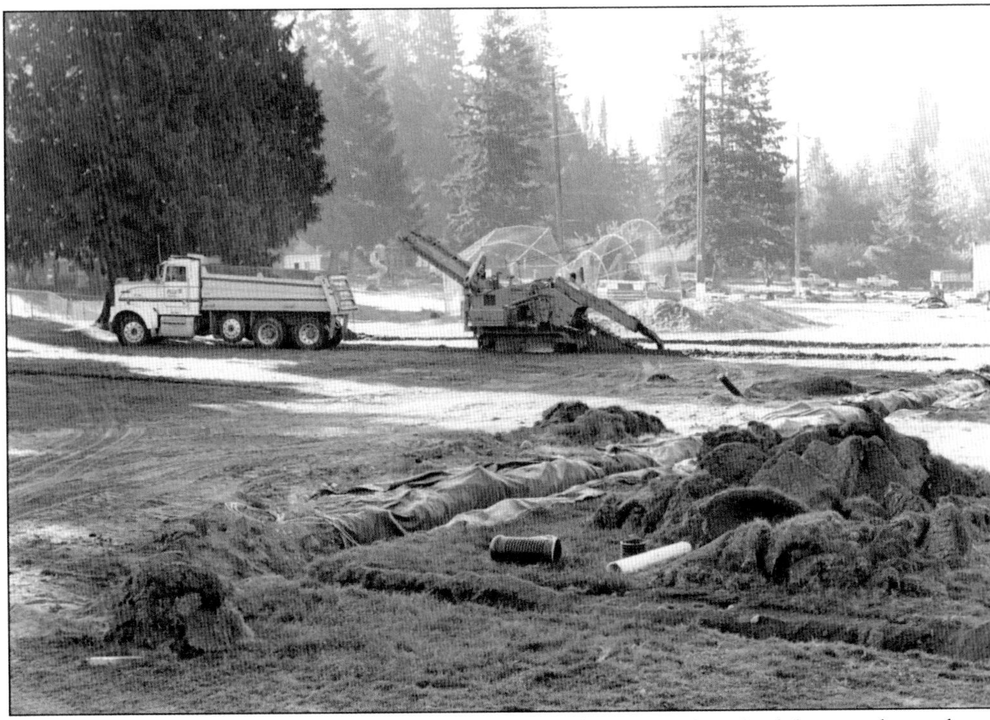

Before becoming Fircrest Park, the area was Spring Lake. Even after the lake was drained and the park was established, the ground remained soggy and unstable, requiring further remediation. These photographs show the drainage field being installed to carry the water away from the area and to make the establishment of the ball fields and play area possible. (Both courtesy of the City of Fircrest.)

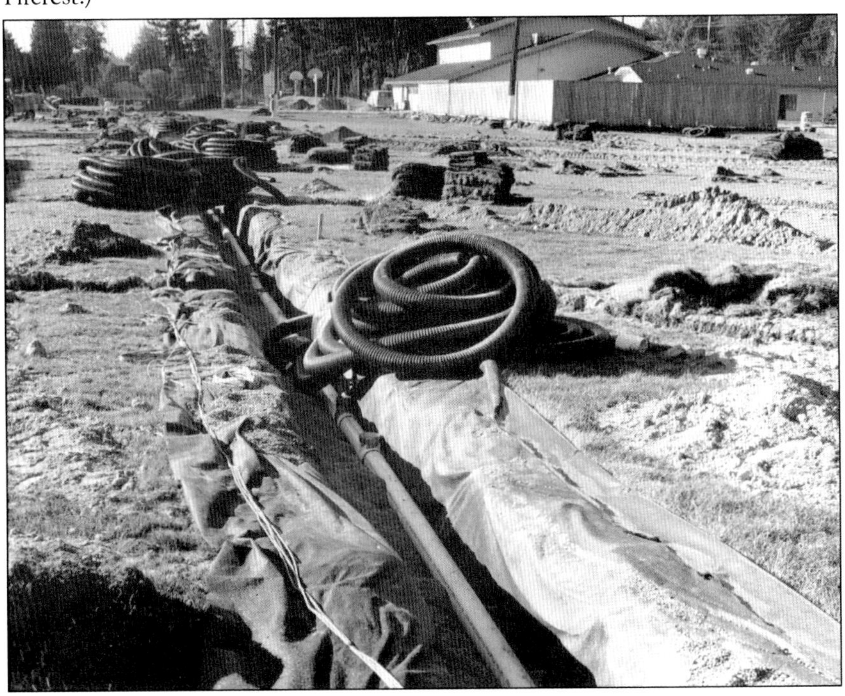

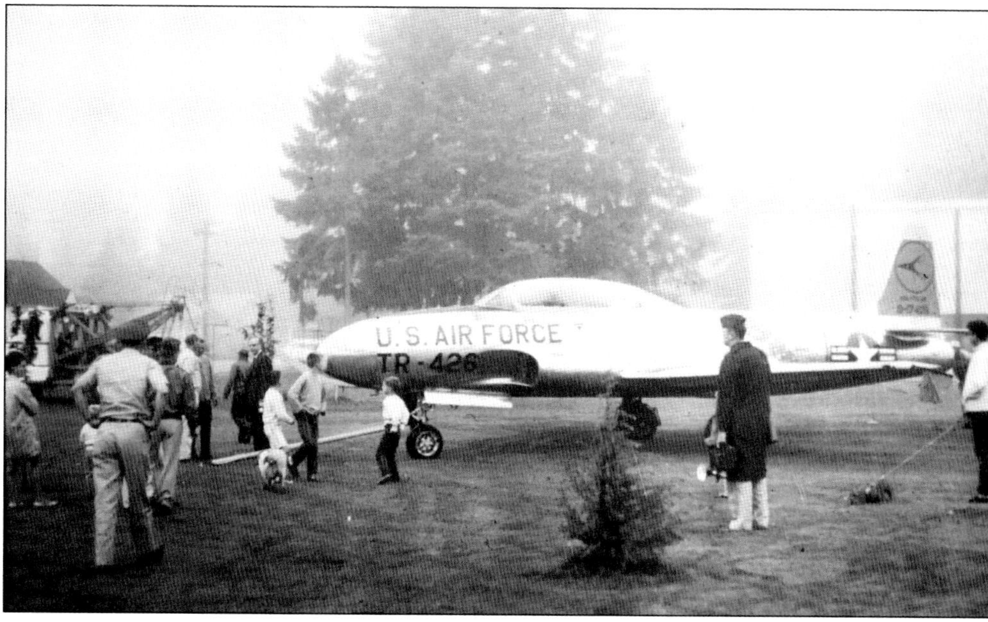

When the City of Fircrest took over Fircrest Park, the park consisted of a wading pool, picnic area, and some donated playground equipment. In 1960, the Community Building was erected at a cost of $65,000. The project was initiated to address the need for a covered and protected play area for the town's children. Park grounds were then developed for football, softball, and baseball. Fircrest citizens provided much of the physical labor and volunteer hours to complete the project. A jet trainer was donated to Fircrest Park by the 325th Fighter Wing, USAF, McCord Field. Although a popular attraction for the children, the jet was later removed due to frequent injuries as well as vandalism. (Both courtesy of the City of Fircrest.)

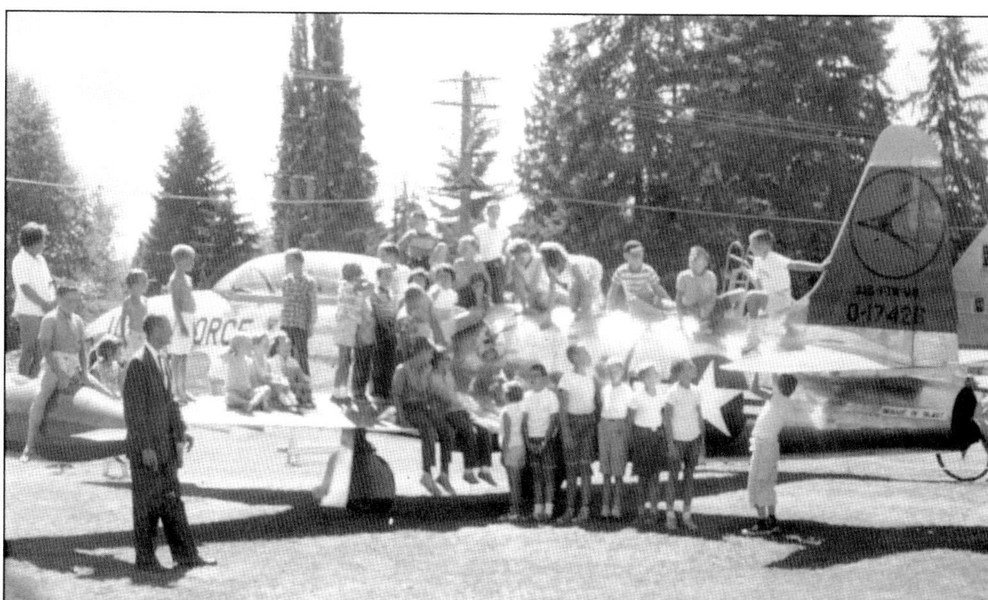

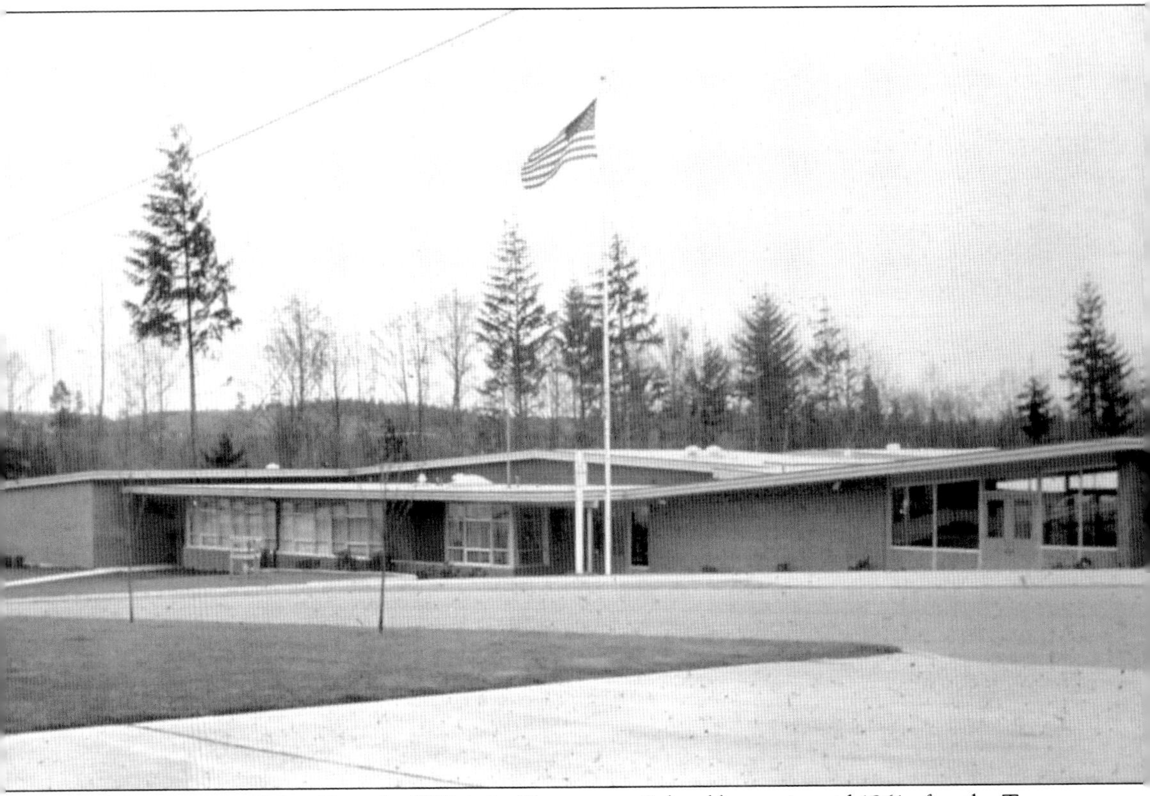

Construction of John Greenleaf Whittier Elementary School began in mid-1961 after the Tacoma School District purchased the land from Fircrest. John Whittier, a Quaker, developed a social conscience early in life. Whittier was an avid supporter of antislavery reforms and petitions, and he was well known for his poetry. (Courtesy of the City of Fircrest.)

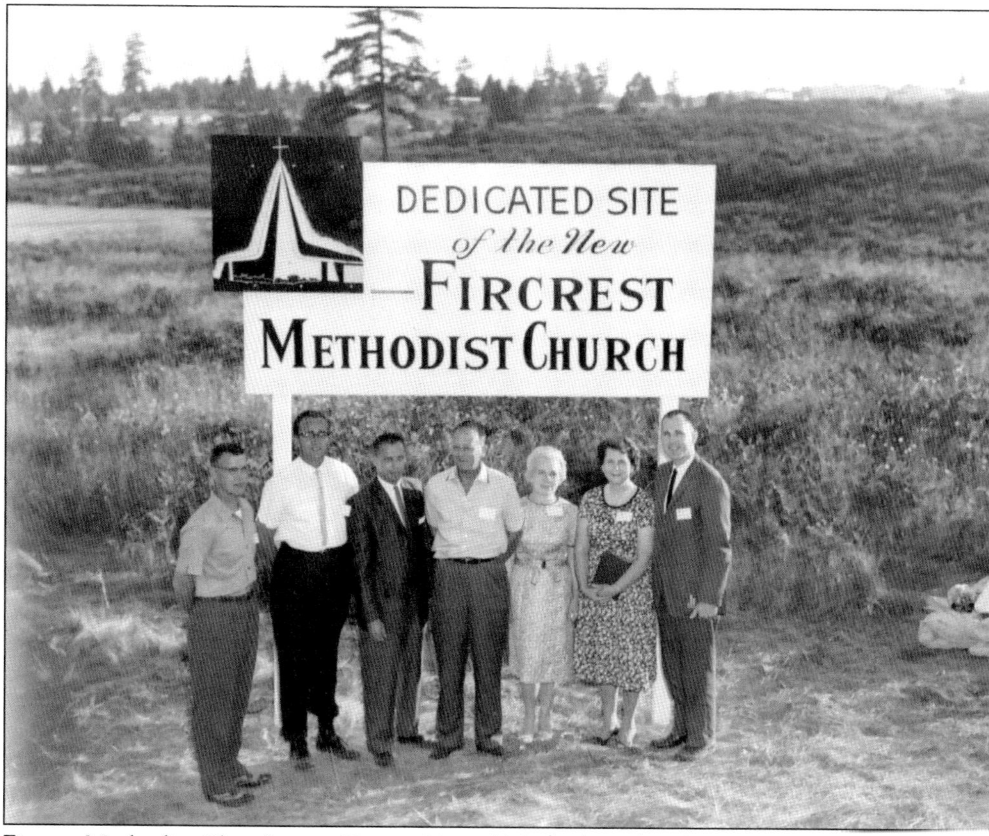

Fircrest Methodist Church, now Fircrest United Methodist Church, is located at 1018 Columbia Avenue. Shown above is a sign announcing its upcoming construction. Fircrest Presbyterian Church, below, was chartered in 1967. The congregation spent several years worshiping at the town hall and the Methodist church before opening its own building at 1250 Emerson Street. (Both courtesy of the City of Fircrest.)

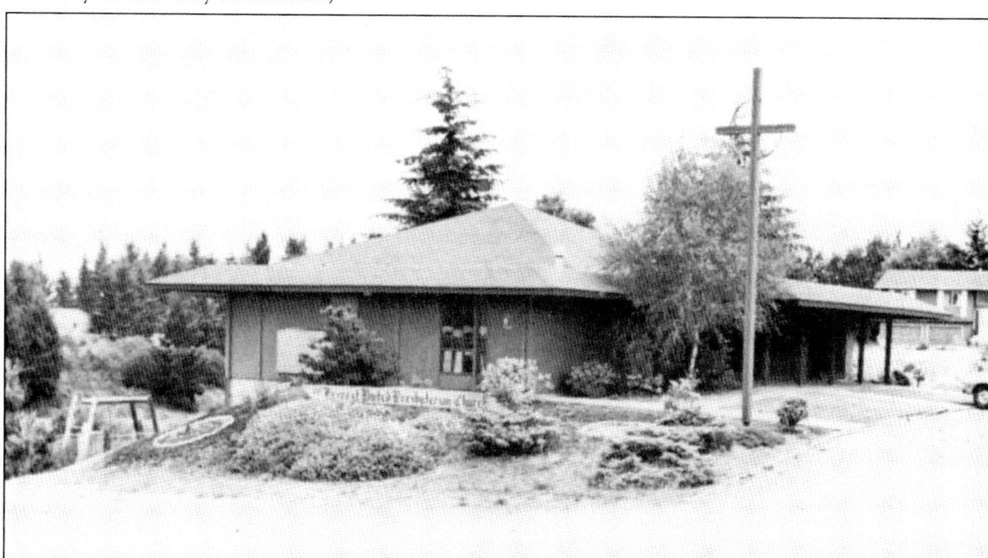

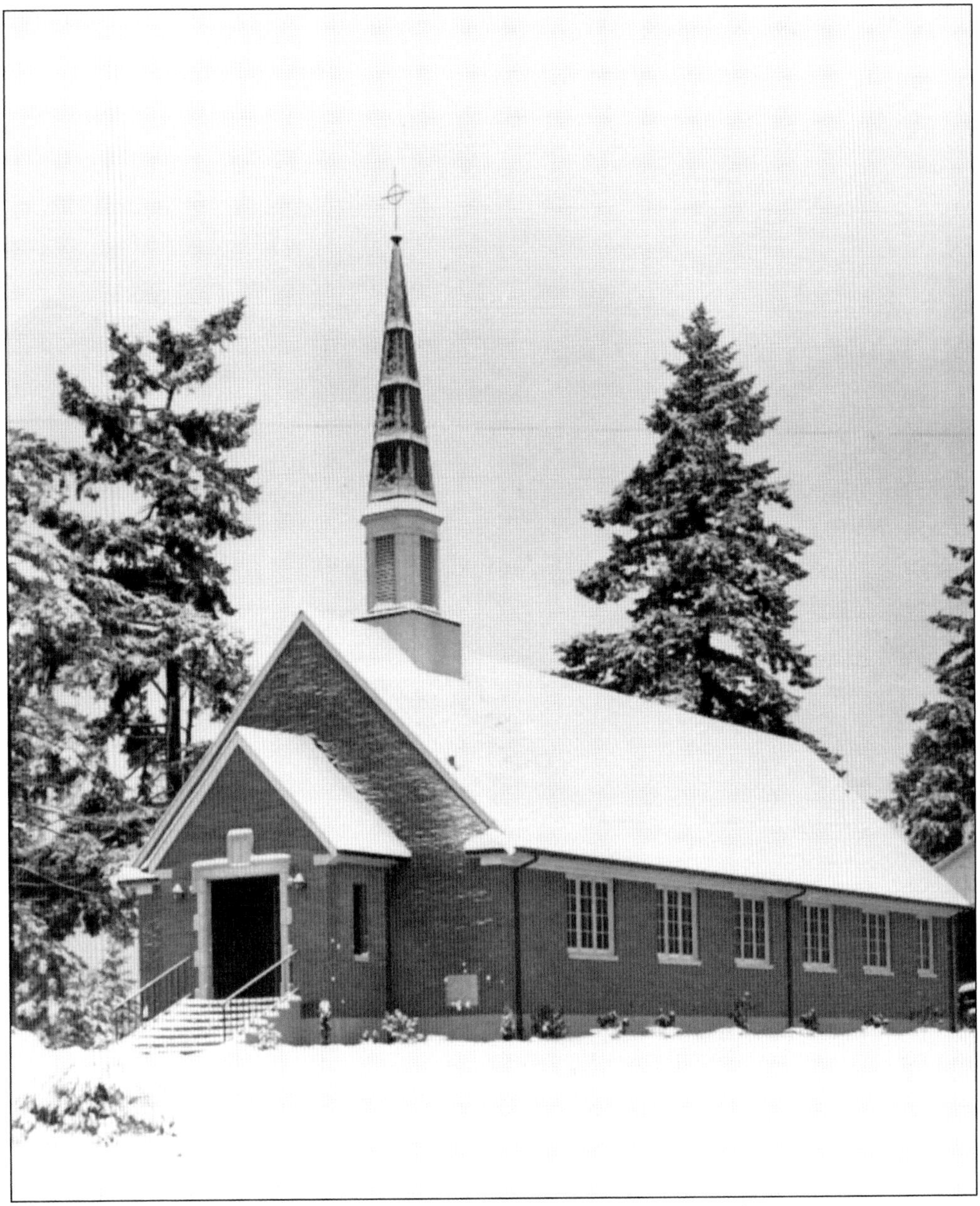

Religious services in Regents Park began formally in 1909 in a tent. A permanent structure was erected on the corner of Dartmouth Street and Alameda Avenue. It was overseen by the Evangelization Union of the Methodist Episcopal Church of Tacoma. By 1912, the church boasted 12 members. As the population grew, so did the representation of denominations and church services. Shown here is Redeemer Evangelical Lutheran Church, located at 1001 Princeton Street. Ground-breaking ceremonies for this church were held in the spring of 1953. (Courtesy of the City of Fircrest.)

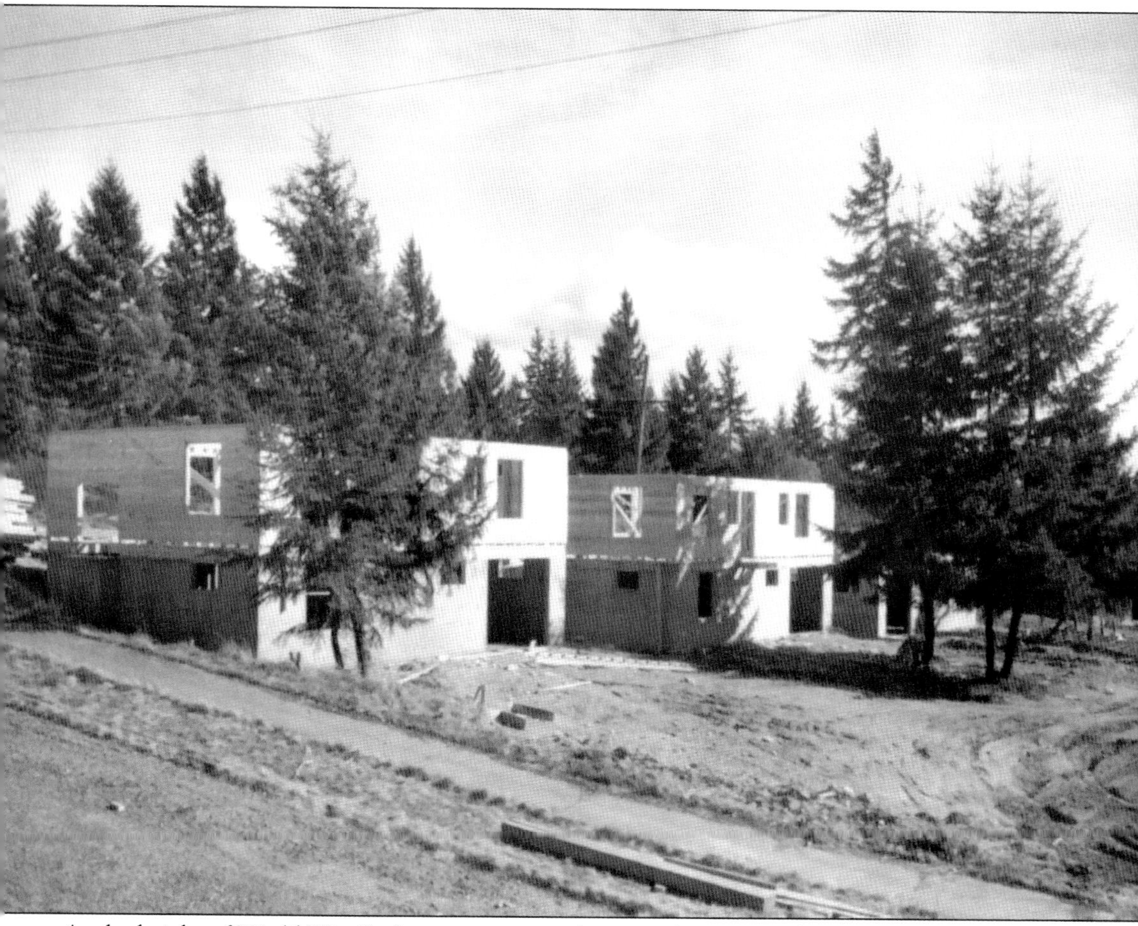

At the height of World War II, there was a severe housing shortage in those parts of the country where military bases and manufacturing facilities were located. The postwar housing boom in Fircrest began in the final years of the war. A 50-home project was expected to be completed in the latter part of 1944. This photograph, showing two of the houses under construction, was taken on March 24, 1944. (Courtesy of the Tacoma Public Library, D17250-9.)

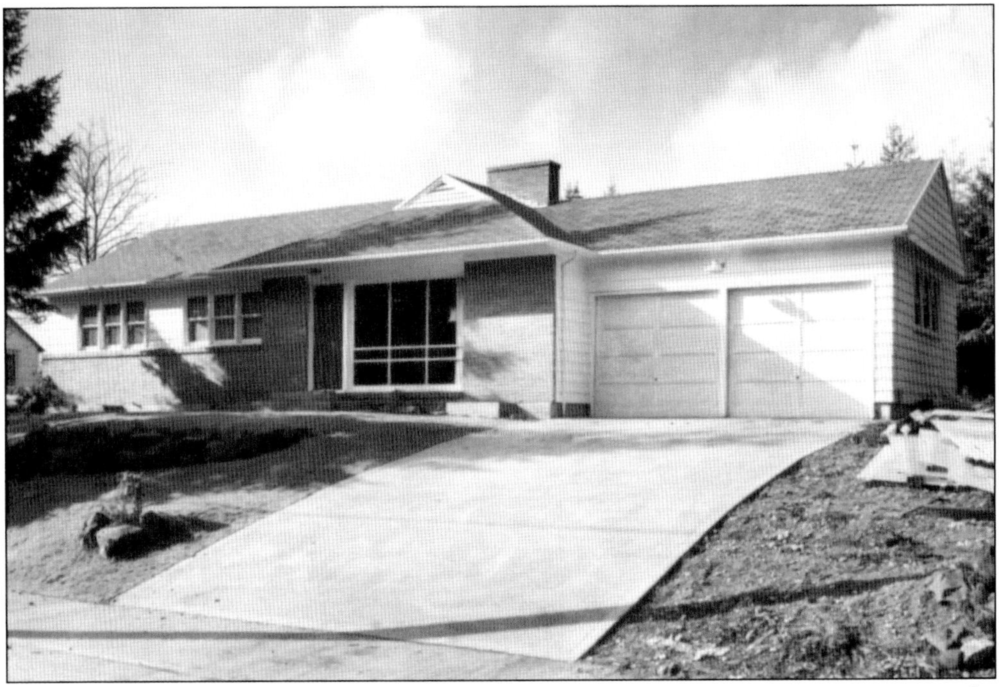

The image above shows a typical rambler, or ranch home, at 226 Del Monte Avenue. It was the residence of the executive secretary of the Tacoma chapter of the Associated General Contractors of America, Clarence Todd, and his wife, Evelyn. The living room of Wally and Elenor Stabbert, below, shows the "modern look" of a mid-century home's interior in Fircrest. Note the iconic mirror above the fireplace and the low-slung, curved furniture, which is making a comeback today. (Both courtesy of the Tacoma Public Library: above, D48000-5; below, A65688-2)

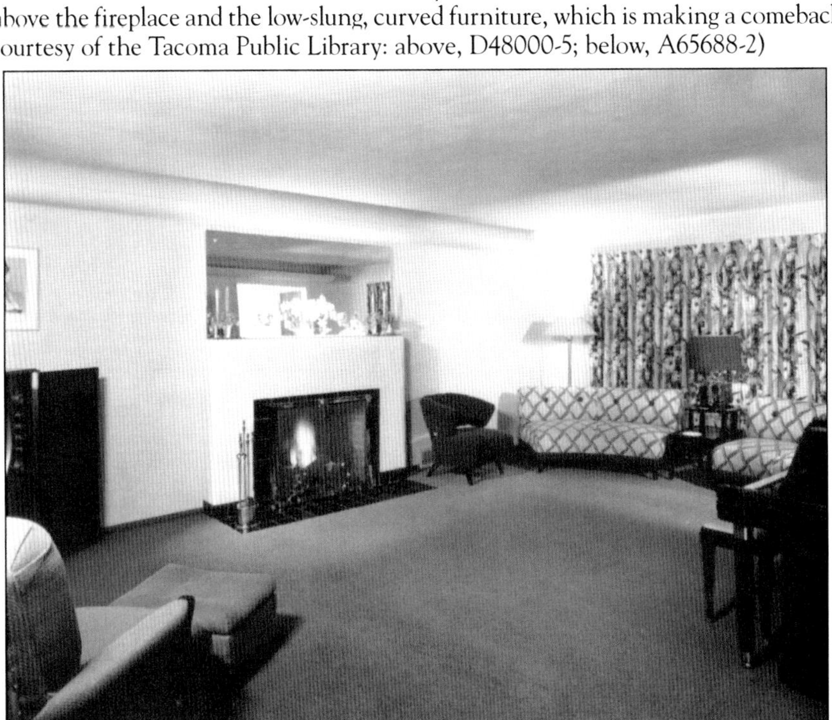

As the Cold War between the United States and the Soviet Union escalated, fear of the atomic bomb and anxiety over the possibility of a nuclear war drove many Americans to dig deep into the earth in an effort to survive what seemed at the time an inevitable nuclear attack from the Soviets. Ordinary Americans built bomb shelters in their backyards, often hiding them from their neighbors. At right, a crane lowers a shelter into a newly excavated hole in a Fircrest yard. Below, a would-be survivor descends into the access hatch of one such shelter. (Both courtesy of the Tacoma Public Library: at right, D131642-14; below, D130549-5.)

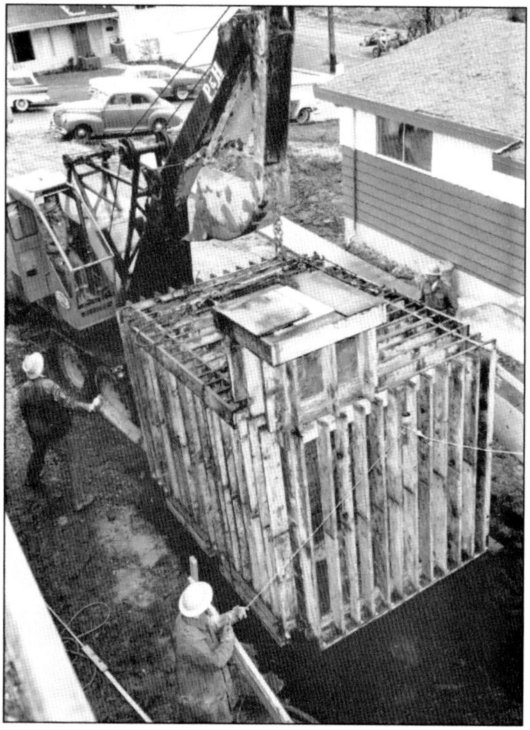

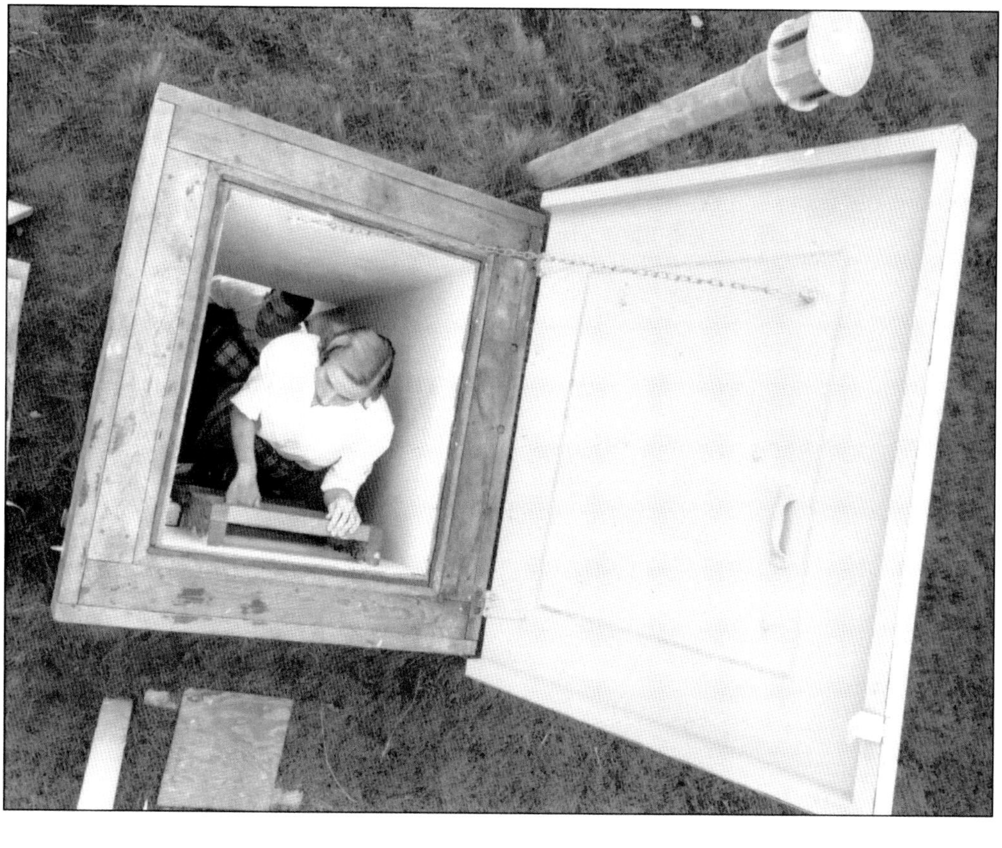

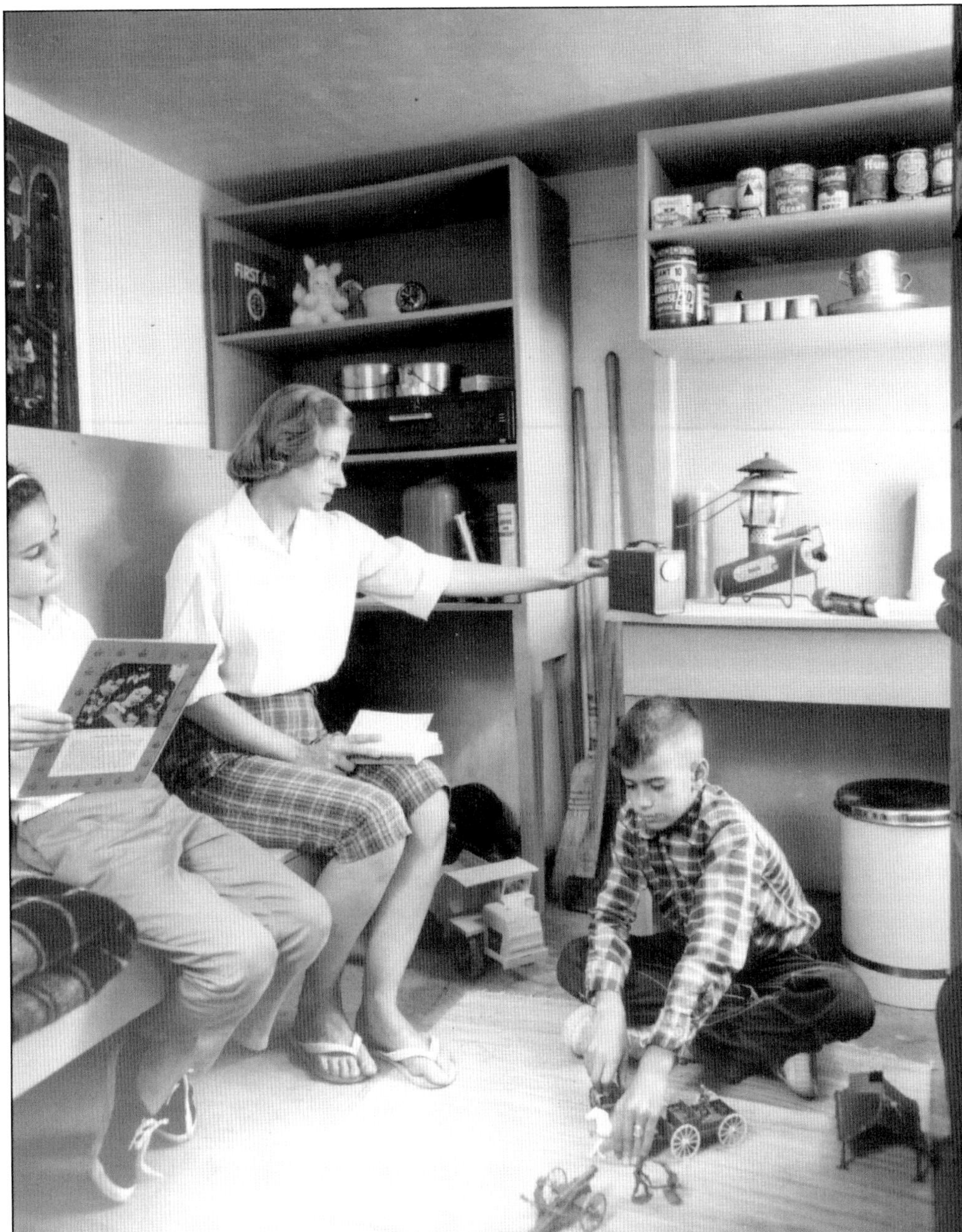

This Fircrest bomb shelter is furnished with many of the supplies recommended by civil-defense authorities, including a battery-operated radio, a gas-fueled lantern, and a first-aid kit, as well as books and toys for the children. The entry of this shelter was shielded from the living area by a sand-filled baffle wall, and the interior was buffered by three feet of dirt covering the roof. (Courtesy of the Tacoma Public Library, D131642-11.)

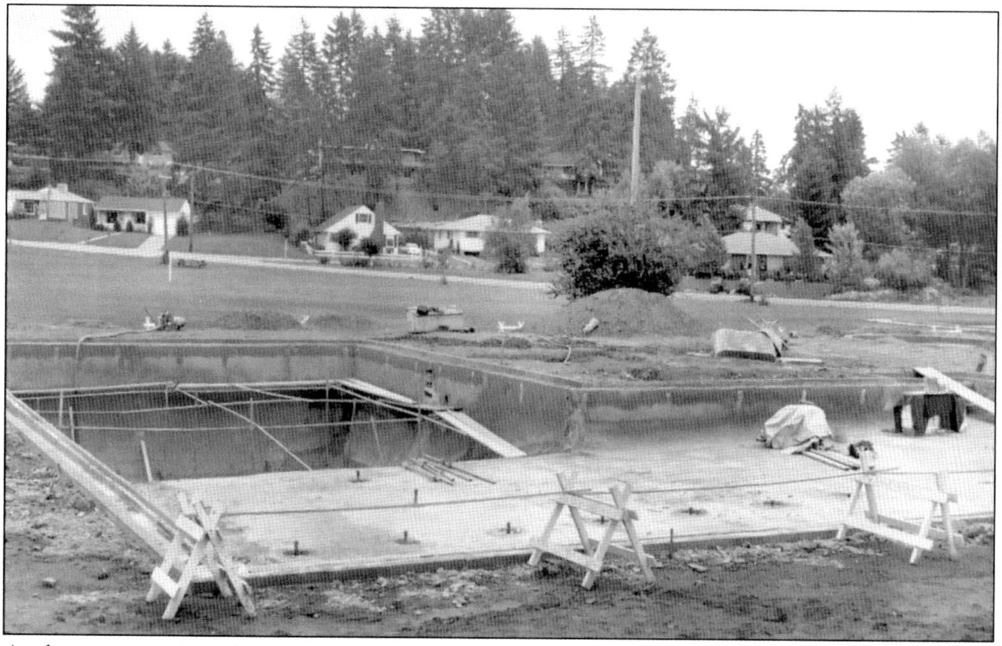

As the town continued to grow, its main recreation area was Fircrest Park, owned and operated by the Tacoma Metropolitan Park District. The dual responsibility for the park, assumed by Fircrest and Tacoma, created many problems. It was decided that Fircrest would drop out of the park district and maintain and develop this land, as well as new properties, for recreational purposes supporting the town of Fircrest. (Courtesy of the City of Fircrest.)

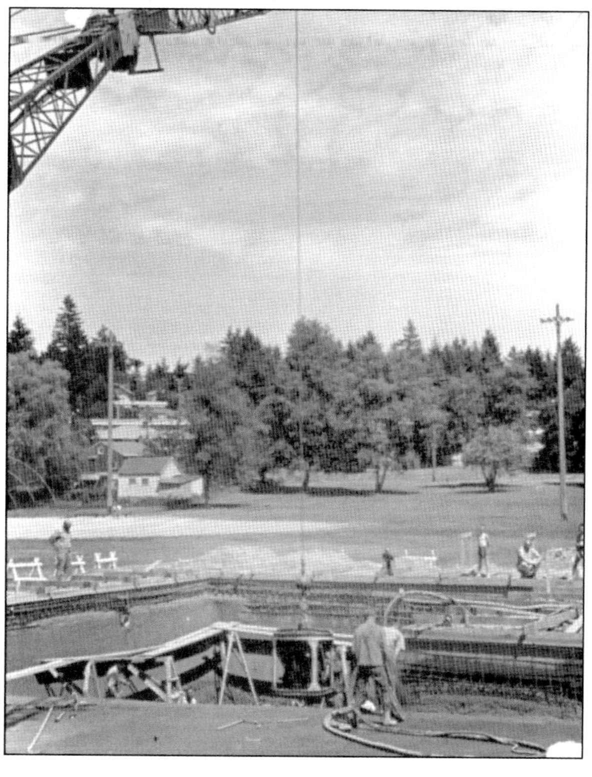

In the early 1960s, a group of Fircrest citizens and councilmen put together a bond to support the building of a community pool at Fircrest Park. Of Fircrest's available voters, 85 percent turned out, and 84 percent of them voted "yes." During construction, an ironworkers' strike threatened to delay the completion date; instead, citizens again pitched in to complete the project. (Courtesy of the City of Fircrest.)

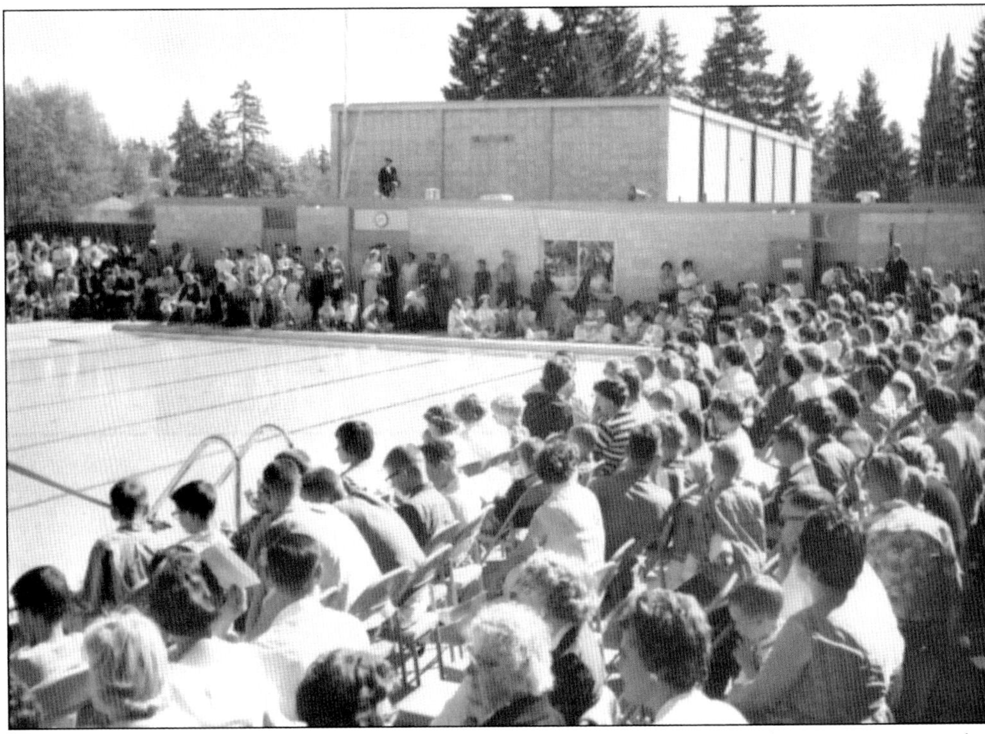

Above, since over 80 percent of Fircrest citizens supported the building of a community pool, it is not surprising that the opening ceremonies at Fircrest Park saw a big turnout. Use of the pool proved to be just as enthusiastic. The photograph below shows an open pool being enjoyed by patrons of all ages. (Both courtesy of the City of Fircrest.)

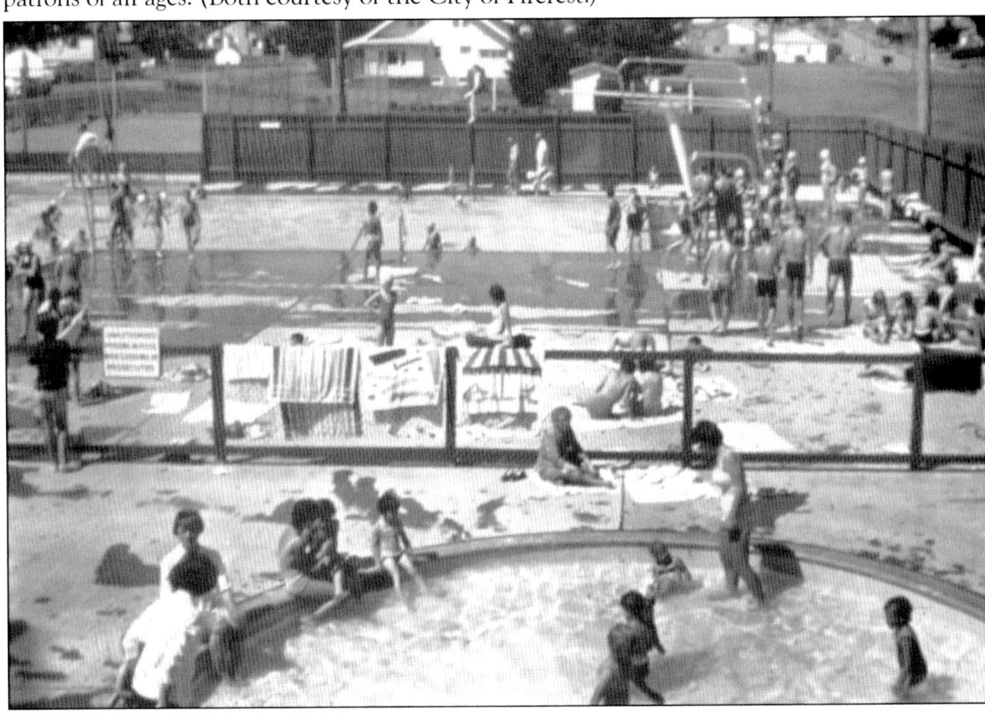

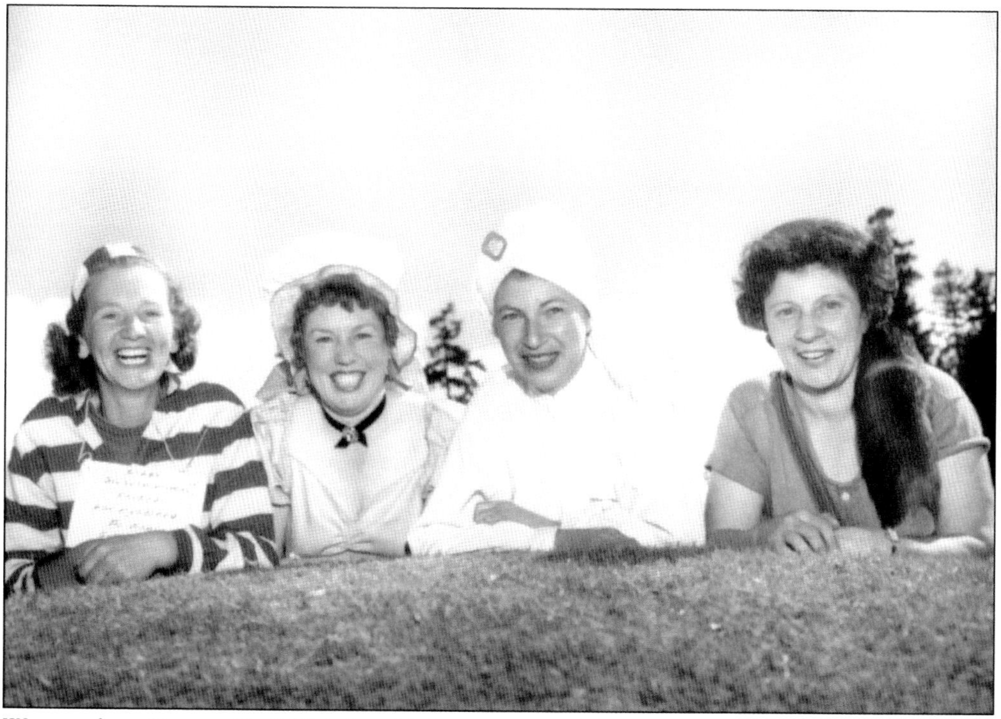

Women from Fircrest Golf Club herald the opening of the summer season on May 1, 1951, by dressing up in costumes. Seen here are, from left to right, Mary Murray (jailbird), Laura McGinn (pioneer woman), Freida Rome (Hindu), and Louise Severson (Daniel Boone). Sadly, none of these women took first prize for the best costume that year. The coveted honor went to Mrs. M.C. Thompson, who was dressed as a Fiji islander, complete with grass skirt. (Courtesy of the Tacoma Public Library, D58207-10.)

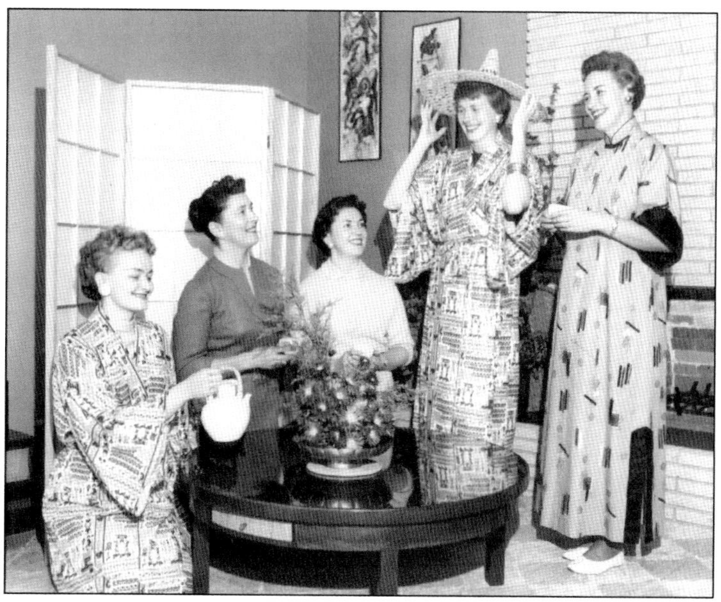

This publicity photograph for Fircrest Golf Club graced the society pages of the *Tacoma News Tribune* in 1959. These festive ladies are posing to advertise a night of "Mandarin Mischief," including dinner, dancing, and games with an Eastern theme. The women are, from left to right, Arla Rohrs, Edith Tollefson, Mrs. Gordon Dowling, Alice Tollefson, and Irene Alskog. (Courtesy of the Tacoma Public Library, D123239-1.)

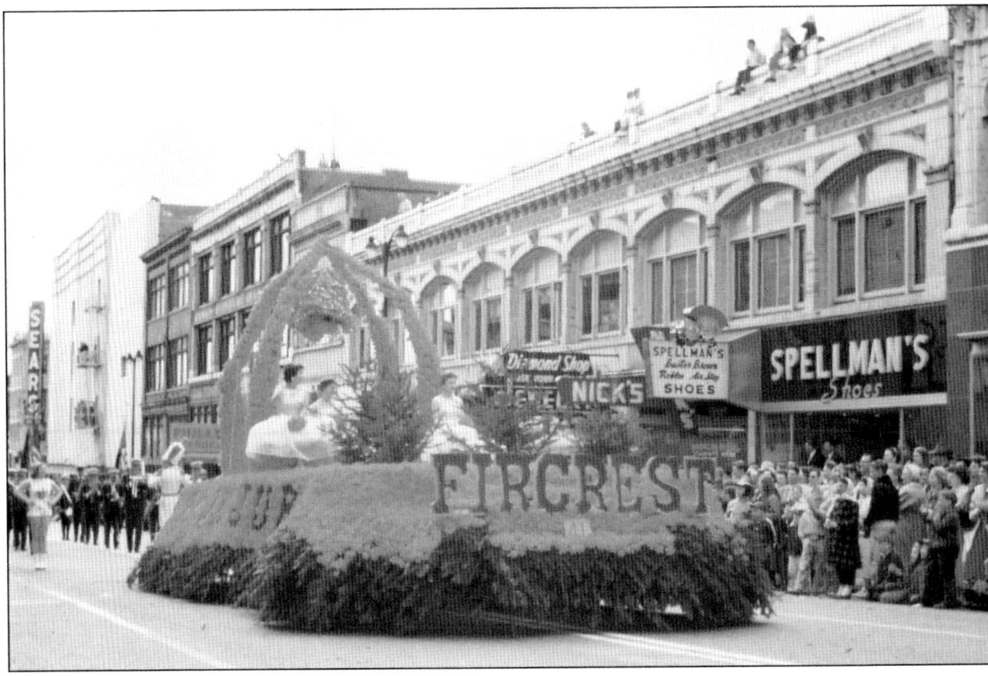

The City of Fircrest sponsored a float for the annual Daffodil Festival Grand Floral Street Parade in 1957. The parade began in 1934. In 1957, it ran through four Pierce County communities. Queen Pat Petterson and Princesses Linda Swanson and Judy Fortune add beauty to the float that celebrates not just the rebirth of spring, but also the 50th anniversary of the Town of Fircrest. (Both courtesy of the City of Fircrest.)

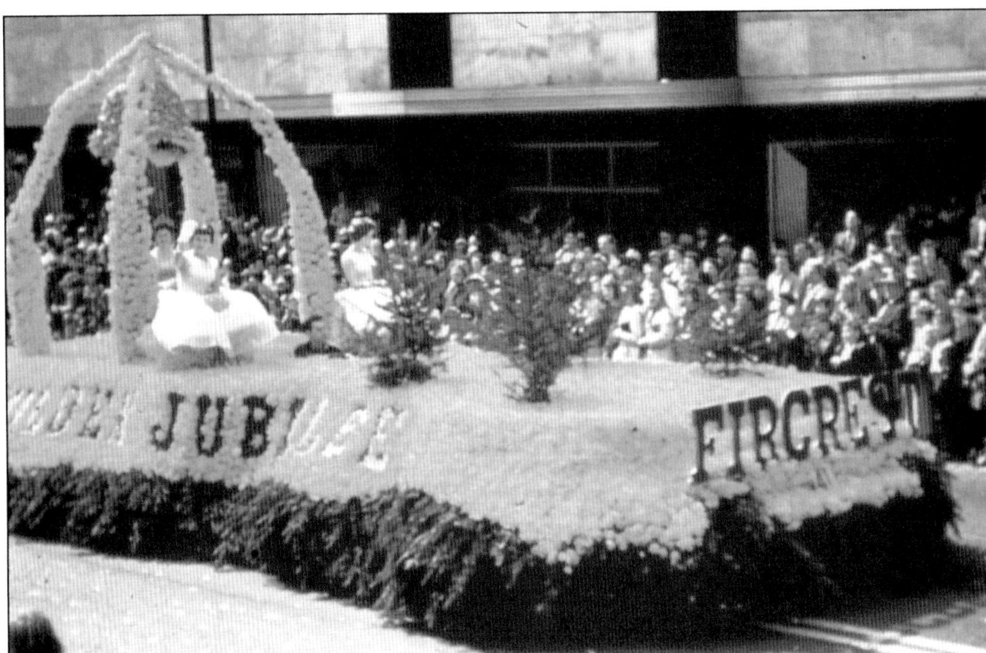

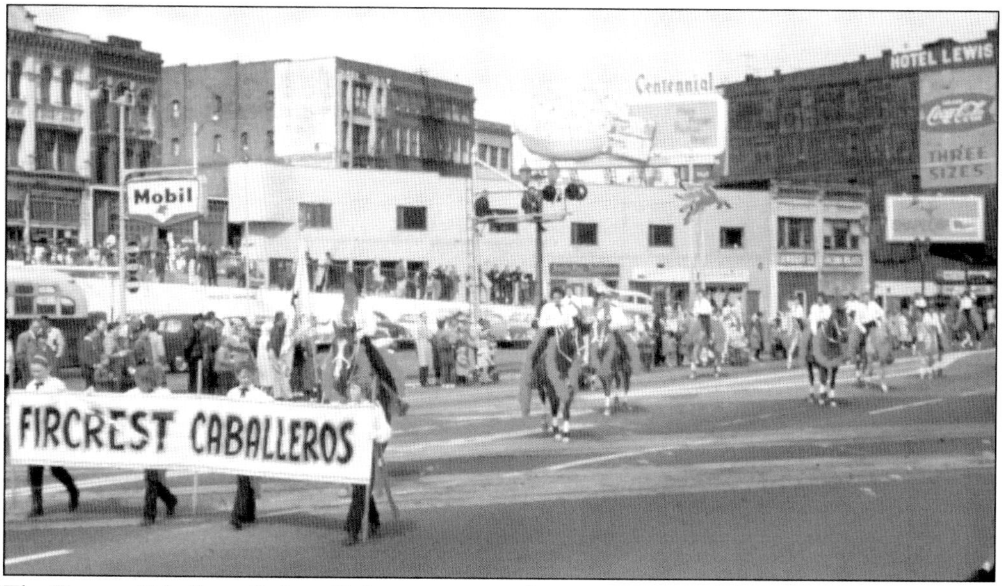

The Fircrest Caballeros Riding Club was a group of men, women, and children who loved to ride horses. Both the riders and the horses wore fancy Spanish garb adorned with daffodils for the 1960 Daffodil Parade. The City of Fircrest sponsored the group, providing them with the spring blooms. The photograph above shows the parade route in downtown Tacoma. The cute little pony seen below follows behind the other horses. Perhaps this little guy aspires to be a caballero, rather than a member of the waste-management team, when he grows up. (Both courtesy of the City of Fircrest.)

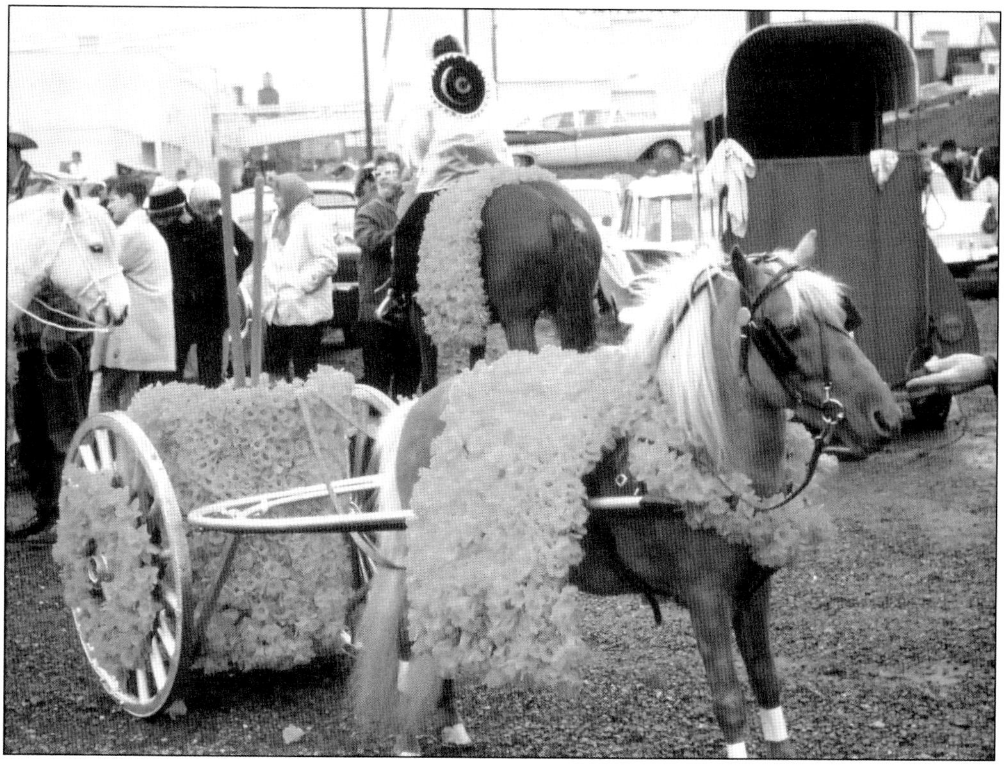

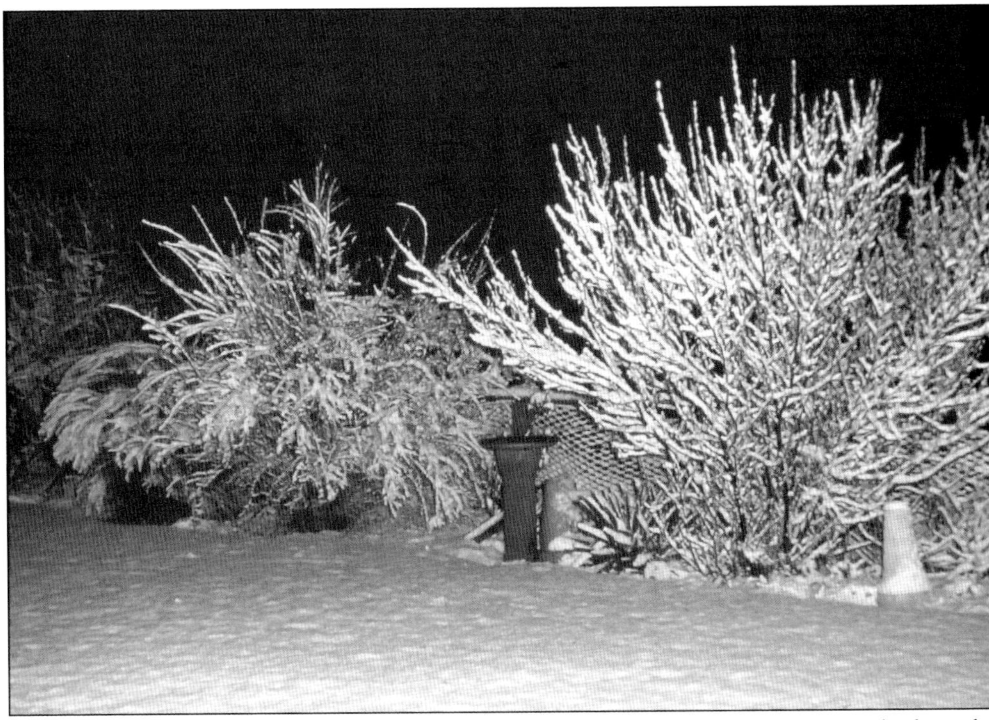

During particularly cold winter snaps, Fircrest shows its Nordic side. These photographs from the 1960s show how wonderful winter can be. The night scene above shows an ice-incrusted tree. In earlier days, Spring Lake froze over, but in the 1960s water was sprayed onto the basketball courts to provide the ice sheet. Below, a father/daughter duo enjoys the temporary ice-skating rink. (Both courtesy of the City of Fircrest.)

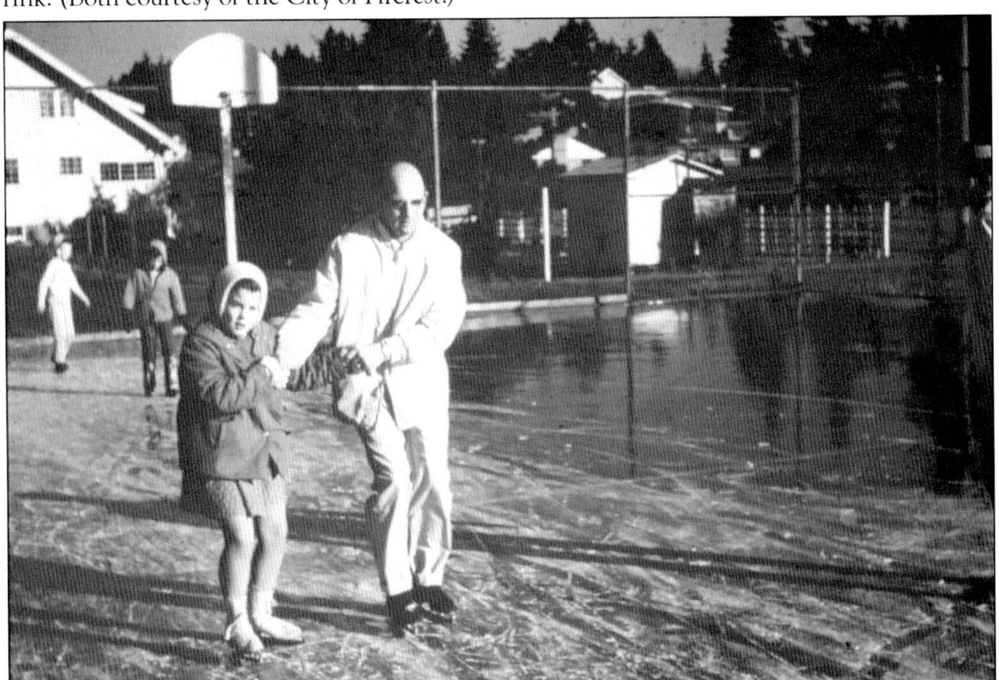

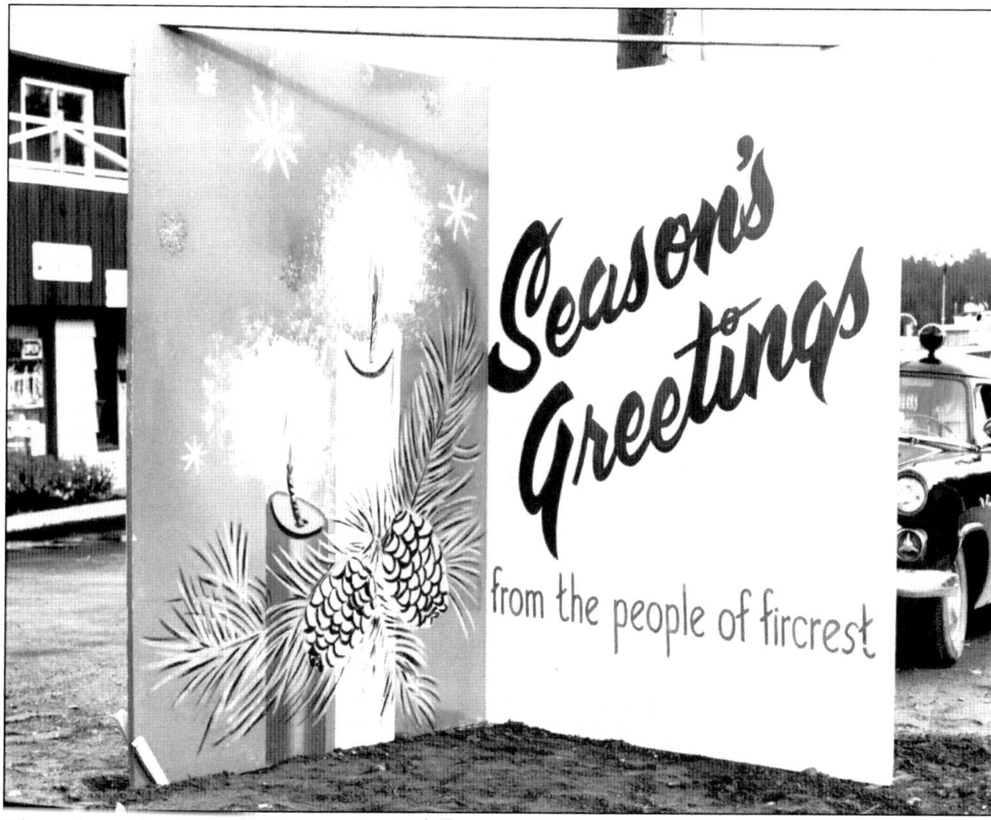

Throughout the years, the Fircrest Council, Fircrest Community Club, and other civic organizations promoted holiday celebrations and decorations. Christmas tree–lighting ceremonies, yard-decoration contests, street decorations, Easter egg hunts, and Fourth of July parades remain favorites. Unfortunately, the city found itself embroiled in the separation controversy when the ACLU sued over the display of a manger scene on public property. A temporary solution, shown below, was to move the crèche to private property near the entrance to the city on Regents Boulevard. (Both courtesy of the City of Fircrest.)

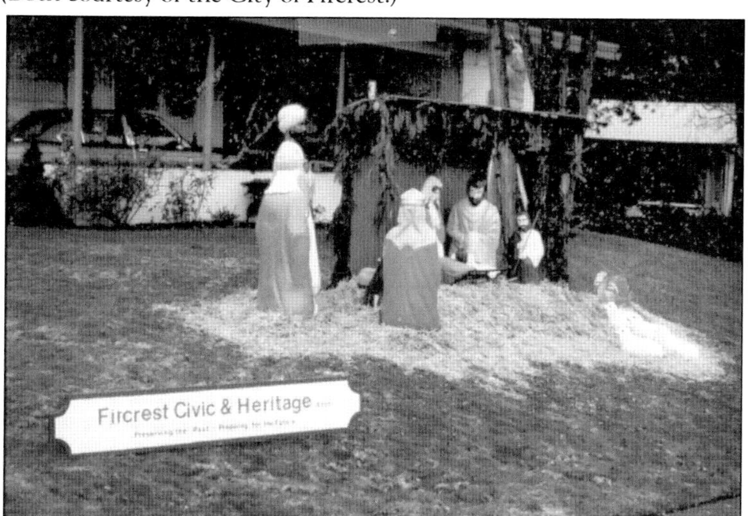

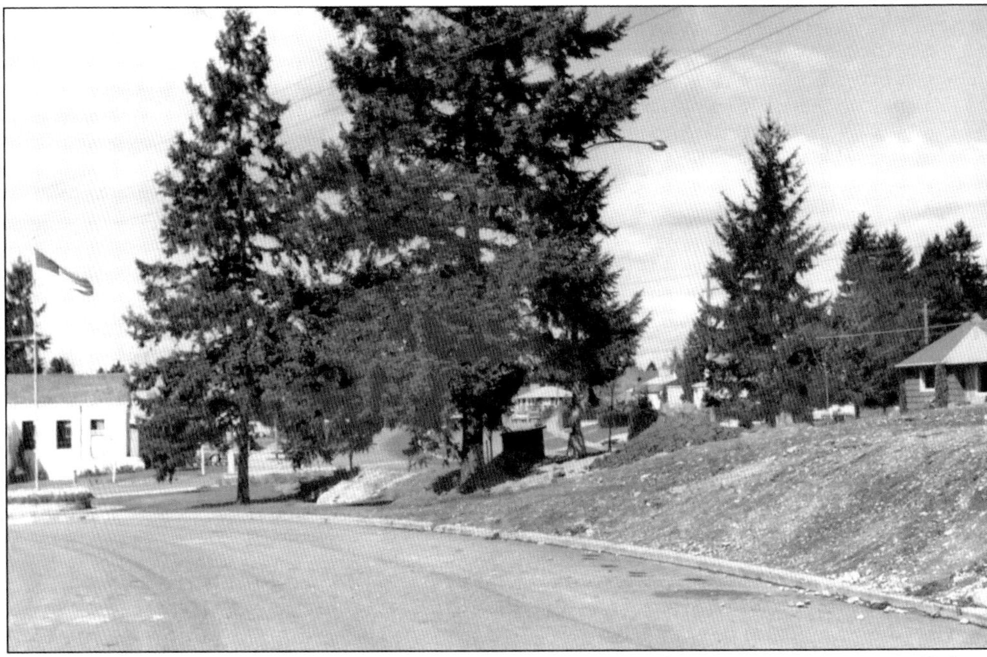

Recreational spaces have always been a priority for the citizens of Fircrest. In 1954, Mayor Helmut Jueling contacted area clubs and challenged them to come up with a plan to beautify the areas that the town had set aside as parklands; thus, the Town Beautification Committee was formed. The first task for the committee was the creation of Alice Peers Park, named after the senior member of the Garden Club. Located at the intersection of Regents Boulevard and Electron Way, the park (below) sports a flagpole, reader board, plants, and flowers. It is lined with trees, including a majestic evergreen in the center—a perfect tree to host the annual Fircrest Tree Lighting Ceremony. (Both courtesy of the City of Fircrest.)

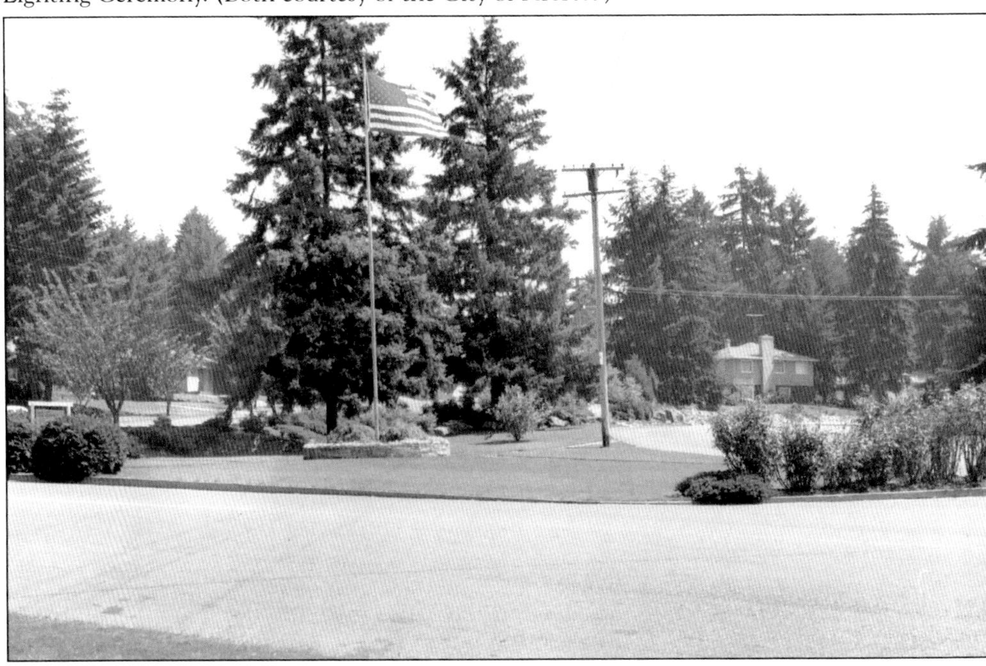

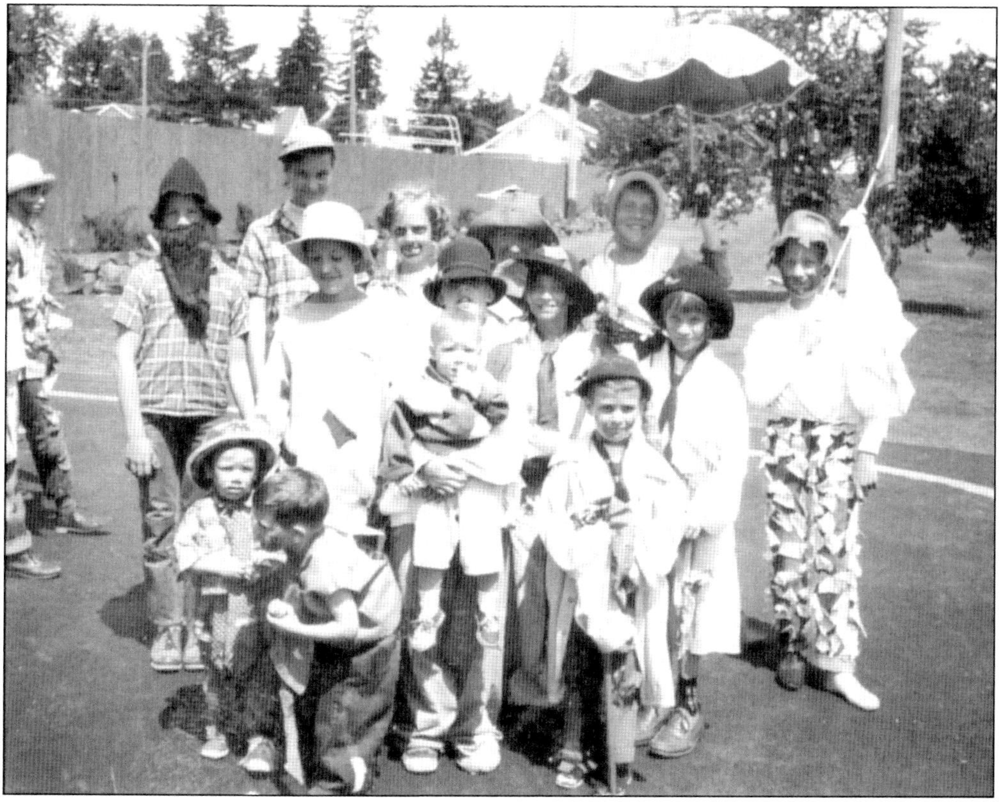

Fircrest has always been a community that values the family unit and works hard to provide fun activities appropriate for all family members. It seems like there is always something to celebrate in this little town. Summer is welcomed with a strawberry feed and a movie in the park. December brings Santa's sleigh, tree lighting, and hot cocoa. Spring finds the parks full of Easter egg hunters. Above, children in the park are dressed as "hobos" for a themed celebration. Cultural dances in the community center were frequent; the one below was for a Scandinavian festival. (Courtesy of the City of Fircrest.)

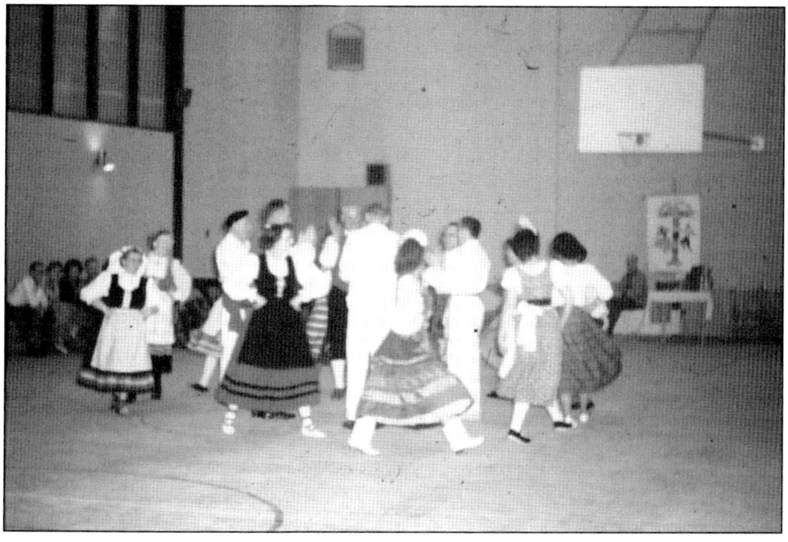

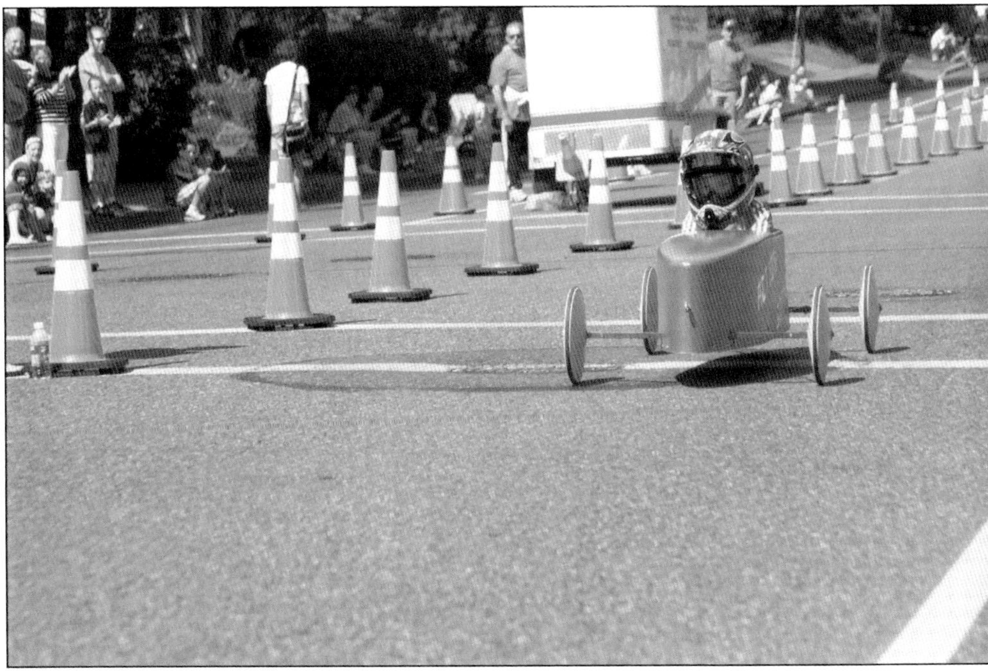

Fircrest Derby Days and the Fircrest Auto Show bring out car enthusiasts, both young and old. The back-to-back events occur annually on the second weekend in July. Above, "Action Jackson" Elliott, in his winning soapbox derby car, speeds down Electron Way on a sunny Saturday morning. Below, Sunday finds Fircrest Park full of some of the area's finest street hot rods and vintage motorcycles. The show and picnic are accompanied by the sounds of classic 1960s rock 'n' roll. (Above, courtesy Juliana Roe; below, photograph by R.R. Colyer.)

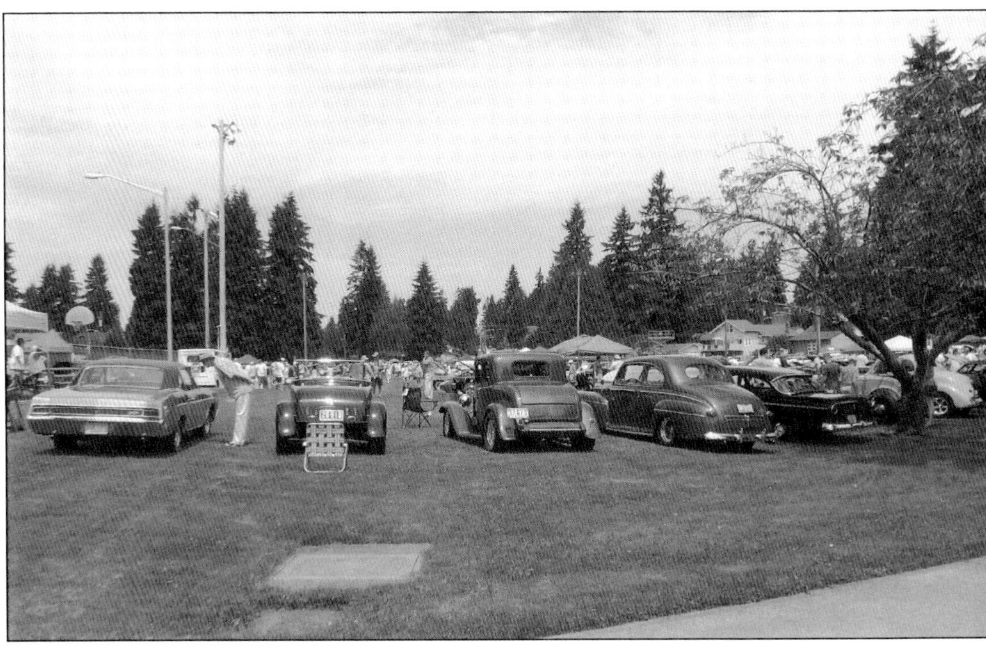

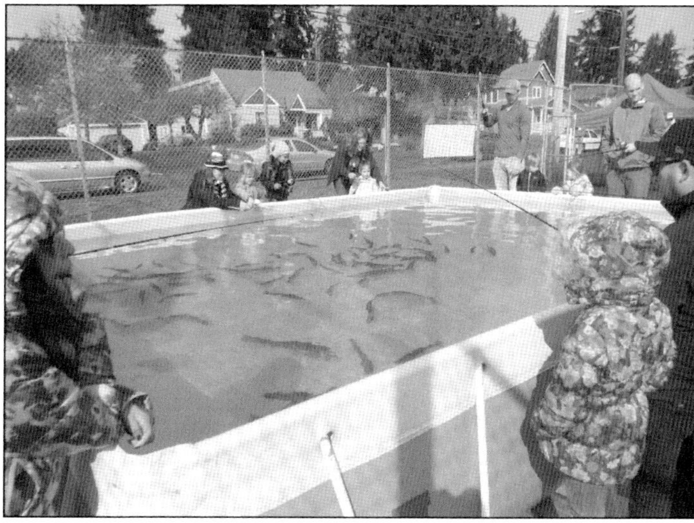

Fircrest Parks and Recreation provides many fun activities for children of all ages. In March 2015, children fish in this temporary "pool" stocked with trout on the grounds of the Roy H. Murphy Community Center. Kids 10 years of age or younger bring their own fishing poles and come prepared to brave the elements in the quest for the elusive "big one." (Photograph by R.R. Colyer.)

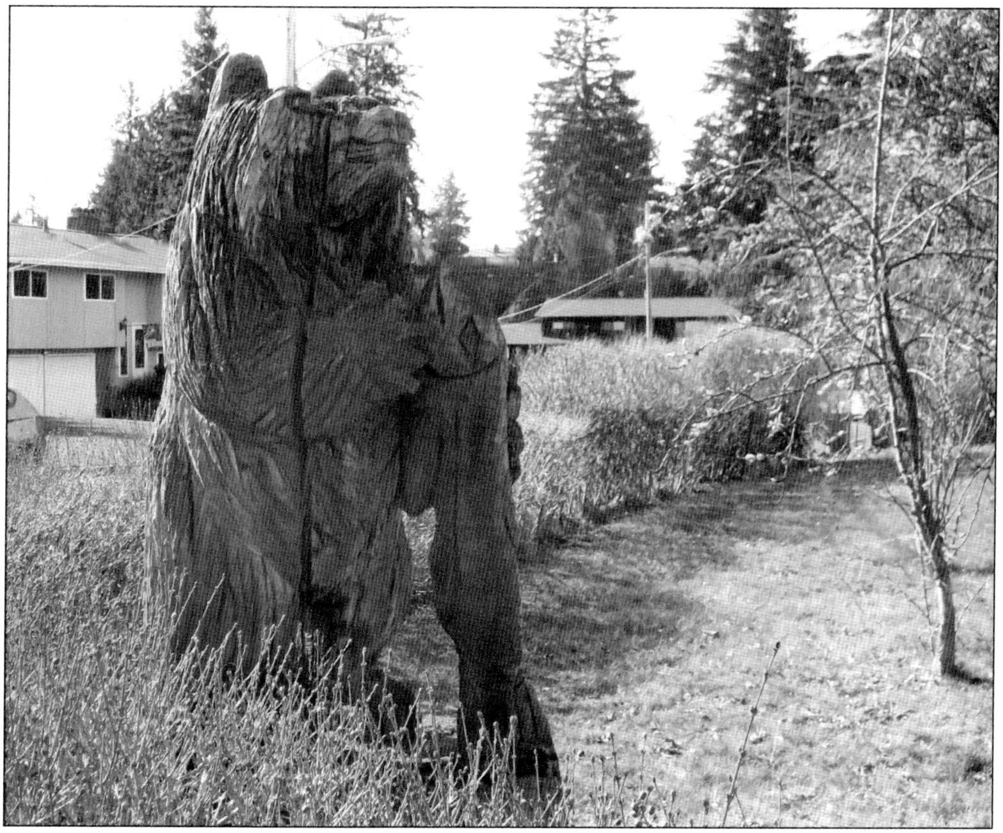

In the 1980s, the art of chainsaw carving hit the airwaves with the national broadcast of the Lumberjack World Championships. This inspired carvers from across the nation to come together to compete and learn from each other. It also inspired a whole new variety of yard art. Country fairs, roadside stands, and even local hardware stores sported these creations, and they soon showed up on the lawns of Fircrest homes. While bears are the clear favorites, one can see birds, fish, mythical creatures, and even pigs. (Photograph by R.R. Colyer.)

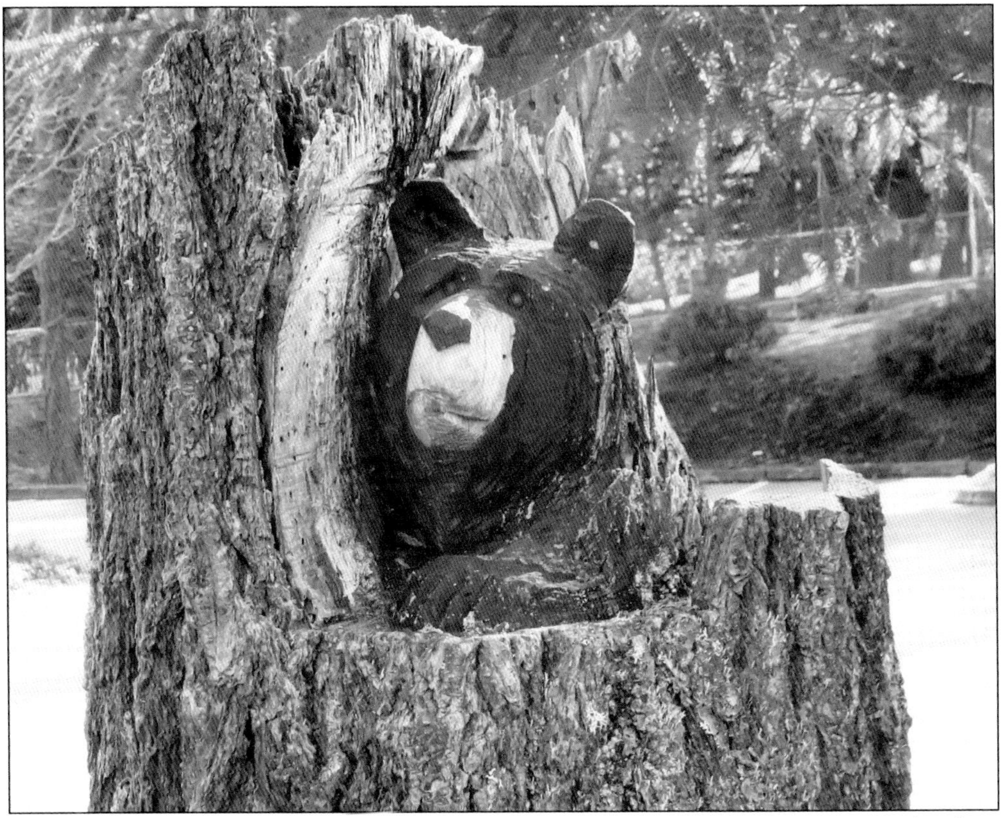

At one time, the locals had a map of every bear in Fircrest. Some carvings have become kindling or termite fodder, while new ones have been installed. Visitors can try to spot as many as possible on a Sunday drive. The count is currently more then 120 around Fircrest. (Both photographs by R.R. Colyer.)

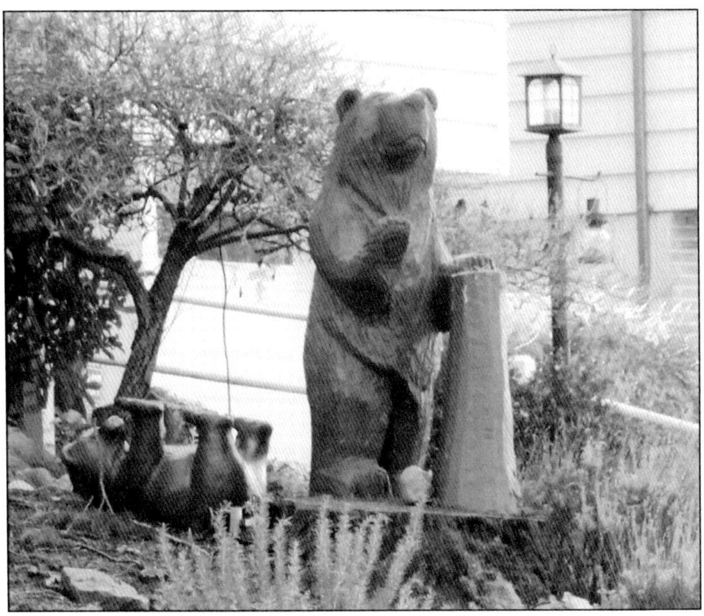

Five

Remnants of the Past

American writer Robert Penn Warren once stated, "History cannot give us a program for the future, but it can give us a fuller understanding of ourselves, and of our common humanity, so that we can better face the future." Fircrest is a unique blend of old and new. In the following pages, readers will witness images from past meld into the future. The photographs are just a few of those to be found throughout this community. As eyes meander down the roads, catch a glimpse of old-style architecture, formal gardens, street markers, and road signs that remind residents of what life used to be like in days gone by. Several houses can still be found sporting historical markers.

It is the author's intent to use the following pages as a starting place of discovery. Readers may gaze at a century-old home during a morning walk and imagine the original owners walking to the trolley or children running to Spring Lake. As new construction pops up, people may pause to consider the beauty of the raw land that existed over a century ago and the foresight, courage, and imagination it took men like Thompson and Bowes to follow their dreams. Carry those visions on to the future. What will the images of tomorrow look like? How will they compare to the past and present? And, perhaps most importantly, what legacy will we leave behind?

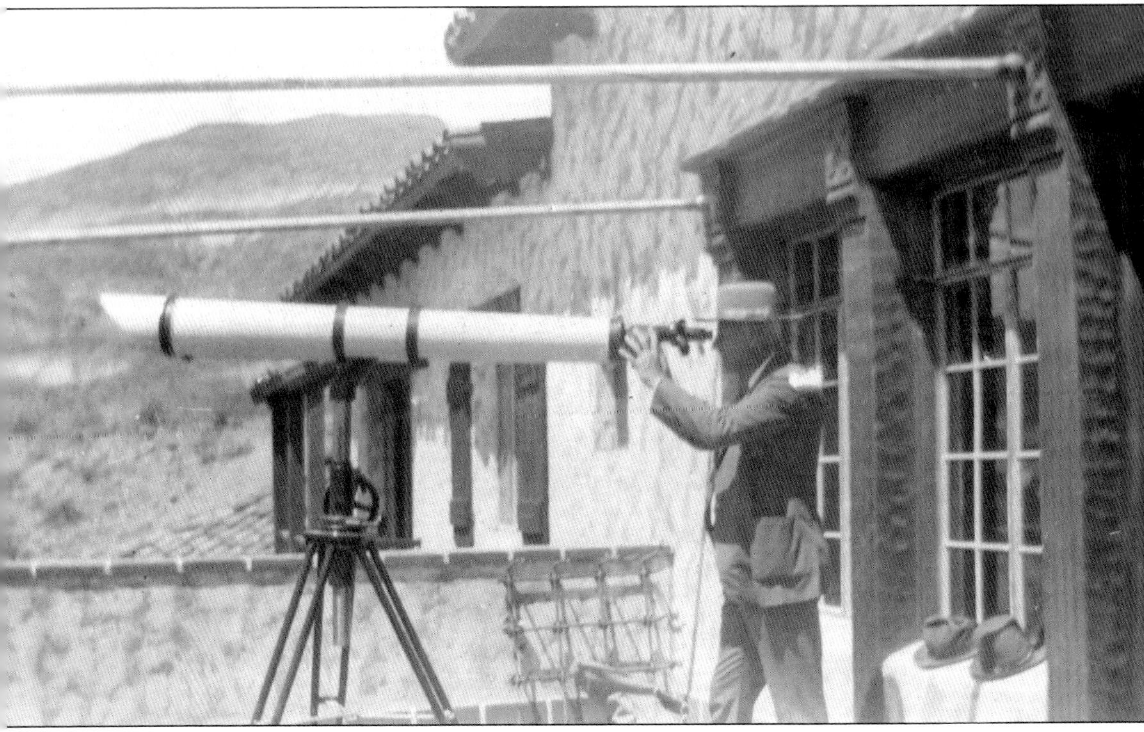

If M. Roy Thompson could have seen into the future and looked upon the city he designed over 100 years ago, it is a safe bet that he would be extremely proud of what has become of the community he had such a hand in shaping. The lots he laid out are filled with homes and families in this fine place to live, learn, work, and play. It truly is the "Gem of the Puget Sound." Much has changed, but much also remains the same. It is extremely interesting and often fascinating in today's age of instant photography to stand in the places where those who came before stood and record an instant in time and place. (Courtesy of the National Park Service.)

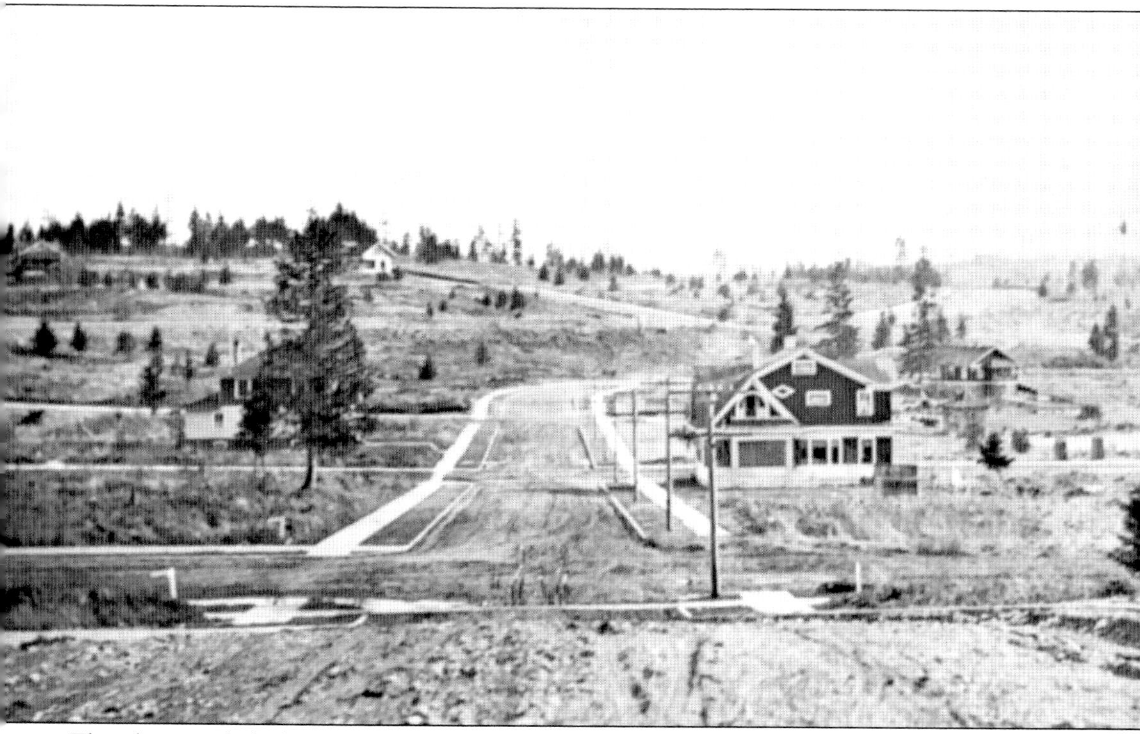

This photograph, looking east down Spring Street, was taken from the intersection of Buena Vista Avenue and Spring in 1913. The prominent home on the right is the Rogers house. Spring Lake is at center right, and the lake's gazebo can just be made out right of the Rogers home. The street at upper center is Golden Gate Avenue. The street in the upper right is Regents Boulevard. The home at left, behind the tree, is the Van De Mark home. (Both courtesy of the City of Fircrest.)

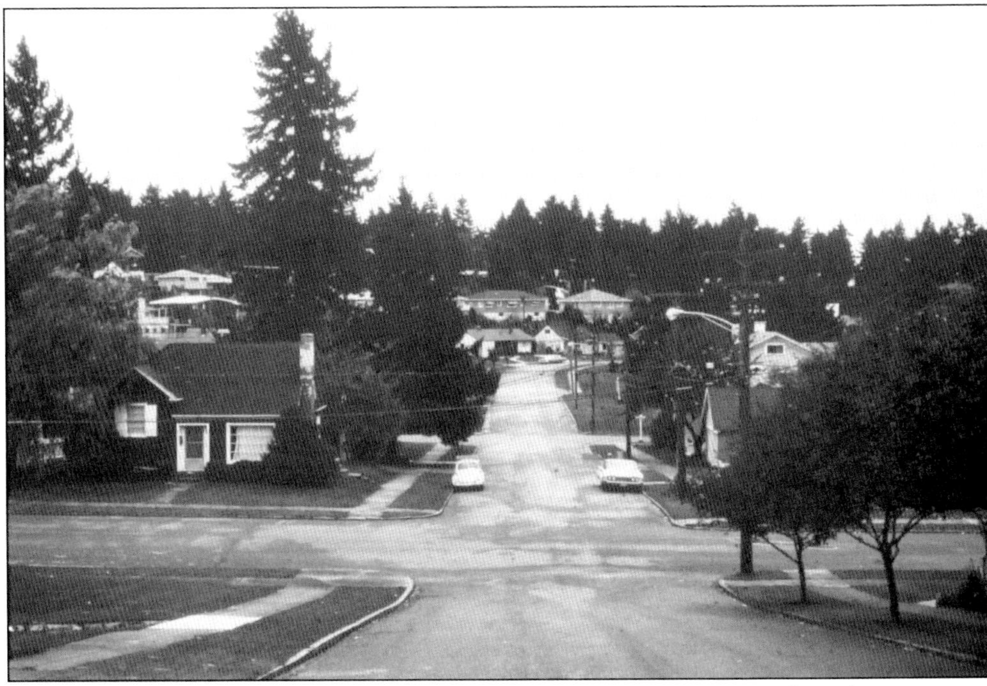

The photograph above was taken about 1970. It looks east down Spring Street from the intersection of Buena Vista Avenue and Spring. Only the top of the Rogers house (now white) and chimney can be seen through the trees right of center. Not only homes fill the lots—note all the fir trees. The image below was also taken from the intersection of Buena Vista Avenue and Spring Street, this time in 2015. Here, the homes can hardly be seen among the trees. The Rogers home (currently blue) can still be seen on the right. The home on the left, on the corner of Spring Street and Berkeley Avenue, replaced the home in the photograph above. (Above, courtesy of the City of Fircrest; below, photograph by R.R. Colyer.)

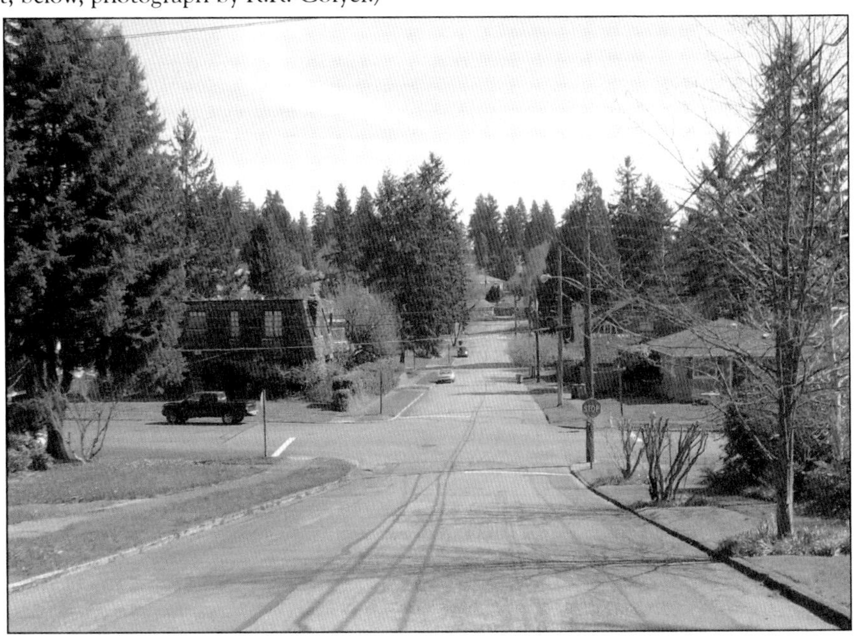

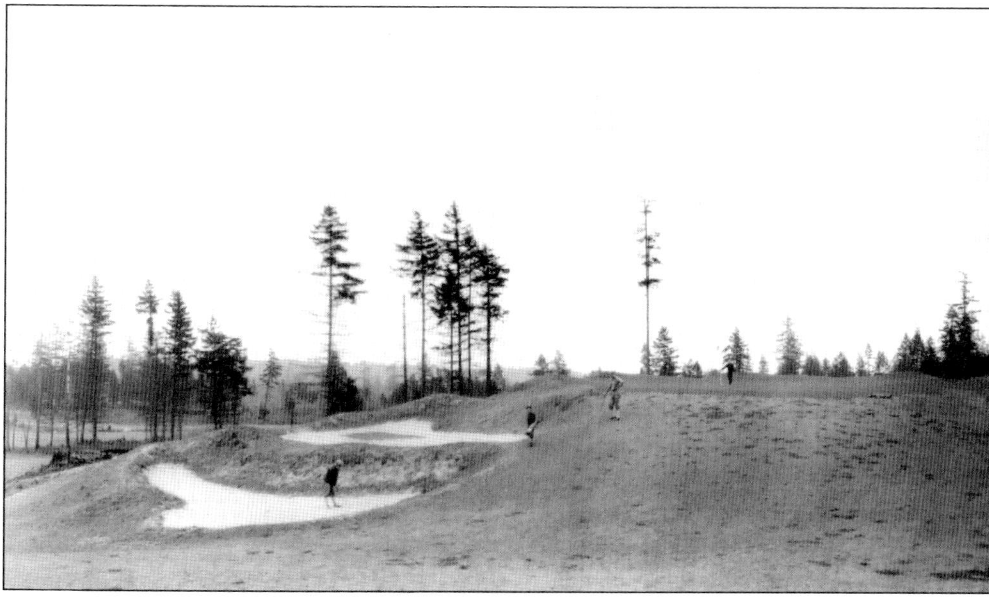

The image above was taken shortly after Fircrest Golf Club opened in 1924. Arthur V. Macan designed the 17th green to mirror Mount Rainier, which could be seen in the distance. One golfer tends the flag, and two look on as a fourth golfer attempts to blast out of a bunker. Partly due to the exploding sand from the bunkers, golfers soon dubbed the 17th "The Volcano Hole." The 17th hole was reconfigured, and the photograph below shows how the green looks today. (Above, courtesy of the Tacoma Public Library, G54.1-031; below, photograph by R.R. Colyer.)

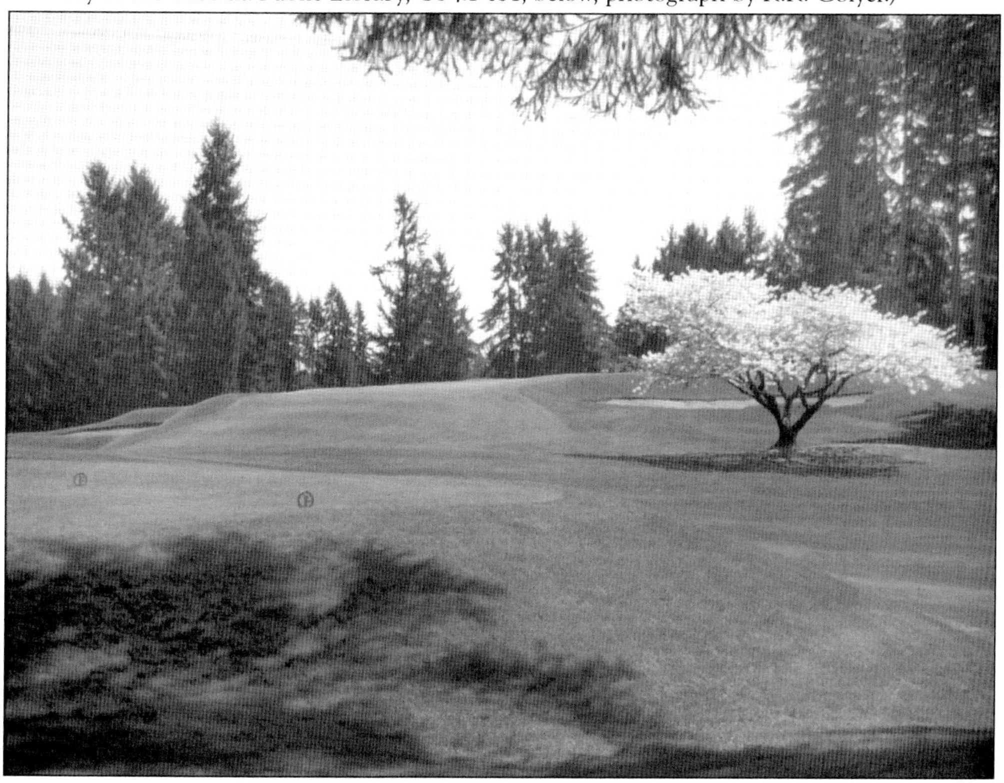

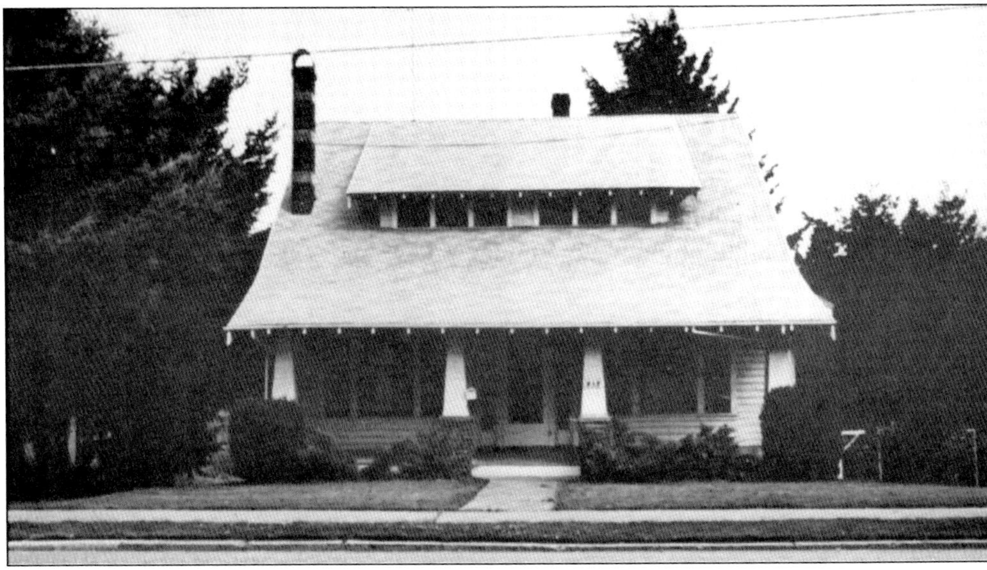

The home shown above was the residence of Ernie Fox, built when Fircrest was still Regents Park. The address was 517 Contra Costa Avenue prior to 1925. It was also waterfront property, facing one of the smaller lakes in the Spring Lake chain. The address of the house is now 528 Ramsdell Street, below, but the original beauty of the home and land is still evident, even without the waterfront view. (Above, courtesy of the City of Fircrest; below, photograph by R.R. Colyer.)

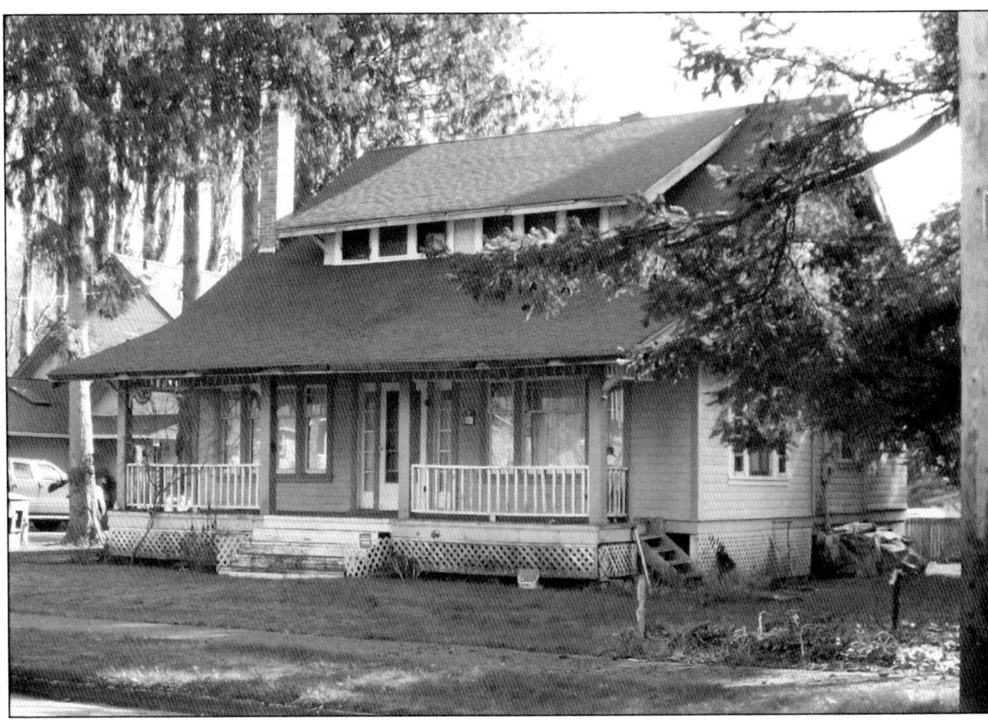

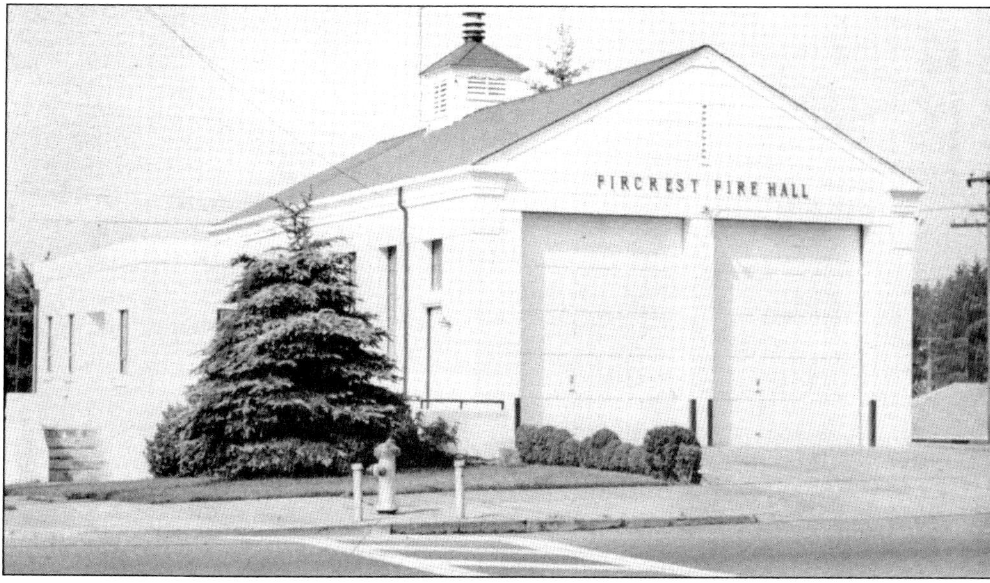

The original Fircrest Fire Hall is seen above in 1948, located on the intersection of Electron Way and Regents Boulevard. The remodeled fire station, below, stands at the same intersection. (Above, courtesy of the City of Fircrest; below, photograph by R.R. Colyer.)

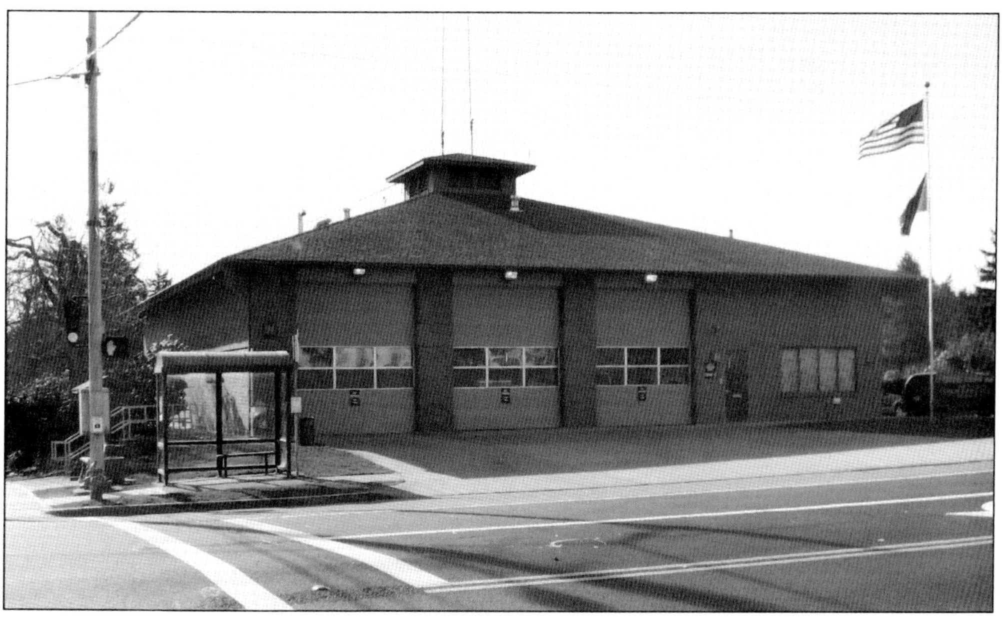

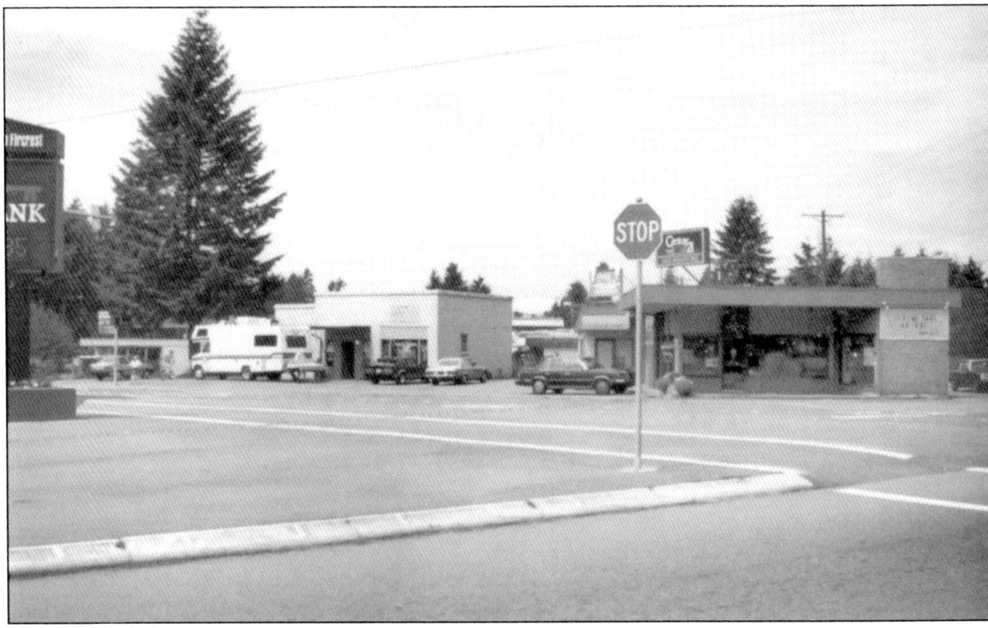

A small triangle of land sits at the intersection of Regents Boulevard and Alameda Avenue. In the 1960s, across the paved intersection with its bank sign showing time and temperature, stood a garage and a Century 21 office. Today, there is a landscaped park. The bank sign has changed sponsors, and the station is now the Espresso Yourself Coffee Shop. Century 21 is still there. (Above, courtesy of the City of Fircrest; below, photograph by R.R. Colyer.)

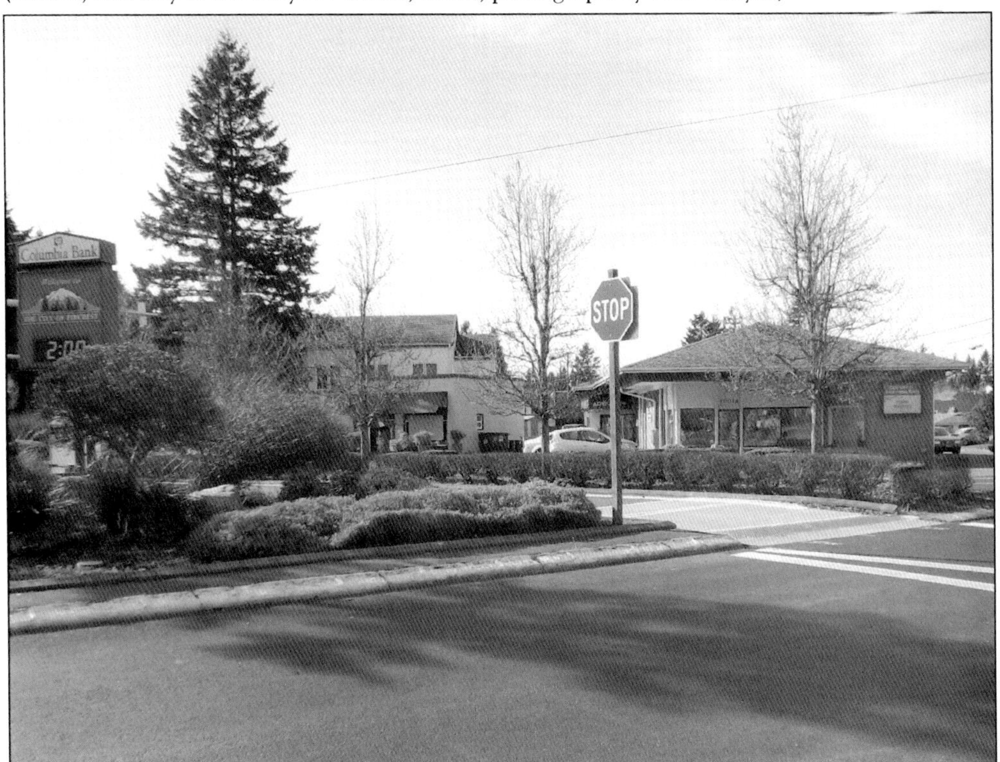

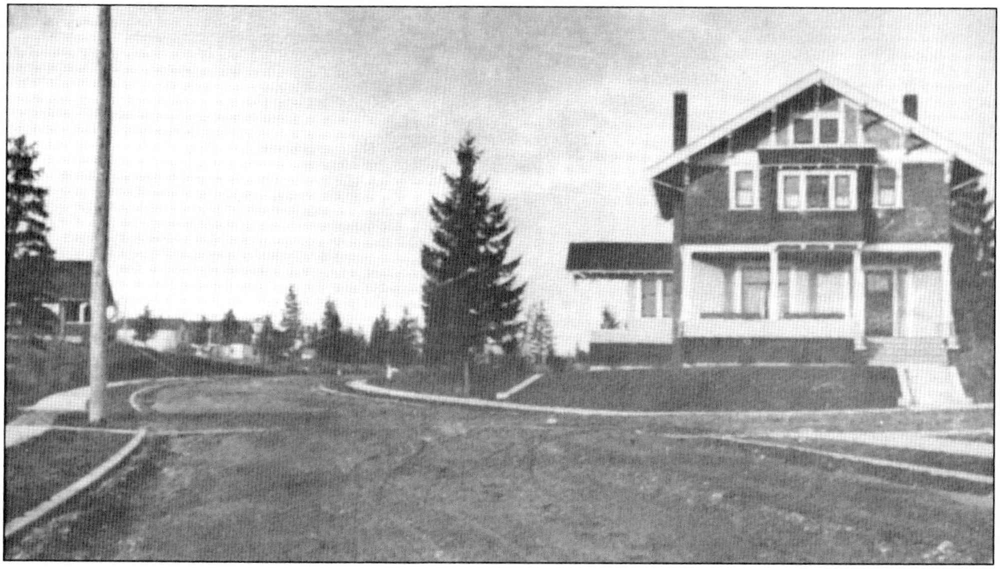

The house at right in the image above originally belonged to Paul Thompson. The photograph was taken from the intersection of Contra Costa Avenue and Princeton Street, looking north. Below, note that the eaves have been removed and the porch has been enclosed. (Above, courtesy of the City of Fircrest; below, photograph by R.R. Colyer.)

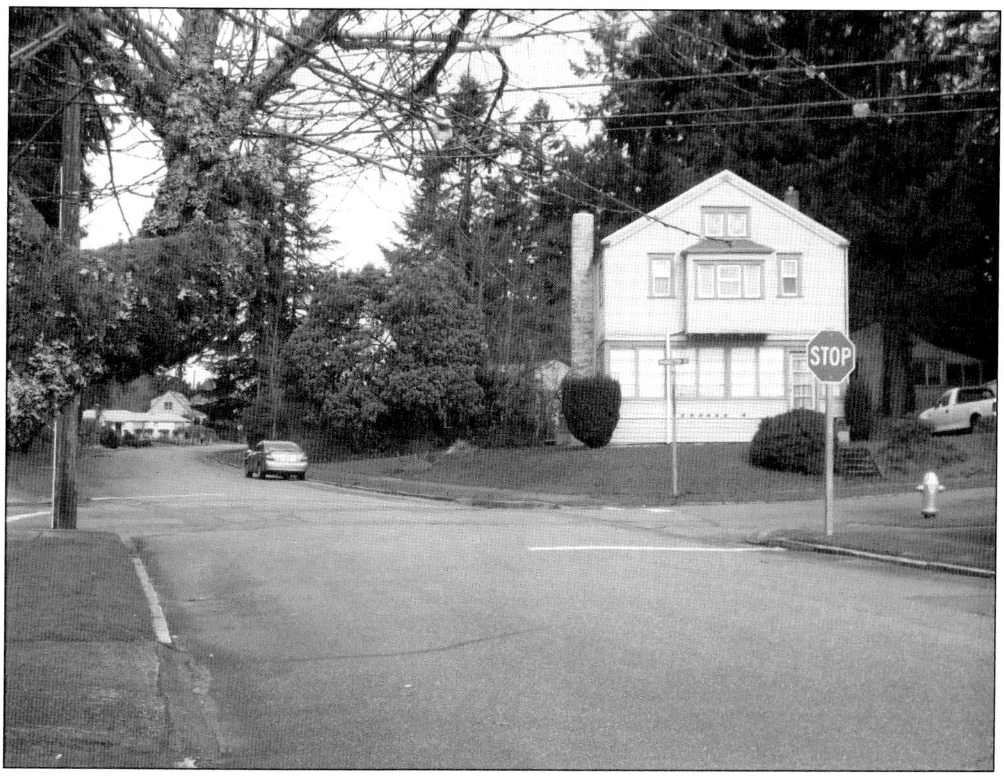

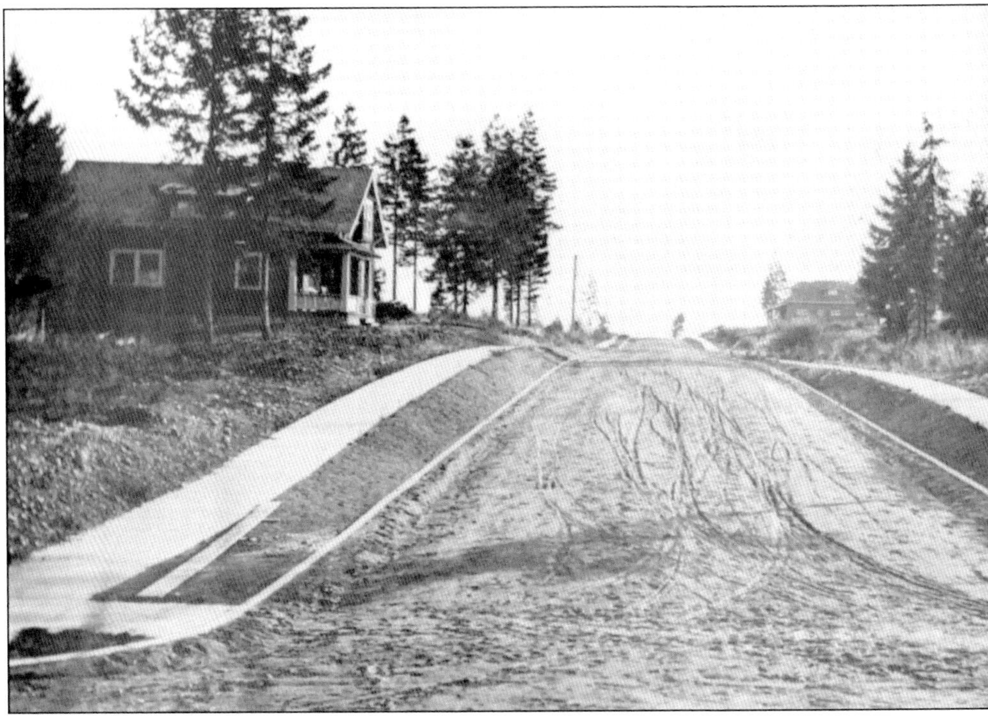

The photograph above of Eldorado Avenue looks south in 1913. Below, the street is seen a century later, in 2015. (Above, courtesy of the City of Fircrest; below, photograph by R.R. Colyer.)

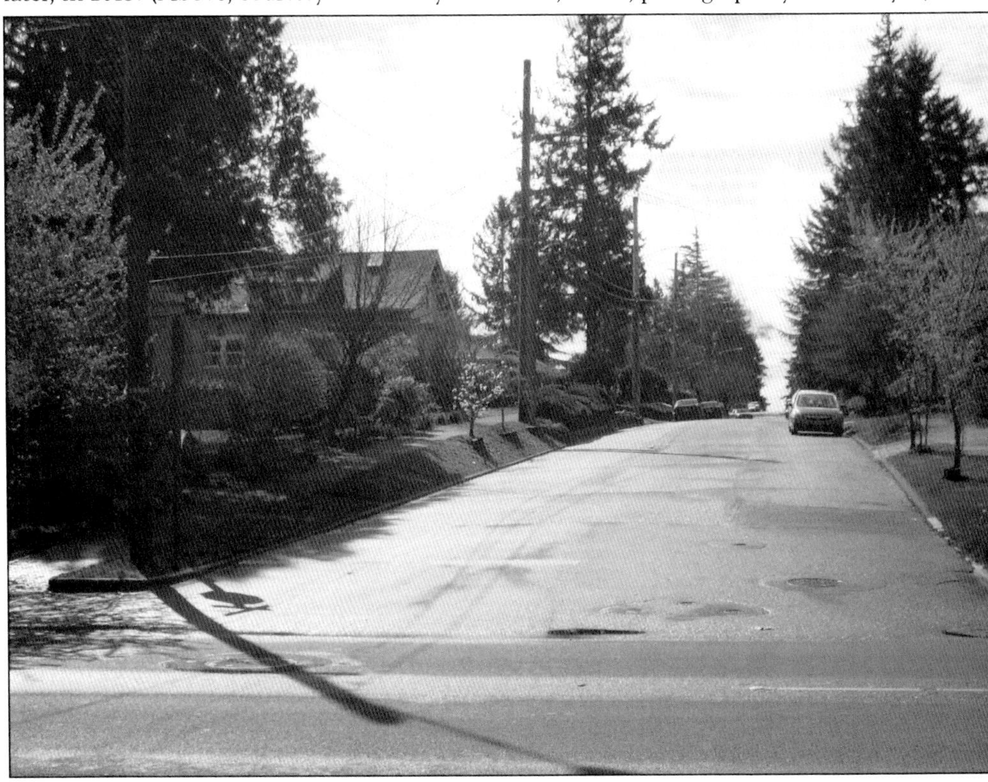

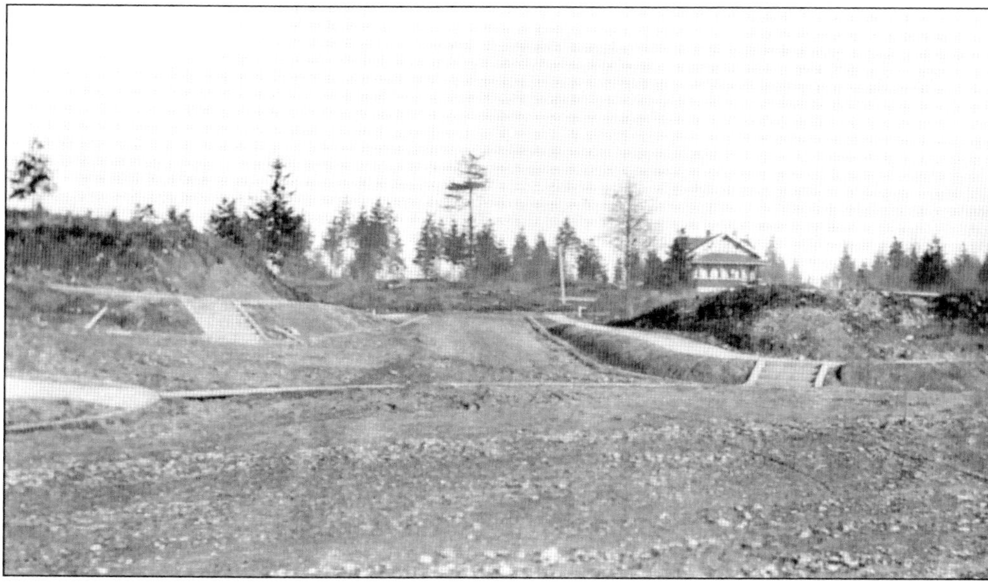

Shown above is Vassar Street, looking east from Regents Boulevard in 1915. A century later, the only thing recognizable from the earlier photograph is the stairs on the left. (Above, courtesy of the City of Fircrest; below, photograph by R.R. Colyer.)

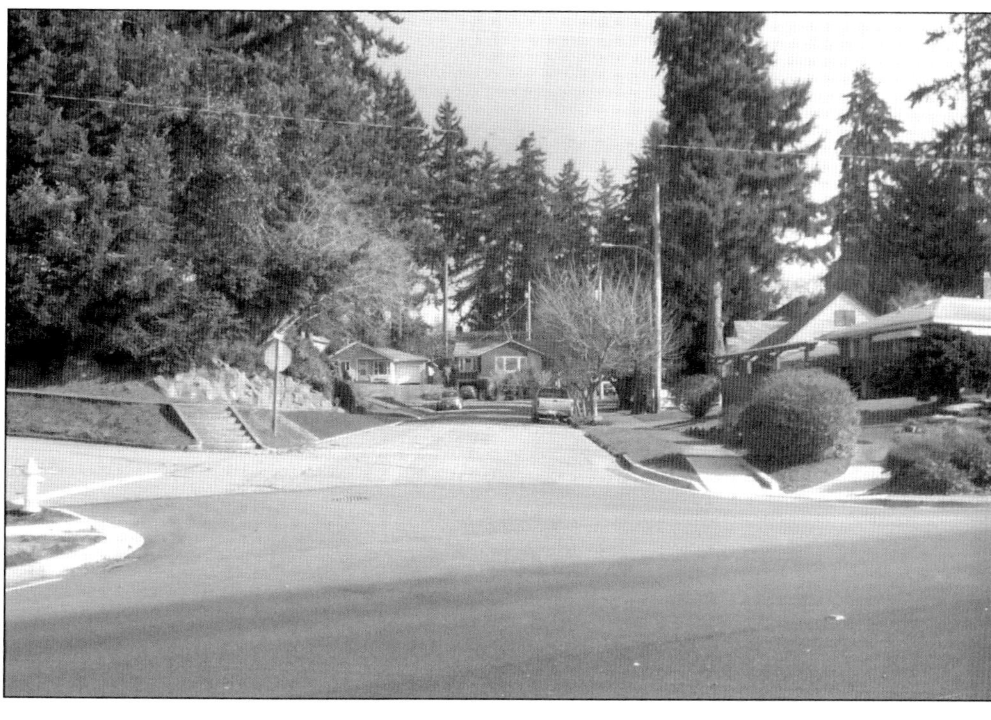

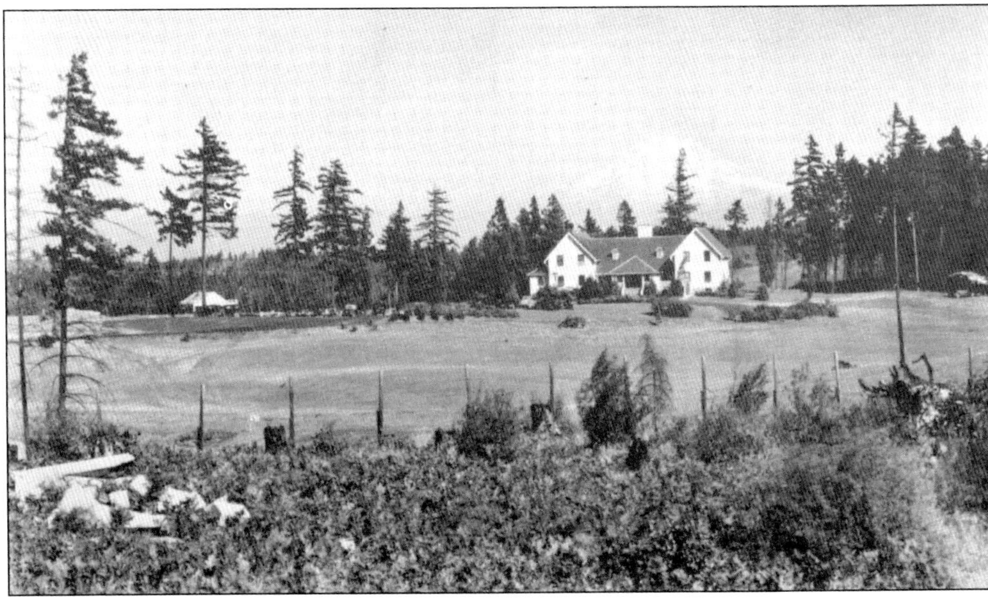

Fircrest Golf Club's clubhouse is seen in a bygone time (above), and in a recent photograph (below). (Above, courtesy of the City of Fircrest; below, the Fircrest Golf Club.)

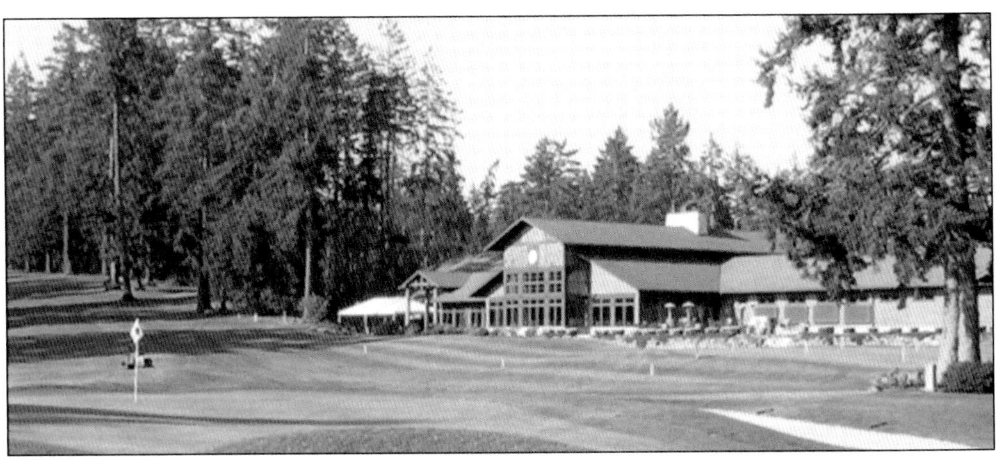

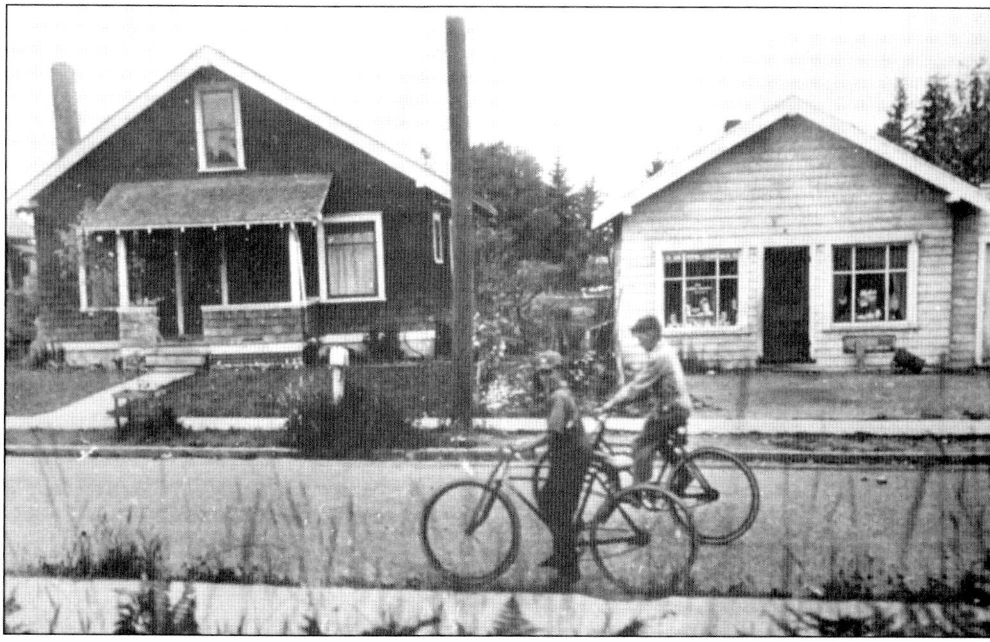

Above, two boys ride their bikes past the Libbey home and store along Farallone Avenue. Regents Park offered many fun activities for local children, with bike riding being a favorite all-season sport. Summer brought swimming and boating. In the winter, if the lake froze over, ice-skating was a real treat. If there was enough snow on the ground, wheels were replaced with runners on the wagons, and kids were pulled along the icy streets. The same street scene is seen today in the image below. (Above, courtesy of the City of Fircrest; below, photograph by R.R. Colyer.)

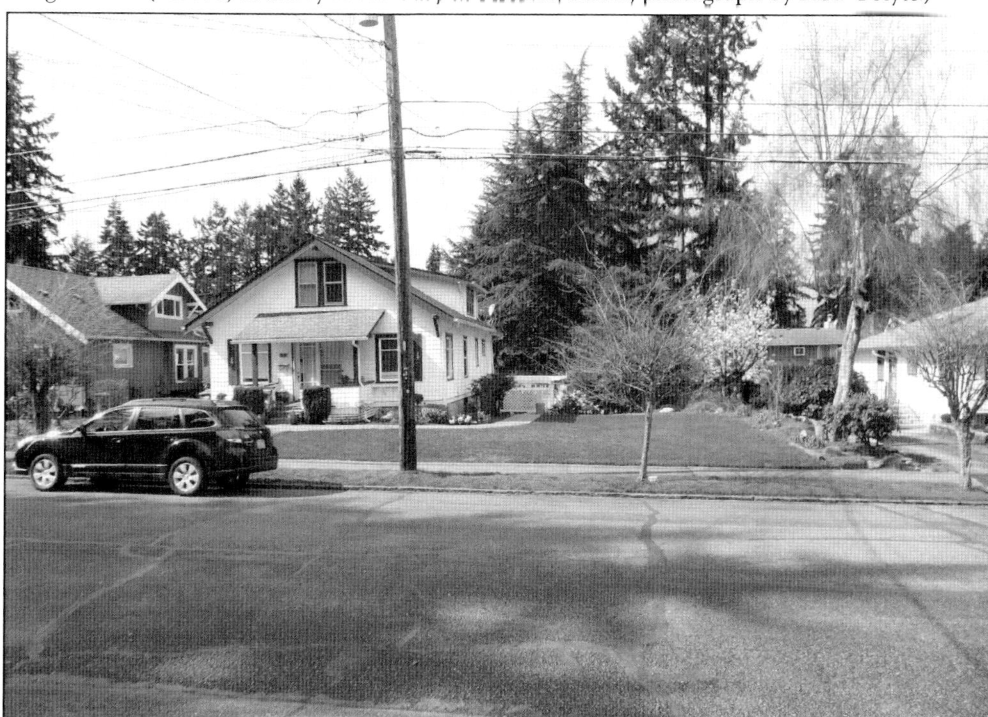

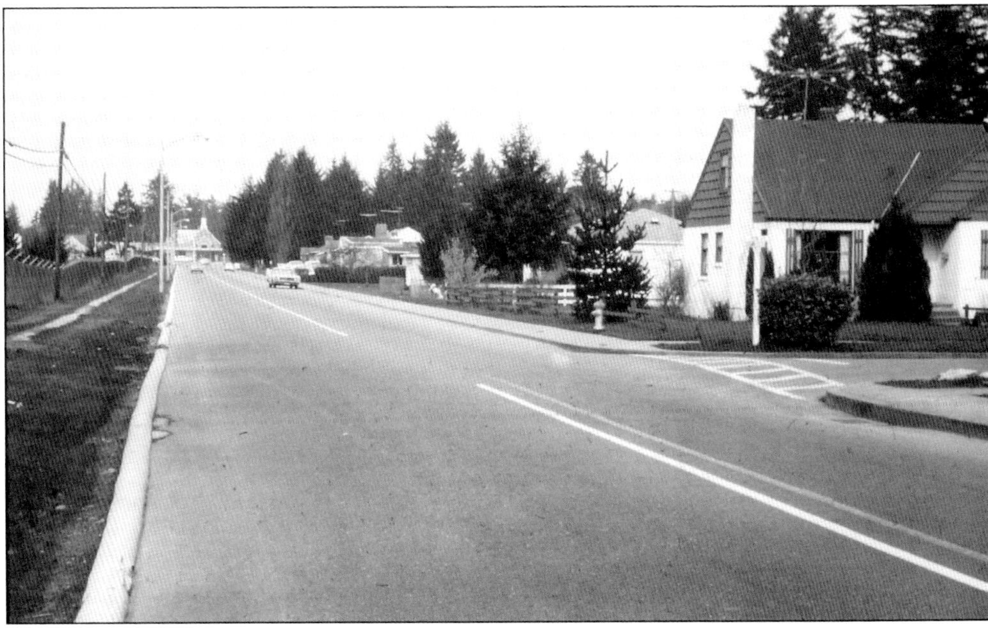

Alameda Avenue, seen today in the photograph below, has not changed much since the 1970s, above. (Above, courtesy of the City of Fircrest; below, photograph by R.R. Colyer.)

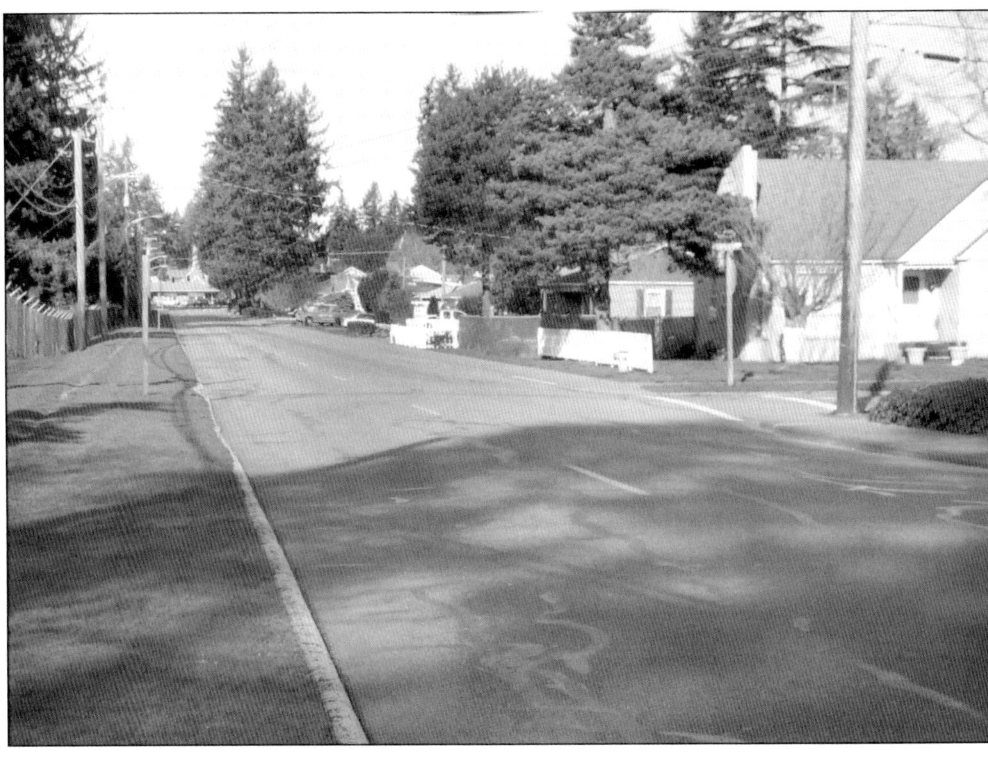

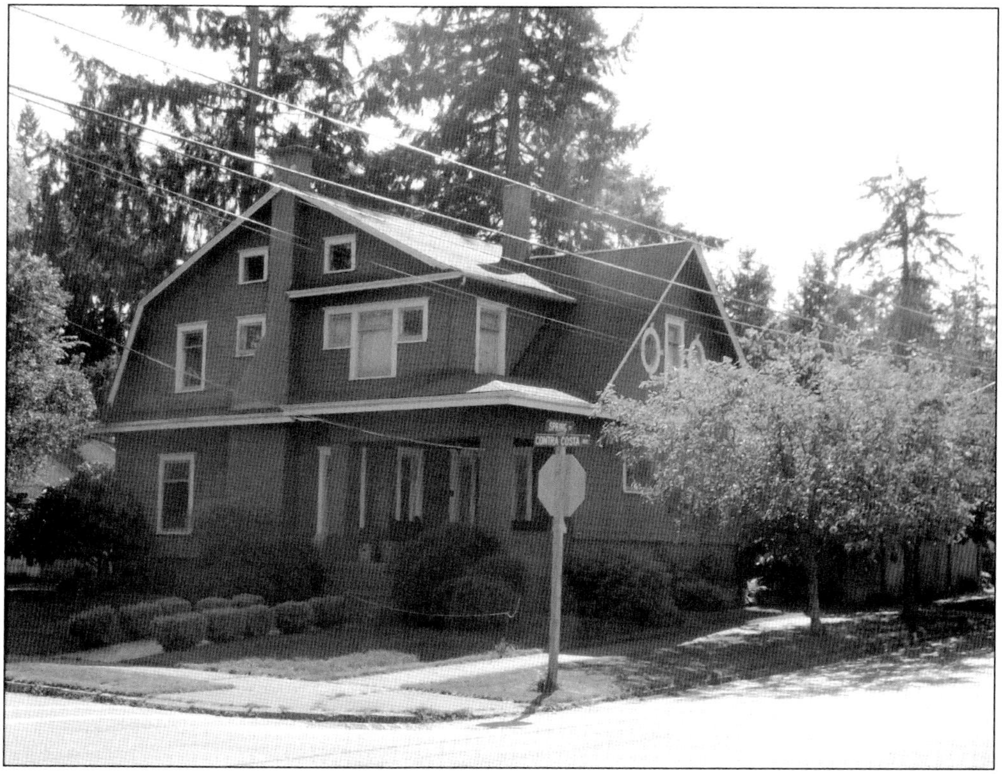

Considered to be one of the most beautiful homes in the area, this residence on the corner of Spring Street and Contra Costa Avenue has changed little (on the exterior) in the last 100 years. (Above, courtesy of the Tacoma Public Library, Boland-B1984; below, photograph by R.R. Colyer.)

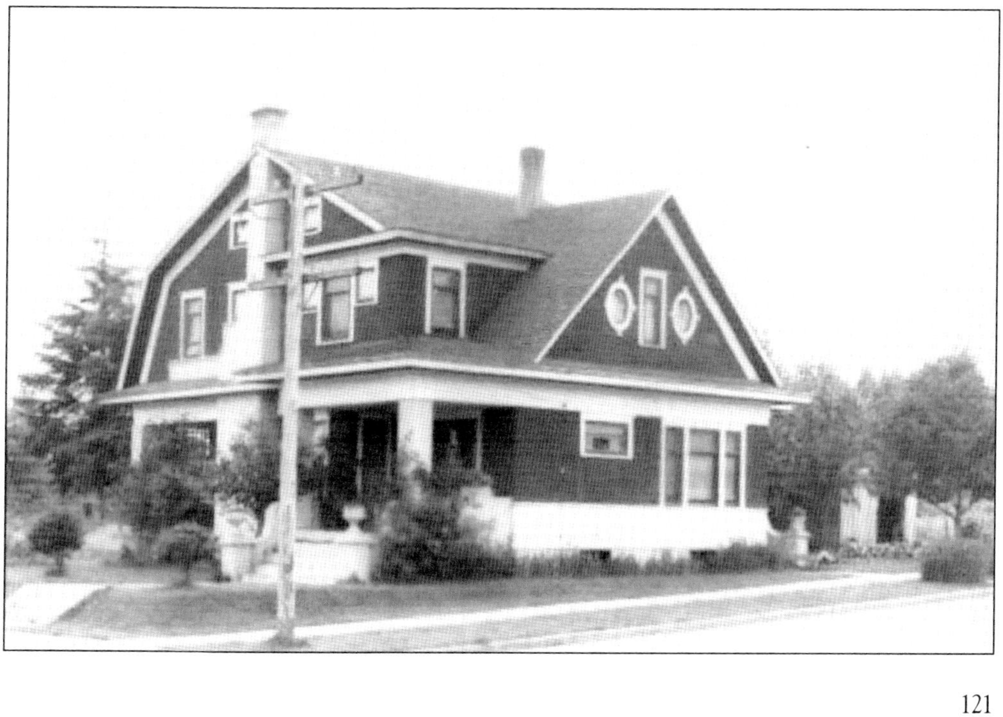

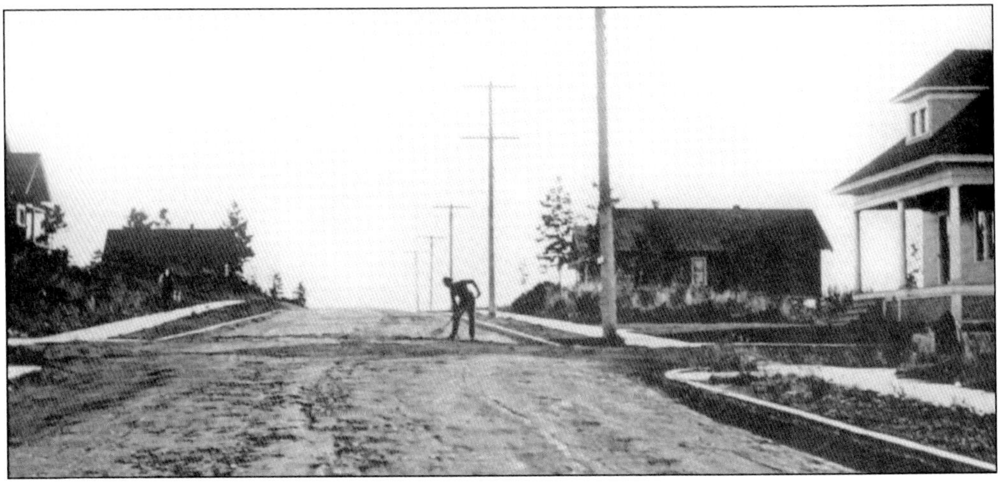

Above, a lone figure repairs a pothole in Farallone Avenue just beyond the intersection with Dartmouth Avenue. The scene today is shown below. Both photographers were looking south down Farallone Avenue. (Above, courtesy of the City of Fircrest; below, photograph by R.R. Colyer.)

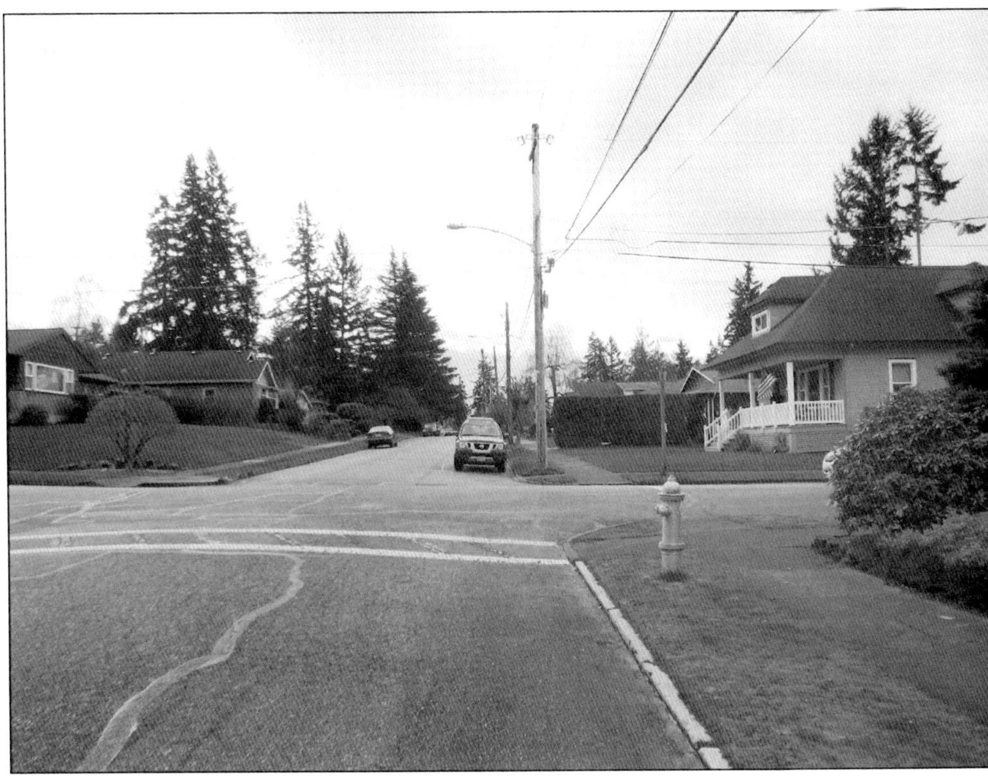

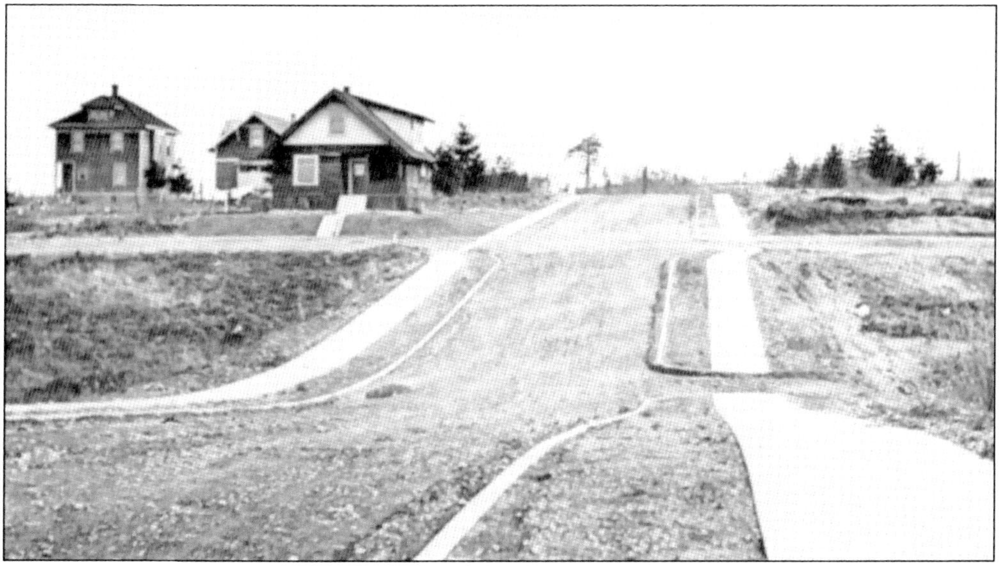

These photographs show Princeton Street looking east from Eldorado Avenue. In the image above, the homes in the distance on the left are the residences of the Conger family, the Browning family, and Gordon Brown, who was a state representative. A current photograph of the street scene is shown below. (Above, courtesy of the City of Fircrest; below, photograph by R.R. Colyer.)

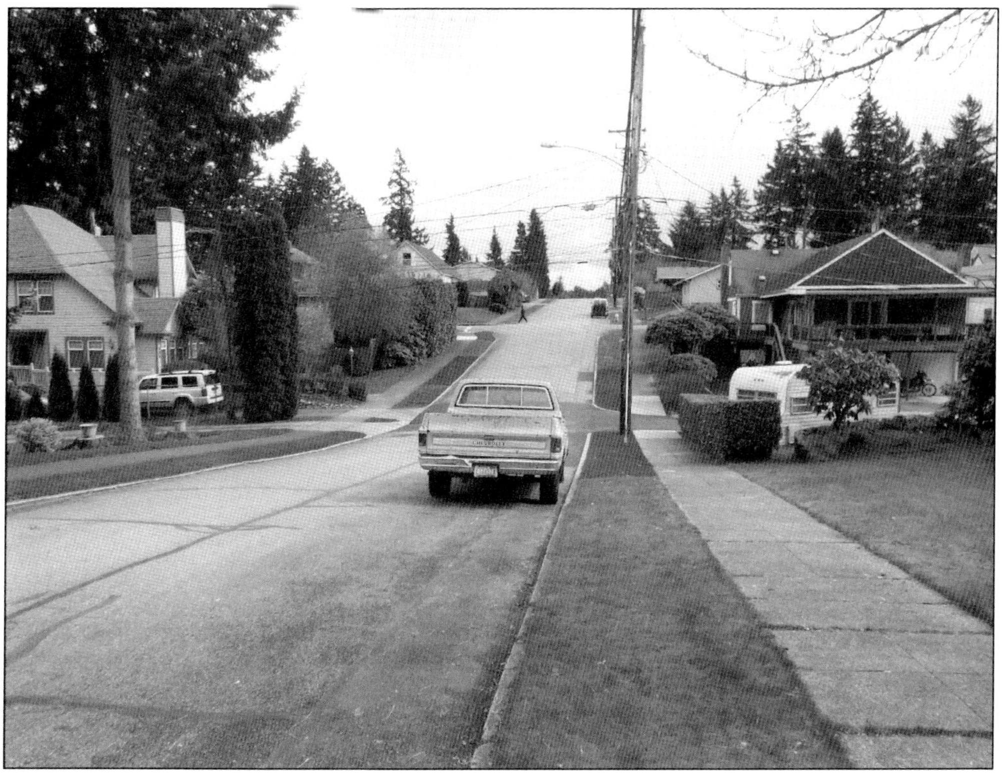

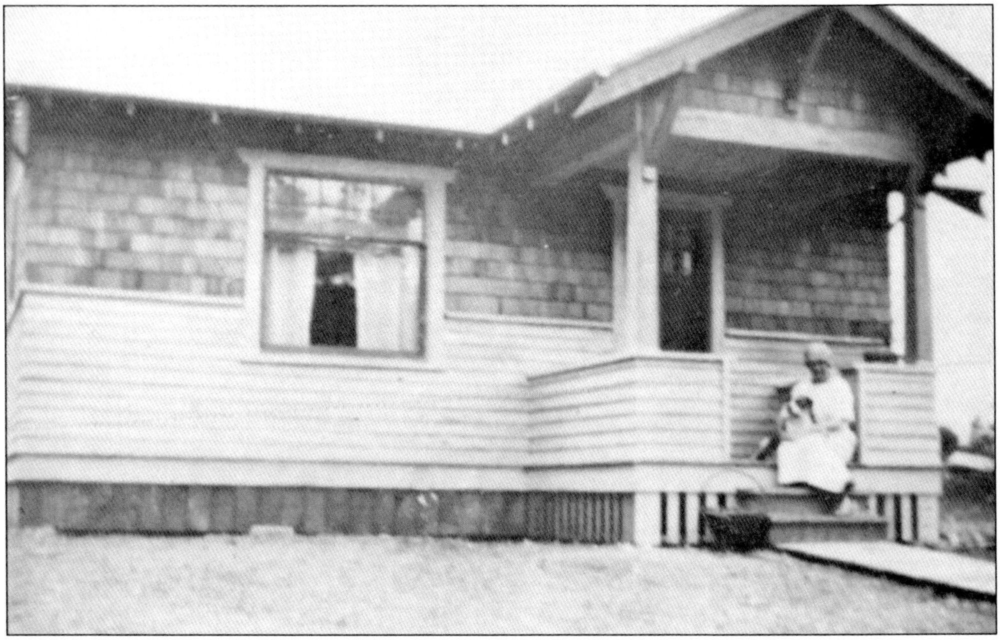

The home at 346 Del Monte Avenue belonged to Floyd World in 1917. The same house is shown below in 2015. (Above, courtesy of the City of Fircrest; below, photograph by R.R. Colyer.)

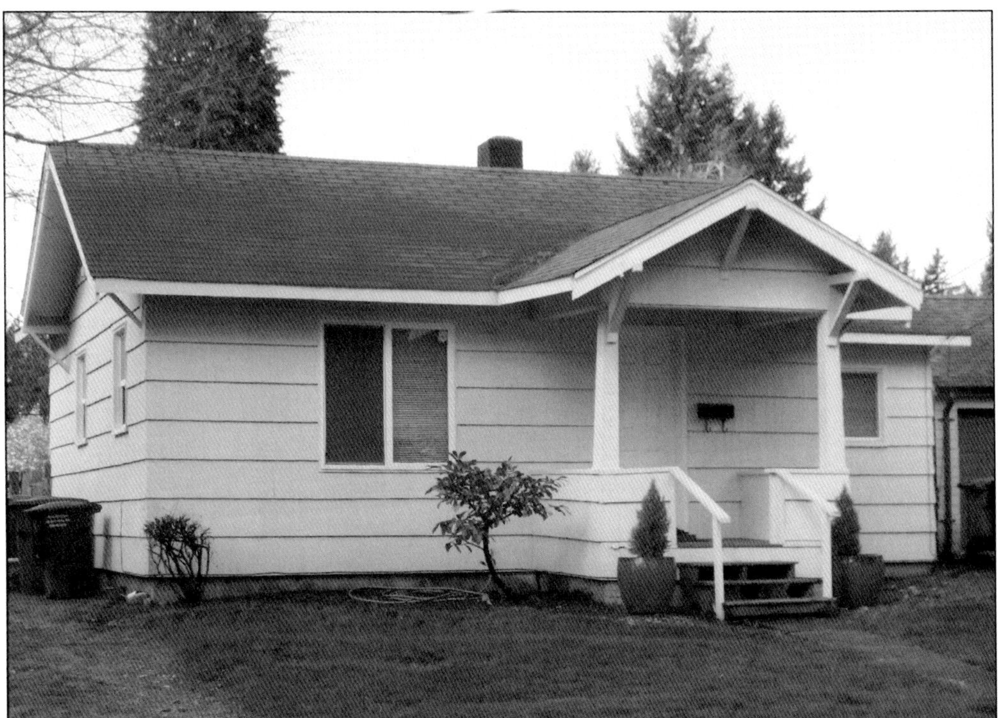

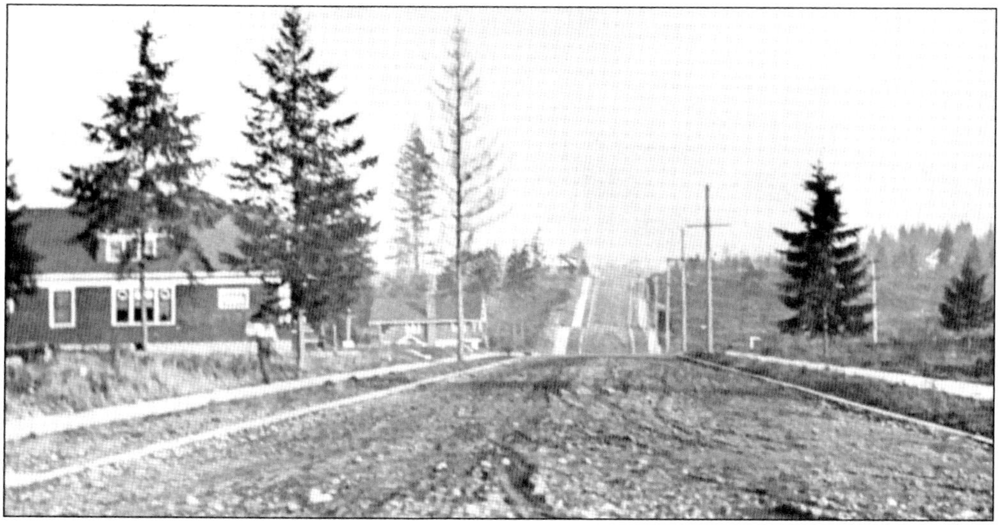

Looking east from Alameda Avenue down Princeton Street, the image above, taken in 1913, shows the home of the Bell family (left). The photograph below offers a current view of the area. (Above, courtesy of the City of Fircrest; below, photograph by R.R. Colyer.)

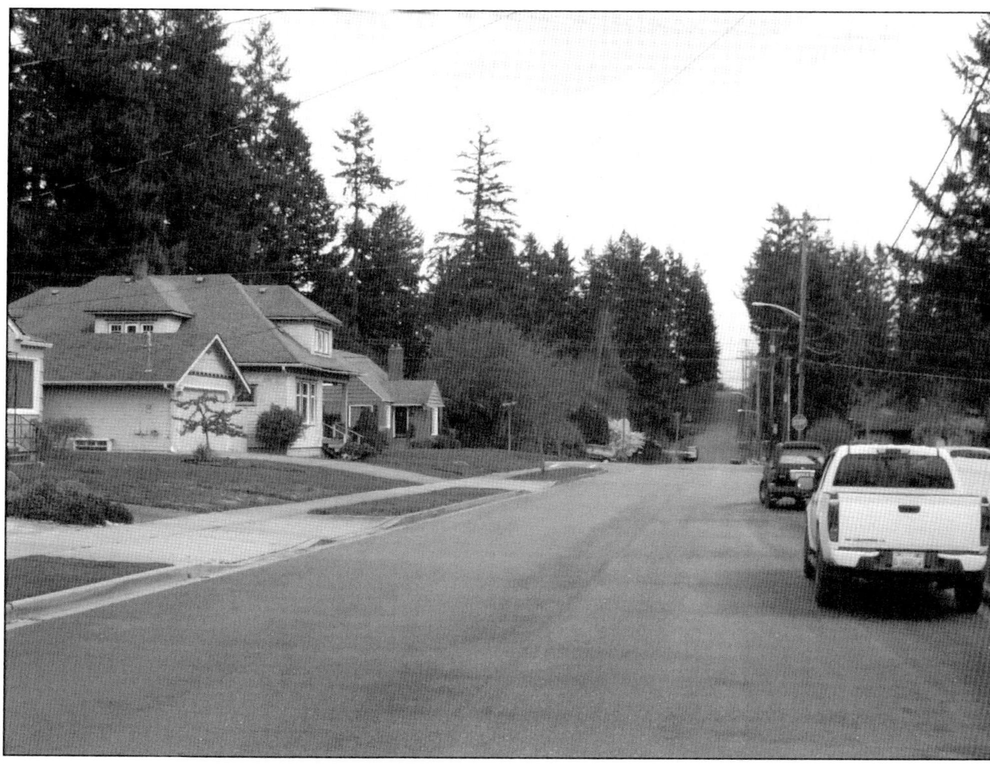

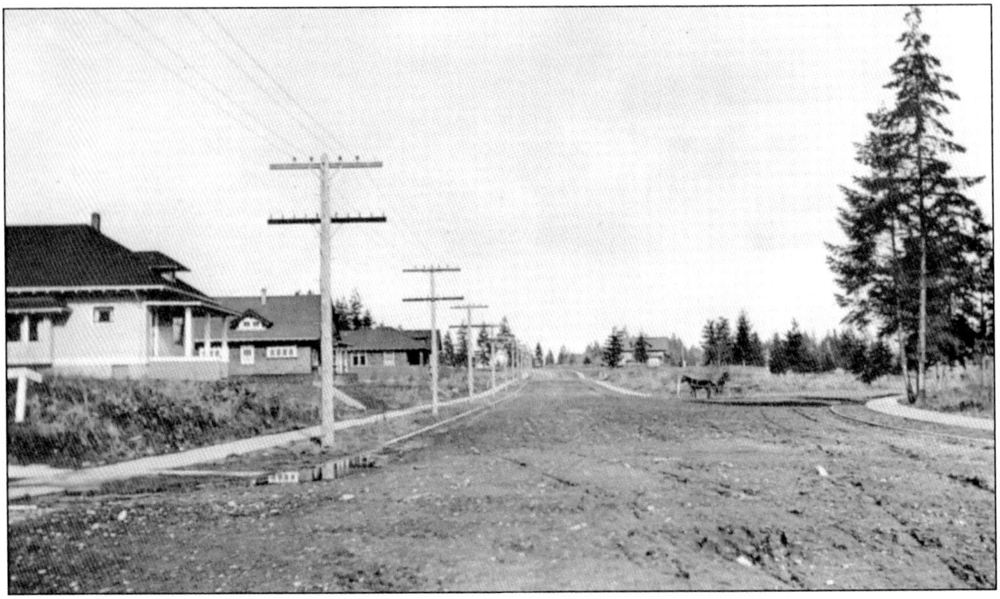

The 1915 photograph above shows the intersection of Berkeley Avenue and Bowes Drive looking north from Spring Street. A similar view of Berkeley Avenue and Bowes Drive is shown in the c. 1970 image below. (Above, courtesy of the City of Fircrest; below, photograph by R.R. Colyer.)

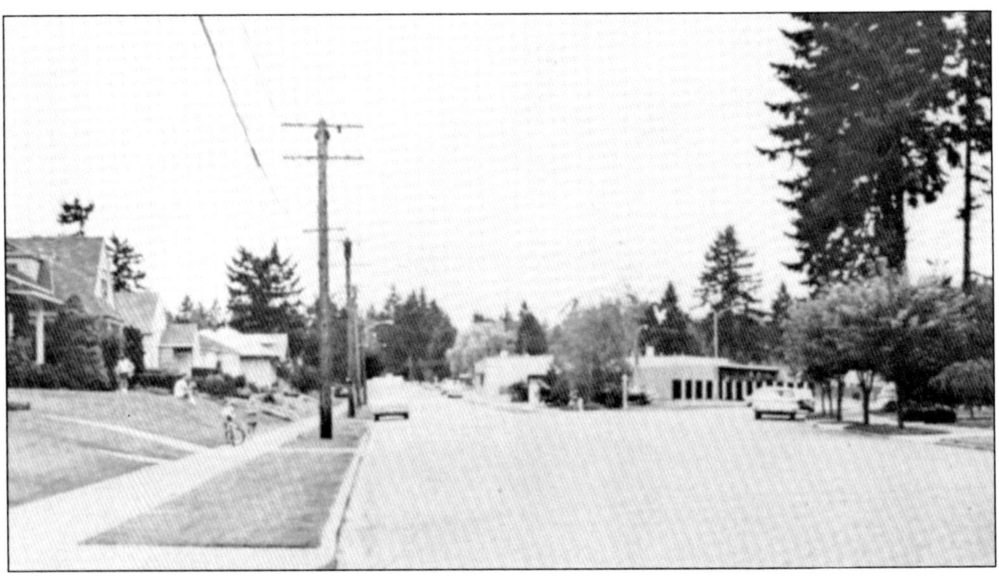

On a hill crowned with fir trees, Edward J. Bowes, famously known later as Major Bowes, envisioned a city of the future: a commuter community where men and women worked in the city and traveled home by automobile or mass transit. In 1907, this was truly visionary. He wanted to invent the quintessential American suburb, where men and women could relax after a stress-filled day and raise a family—he succeeded. The city of Fircrest and the people who reside there owe Major Bowes their gratitude. (Courtesy *The Original Amateur Hour.*)

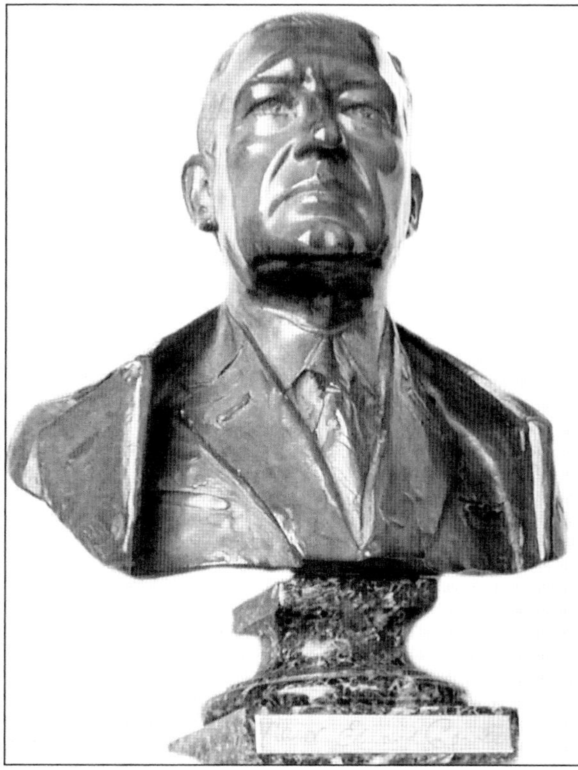

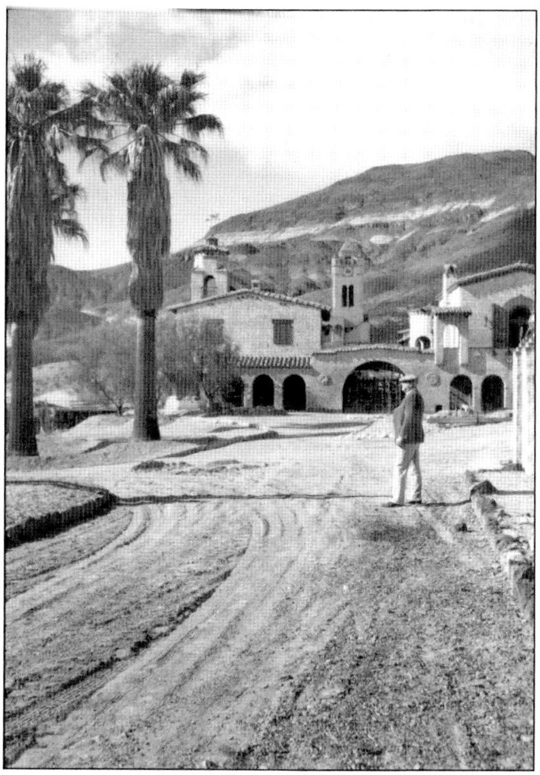

Regents Park, later the city of Fircrest, would not be the community it is today, much less the groundbreaking suburban plan envisioned by Major Bowes, were it not for the genius of a brilliant civil engineer from Tacoma, Washington, M.R. Thompson. Thompson is shown here at another of his innovative projects, in a National Park: Scotty's Castle in Death Valley. Providence brought Bowes and Thompson together for a project that would forever impact both men's lives as it continues to impact the lives of residents of the city of Fircrest today. (Courtesy of the National Park Service.)